THE SWISS LABYRINTH

BOOKS OF RELATED INTEREST

THE SWISS LABYRINTH

Institutions, Outcomes and Redesign

Editor

JAN-ERIK LANE

Routledge
Taylor & Francis Group

LONDON AND NEW YORK

First Published in 2001 by
FRANK CASS PUBLISHERS

Published 2013 by Routledge
2 Park Square, Milton Park, Abingdon, Oxfordshire OX14 4RN
711 Third Avenue, New York, NY 10017

First issued in paperback 2016

Routledge is an imprint of the Taylor & Francis Group, an informa business

Copyright © 2001 Taylor & Francis.

British Library Cataloguing in Publication Data

The Swiss labyrinth : institutions, outcomes and redesign
    1. Switzerland – Politics and government – 1945 –
    I. Lane, Jan-Erik
    320.9′494

Library of Congress Cataloging-in-Publication Data

The Swiss labyrinth : institutions, outcomes, and redesign / editor,
Jan-Erik Lane.
    p. cm.
    "This group of studies first appeared in a special issue of West
European politics (ISSN 0140-2382) vol. 24, no. 2 (April 2001)" –T.p.
verso.
    Includes bibliographical references and index.
    1. Switzerland – Politics and government – 1945-. 2.
Switzerland – Economic policy. I. Lane, Jan-Erik.
    JN8781 .S95 2001
    306.2′09494–dc21

                                                        2001028471

ISBN 13: 978-1-138-98344-1 (pbk)
ISBN 13: 978-0-7146-5142-2 (hbk)

This group of studies first appeared in a Special Issue of
West European Politics (ISSN 0140-2382) Vol.24, No.2 (April 2001),
[The Swiss Labyrinth: Institutions, Outcomes and Redesign].

Contents

MAP OF SWITZERLAND

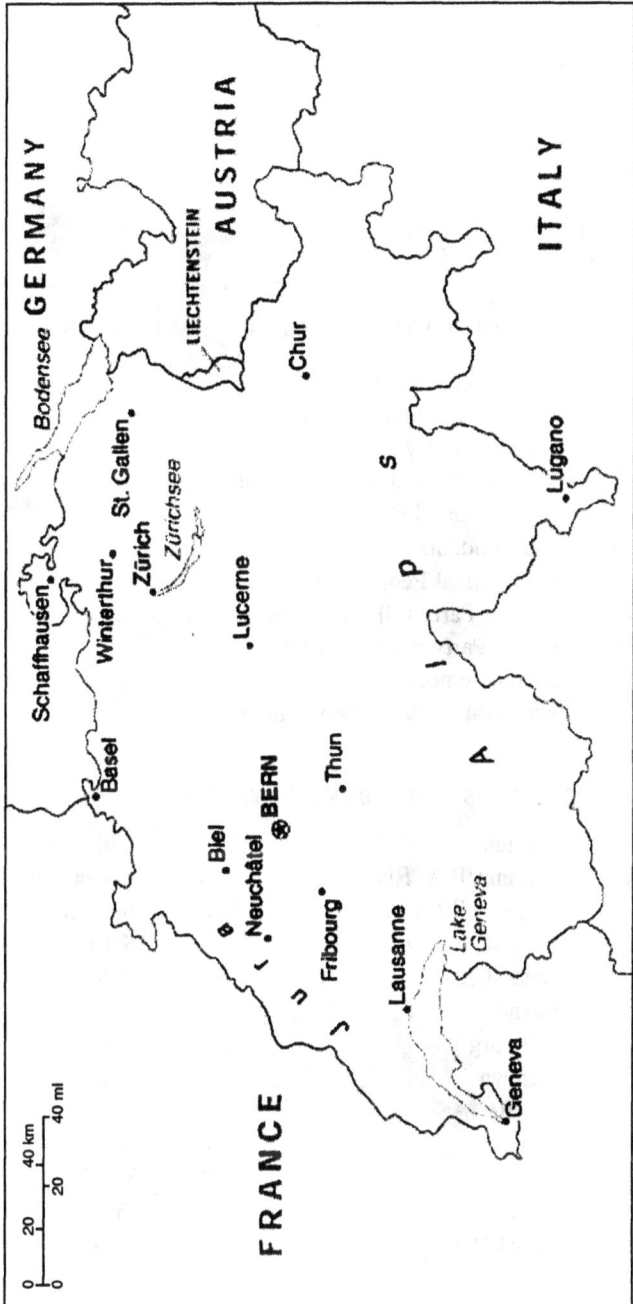

Glossary

THE SWISS PARTY SYSTEM AND ABBREVIATIONS

FDP	Liberal Democratic Party
CVP	Christian Democratic Party
SPS	Socialist Party
SVP	Democratic Union of the Centre
LPS	Swiss Liberal Party
LdU	Independents
EVP	Evangelical People's Party
PDA	Labour Party (GE incl. Solidarités)
GPS	Green Party of Switzerland
SD	Swiss Democrats
FPS	Freedom Party of Switzerland

SWISS CANTONS AND ABBREVIATIONS

AG	Aargau	NW	Nidwalden
AR	Appenzell A. Rhein	OW	Obwalden
AI	Appenzell I. Rhein	SH	Schaffhausen
BL	Basel-Country	SZ	Schwyz
BS	Basel-City	SO	Solothurn
BE	Berne	SG	St Gallen
FR	Fribourg	TI	Ticino
GE	Geneva	TG	Thurgau
GL	Glarus	UR	Uri
GR	Graubünden	VS	Valais
JU	Jura	VD	Vaud
LU	Lucerne	ZG	Zug
NE	Neuchâtel	ZH	Zurich

MAP OF CANTONS

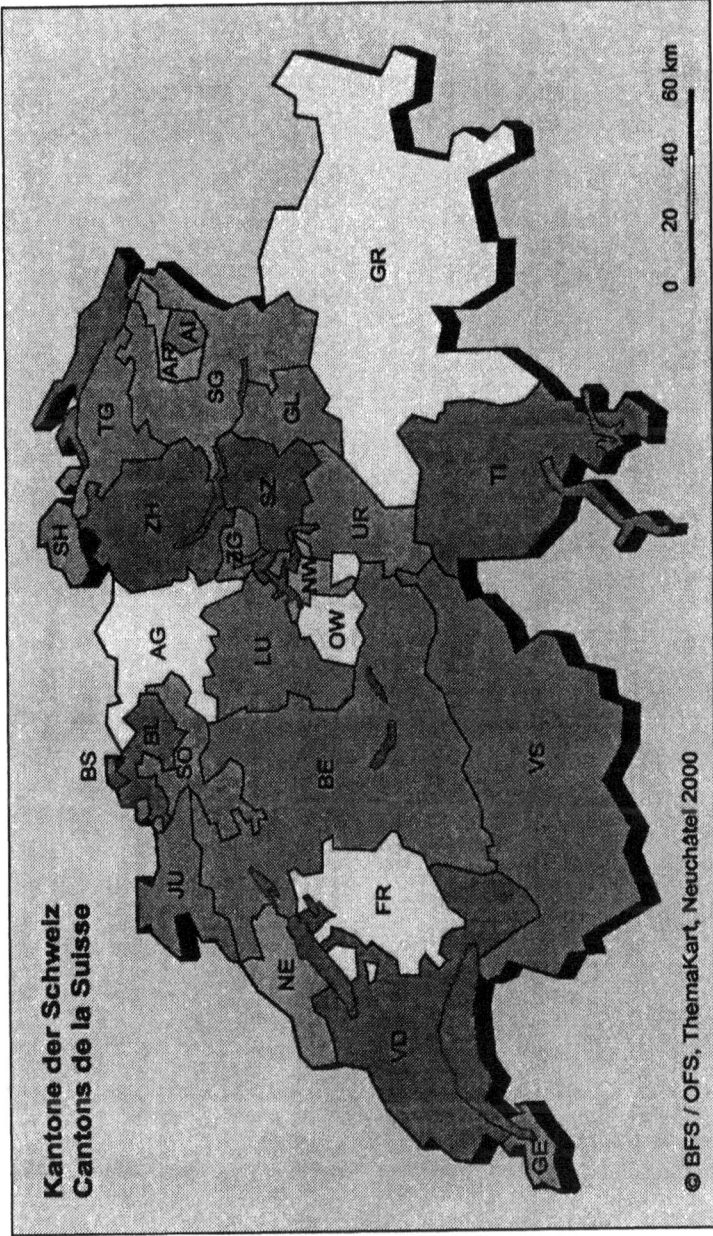

Kantone der Schweiz
Cantons de la Suisse

SH

TG

AR

AI

SG

ZH

GL

ZG

SZ

BS

BL

SO

AG

NW

OW

UR

GR

JU

LU

BE

TI

NE

VS

FR

VD

GE

0   20   40   60 km

© BFS / OFS, ThemaKart, Neuchâtel 2000

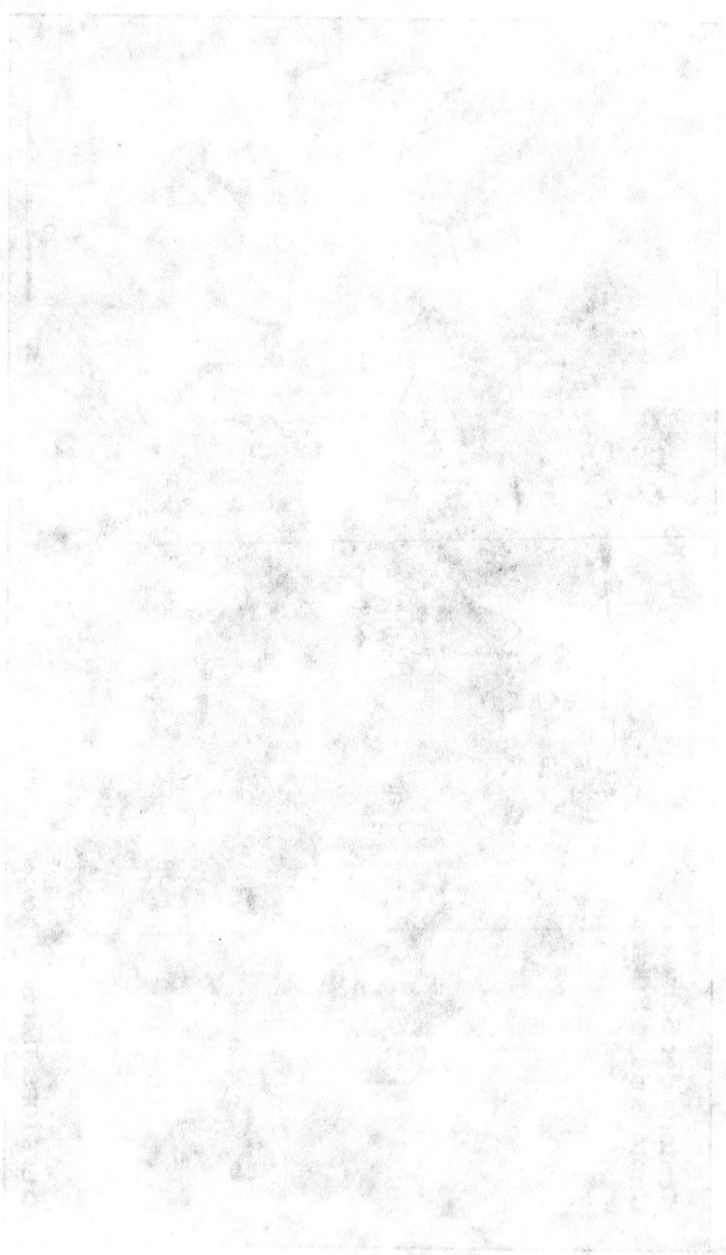

Introduction:
Switzerland – Key Institutions and
Behavioural Outcomes

JAN-ERIK LANE

Switzerland, a labyrinth of political institutions, is an interesting laboratory for institutional research. There are so many political institutions in use that each one is enough for a book. Thus, the referendum, Swiss federalism and the grand coalition have been much discussed. Equally interesting are Swiss corporatism, the Central Bank and the Federal Supreme Court as well as the electoral system, which has both proportional and majoritarian techniques.

'What does it all add up to?' we have to ask when interpreting Swiss politics from a macro perspective. We are all familiar with the key concepts that scholars have suggested: 'plebiscitary democracy' (Hastad), 'amicable agreement' (Steiner), '*Konkordanz*' (Lehmbruch), 'consociationalism' or 'consensus democracy' (Lijphart), 'liberal corporatism' (Katzenstein). Today, these extremely general characterisations are less helpful when approaching Swiss politics in a process of transition from splendid isolation towards a post-modern society. One leading Swiss political scientist, Hanspeter Kriesi, has even described the Swiss political system as an 'anachronism'.

The time has come to analyse Swiss politics in terms of the new institutional paradigm in the social sciences. One should no longer treat Switzerland as a peculiar country in Central Europe pursuing its own model as if it were an ideal-type in itself. Instead, one must analyse its institutions in terms of general social science models, assessing the outcomes of the operation of these institutions. What is especially important in order to understand Switzerland is how its institutions interact, each conditioning the operation of the others – *institutional bending*. Examining how Swiss institutions really operate with the help of new research over the last decade we can replace general and superficial labels with an assessment of the pros and cons of these world-famous institutions. This opens the way to discuss the possibilities of institutional

Jan-Erik Lane, University of Geneva

reform, as practice moves further away from the ideal-type than that recognised in comparative research.

In this volume we examine how the characteristic Swiss political institutions operated during the 1980s and 1990s. We examine institutional change as well as institutional outcomes. The key question in institutional analysis: 'Do Institutions Matter?' should be raised in relation to the country with the most special set of political institutions among European democracies. This will both improve new institutional theory and broaden comparative institutional enquiry from an empirical perspective. Analysing the Swiss case in detail helps to improve our understanding of *institutional integration* and *institutional contradictions*, especially as one much-discussed theme in relation to the Swiss political institutions is the compatibility of the various institutions that make up the political system. Probing more deeply into how Switzerland operates politically will allow entry into the difficult and often neglected question in institutional theory of how the operation of one institution conditions the operation of another institution.

THE SWISS INSTITUTIONS

Switzerland has long had a set of stable and special political institutions. There are at least six very important institutions when examining politics during the post-war period:

(1) decentralised real federalism;

(2) active referendum democracy at the federal and cantonal levels;

(3) a seven headed presidency (directorial system);

(4) *la formule magique* (permanent grand coalition);

(5) hidden corporatism (or quasi-corporatism);

(6) a highly independent central bank; as well as a seventh feature –

(7) neutrality in international politics.

Each one of these institutions would be worth an examination, but what creates the exceptionalism of Swiss politics is the combination of the six institutions during the post-war period. This exceptional mix of political institutions has been claimed to contain the secret of the country's success in terms of economic prosperity and political stability despite its high degree of social heterogeneity, ethnically and religiously speaking.

Thus, Switzerland is special because it is the most decentralised of all federal systems, the country with the most use of referendum democracy, the country which mixes presidentialism and parliamentarism in its so-called directorate model of government, and the country that consistently employs oversized coalitions. In addition, it practises a form of corporatism that is more implicit but still strong. There is nothing mysterious at work here. One can evaluate the impact of this institutional set-up and discuss institutional redesign.

Actually, what is unique about Switzerland is not each one of the institutions listed above. They can be found in other countries too. What creates Swiss exceptionalism is the constellation of all of them at the same time. This no other country in the world displays. However, they must be analysed by means of ordinary institutional research, targeting not only how one institution operates and what outcomes it promotes but also how a set of institutions functions.

The special set of Swiss political institutions is the outcome of the historical evolution of the country – path dependency no doubt. Its decentralised structures reflect the evolution from a loose confederation to a modern state. We may go as far back as feudal times, when various provinces were part of the Holy Roman–German Empire up until 1648. Yet, historical legacy explains only so much. It is the present constellation of forces that decide how institutions function. The operation of each one of these institutions depends upon how the others function. And the way these operate is in a process of change at the turn of the century, as Switzerland copes with the requirements of a post-modern society in the period of globalisation.

The purpose of this volume on Swiss politics today is twofold. First, we wish to present an analysis of institutional change and institutional outcomes employing the peculiar Swiss political institutions as our reference point. Second, we wish to make available an up-to-date text for scholars and students in Switzerland as well as to an international readership that may not be informed about the country, but are interested in the present process of institutional change. Thus, this account provides a new perspective on the most recent trends towards change in Switzerland, and complements single-authored books such as *Schweizerische Demokratie, Institutionen, Prozesse, Perspektiven*, Wolf Linder (1999); *Le Système Politique Suisse*, Hanspeter Kriesi (1998), as well as the multi-authored volume *Handbuch der Schweizer Politik*, ed. Ulrich Klöti *et al.* (1999). This volume presents a concise and up-to-date English presentation of Swiss politics to an international audience by scholars researching in the area.

When assessing institutional performance one may look at either how an institution affects another institution or how institutions condition behaviour. The analyses of the Swiss political institutions in this volume contain both perspectives on institutional outcomes. Thus, there is much discussion about the coherence of the six institutions in relation to each other, but the outcome analysis also comprises the effects of these institutions upon political behaviour such as participation, the party system and public policy. One can identify systematically the four following possible relations between institutions when one is confronted by a set of institutions comprising no fewer than six elements:

(1) consistency

(2) compatibility

(3) independence

(4) contradiction

This volume shows that all these relationships occur among the Swiss political institutions. It is not tenable to regard Swiss democracy as a close approximation to a logically consistent ideal-type called 'consociational' or 'consensus democracy'. The situation is rather one of tension among the Swiss political institutions, and that becomes apparent when one examines institutional contradictions and outcomes.

OUTCOMES

Switzerland is first and foremost recognised as the referendum democracy *par preference*. Most political scientists are well informed about the frequent employment of the referendum on a national level, where there have been some 250 such referenda since 1945. However, the frequent use of the referendum in politics at the cantonal level is far less well known. As Papadopoulos emphasises, the Swiss referendum includes two elements, one '*von oben*' and one '*von unten*'. Obligatory referenda on constitutional matters belong to the former category, whereas the latter refers to the ability of citizen groups to demand a referendum on any issue – the *optional referendum*.

Mandatory referenda have occurred often because the expansion of the federal government tasks in relation to the welfare state, for instance, has often necessitated a minor constitutional revision. One would be inclined to conclude that frequent mandatory referenda increase democratic control over policy-making. But one must remember that the level of participation

TABLE 1

PARTICIPATION IN ELECTIONS AND REFERENDA 1919–99 (%)

Year	Elections	Referenda
1919	80.4	56.6
1922	76.4	66.1
1925	76.8	65.7
1928	78.8	61.9
1931	78.8	63.5
1935	78.3	73.5
1939	74.3	58.7
1943	70.0	54.3
1947	72.4	58.8
1951	71.2	52.2
1955	70.1	50.4
1959	68.5	50.2
1963	66.1	44.1
1967	65.7	38.6
1971	56.9	42.9
1975	52.4	41.6
1979	48.0	41.6
1983	48.9	37.7
1987	46.5	42.1
1991	46.0	47.5
1995	42.2	40.5
1999	43.5	41.8

Note: This is an average for the referenda and elections that took place 1.5 years before or after
the time point.

Source: Statistisches Jahrbuch der Schweiz, 2000, p.446.

in referenda has been low, often below 50 per cent of those eligible to vote.
The figures presented in Table 1 should be enough to shatter any naive
view of Swiss politics as a populist democracy according to Rousseau's
ideas.

Looking at the secular trend in Figure 1 concerning participation in
referenda, one observes that less than half of those eligible now participate.
Perhaps one would dare to suggest a drastic institutional outcome
hypothesis: namely that too many referenda kill democracy. In any case,
Switzerland is far from a populist democracy because of the heavy
institutionalisation of its politics.

Another much-discussed institutional outcome of the Swiss referendum
democracy is the hypothesis of a fundamental impact of the referendum
upon the other institutions, especially the grand coalition. The threat of
popular action by means of the referendum institutions has led to a strong

reinforcement of consensus-making by the political elite in the country, as argued Leonhard Neidhart in *Plebiszität und pluralitäre Demokratie*, published in 1970. This is a most interesting institutional-outcome interpretation of Swiss politics that recurs in several of the contributions here.

The Neidhart argument focuses upon a contradiction between the referendum being a majoritarian mechanism and the grand coalition, which is a unanimity mechanism. It goes against any image of Switzerland as having reached full institutional integration, meaning that all the six institutions pull in the same direction. This would make the country come close to an ideal-type of consociational democracy with harmony between the various institutional parts. Yet the Neidhart argument points in the direction of *institutional contradiction*.

This conclusion takes us to another interpretation of the Swiss referendum, which states that the general spirit of the Swiss political institutions – the emphasis upon the capacity to veto decisions – bends the referendum to serve exactly this function. Thus, the Swiss referendum is less a set of rules for majorities to get things done but rather a blocking mechanism for minorities to undo decisions by majorities. This is the institutional hypothesis suggested by Heidrun Abromeit in *Interessenvermittlung zwischen Konkurrenz und Konkordanz* (1993). It emphasises less institutional contradiction, but more how one institution is made to operate in accordance with the other institutions – *institutional bending*.

Papadopoulos himself offers yet another hypothesis, namely that the way the referendum is employed today is conducive to a legitimation crisis in Swiss politics. Although he underlines the inefficiencies that the frequent employment of the referendum results in, one could also link the *legitimation crisis* argument with the two other hypotheses. Too much blocking incapacitates democracy, which is true of many contradictions.

What could limit the disruptive consequences of the referendum institution? One possibility is that judicial review expands in Switzerland, which entails that judges take over some of the powers of the people to decide in politics. The institutions for a future judicialisation of Swiss politics can easily be created, as the Federal Supreme Court in Lausanne has long experience with handling constitutional disputes between the federal government and the cantons. But what is missing is the permission for the court to test generally the constitutionality of referendum decisions.

Here we have a most interesting case of *institutional compatibility*, often not recognised in the comparative literature. The lack of strong judicial review in Switzerland is clearly compatible with the nature of its referendum institutions, as judges could not be allowed to test the correctness of the will of the people – at least not comprehensively. The absence of legal review in Switzerland has not been fully taken into account in general models of political institutions and decision-making.

Yet, as Rothmayr shows, the process of institutional change in Switzerland is in accordance with world trends, meaning increased judicialisation of politics. However, she also maintains that Switzerland is in no way prepared to move to a full acceptance of judicial review. The Federal Supreme Court has moved to emphasise more and more the protection of individual liberties, linking up with general developments in Europe in relation to the Council of Europe of which Switzerland is a member. Its European Convention of Human Rights of 1950 as well as its application in numerous cases at the European Court on Human Rights has served as somewhat of a model for the Lausanne court. When the new constitution came into force in April 1999, then this up-dating of the 1874 constitution did not involve any change of the restriction upon using judicial review as a political instrument. At the same time, the new constitution reinforces individual rights by making the list of basic rights more compact than earlier. It includes both negative and positive rights in the language of jurisprudence.

Here one may argue that we have a case of *institutional consistency*, that is, the strong referendum negates the full utilisation of judicial review. It seems much more difficult to argue that the referendum, logically speaking, requires federalism. But federalism is, of course, compatible with the referendum, especially as the latter is based upon both federal and cantonal referenda.

Linder and Vatter extensively cover the recent changes in Swiss federalism in their contribution. If direct democracy is the primary political institution in Switzerland, then surely federalism is the second major institution in the country. One can have direct democracy and unitarism as well as federalism and only representative democracy. Thus, these two institutions are in principle independent of each other, but how do they interact in the Swiss case? Swiss federalism is one of the few examples of real federalism in the world, as many countries operate federalism merely on paper.

The federal government in Bern has increased considerably in power and resources over the years. Thus, it operates a number of policies in relation to both service provision and social security. However, the slow process of centralisation has not been a continuous movement, as the cantons have formidable blocking powers. Swiss centralisation requires constitutional changes, which in turn must be backed by both Chambers of Parliament and a majority of the population as well as of the cantons. It is the Swiss federal dualism which creates this inertia. The basically *dualistic nature* of Swiss federalism dates back to the establishment of the federation in 1848 when a very limited list of competences were provided to central government by the provinces. As more competences have been given to the federal government over time, Swiss federalism has developed more towards German federalism, that is, *co-operative federalism*. Given the size of the Swiss public sector, it is not surprising that all three players – the federal government, the cantons and the communes – are involved and interlocked in policy-making and policy implementation. In terms of resources allocated these three players are of about equal size.

Yet Swiss federalism does not breathe smoothly. The fundamental problem is the population imbalance between the cantons, which are of very different sizes (see Table 2). Although there is a complex policy of fiscal federalism in Switzerland involving transfers of money from the federal government to the cantons as well as from one canton to another, these imbalances have become such a burden for the system that Linder and Vatter call for a major revision of the cantonal division. What is taking place in Switzerland is not that the very large cantons dominate the small ones, but rather the opposite problem, namely free-riding by the small ones on the large ones. The small rural cantons are overrepresented in the Senate whereas the large urban cantons carry the major burden of the Swiss welfare state, especially in relation to higher education and advanced health care. However, the small cantons are sometimes too small to be able take on tasks that the bigger cantons can handle. This is the paradoxical situation today, as the small cantons guard their power but fail sometimes to deliver on their obligations.

It is true that Swiss federalism has experienced changes that move it away from strict dualism between the centre and the provinces. Several programmes are jointly financed or executed. The cantons have put up a variety of intercantonal collaboration mechanisms, seeking even to influence the EU directly and not via Bern. Yet Swiss federalism, however unbalanced it may be today, still involves a strong dose of decentralisation typical of classical dualist federalism. The various cantons display numerous differences in public law, including education, health care and income maintenance.

TABLE 2
POPULATION IN THE CANTONS, 1998

Kanton / Canton	Total			SWISS			FOREIGNERS		
	Total	Men	Women	Total	Men	Women	Total	Men	Women
Zürich ZH	1,187,609	578,481	609,128	936,093	442,231	493,862	251,516	136,250	115,266
Bern BE	941,144	457,061	484,083	832,936	398,578	434,358	108,208	58,483	49,725
Luzern LU	343,254	169,109	174,145	292,925	142,074	150,851	50,329	27,035	23,294
Uri UR	35,612	17,818	17,794	32,609	16,236	16,373	3,003	1,582	1,421
Schwyz SZ	126,479	63,561	62,918	107,239	53,367	53,872	19,240	10,194	9,046
Obwalden	31,989	15,984	16,005	28,608	14,201	14,407	3,381	1,783	1,598
Nidwalden, NW	37,320	18,847	18,473	33,862	16,980	16,882	3,458	1,867	1,591
Glarus GL	38,698	19,091	19,607	31,029	14,964	16,065	7,669	4,127	3,542
Zug, ZG	96,517	48,028	48,489	78,442	38,353	40,089	18,075	9,675	8,400
Fribourg FR	232,086	115,516	116,570	199,953	98,240	101,713	32,133	17,276	14,857
Solothurn SO	243,450	119,813	123,637	204,461	98,951	105,510	38,989	20,862	18,127
Basel-Stadt BS	190,505	89,714	100,791	140,242	62,844	77,398	50,263	26,870	23,393
Basel-LandschafT BL	256,761	125,902	130,859	214,972	103,420	111,552	41,789	22,482	19,307
Schaffhausen SH	73,725	35,657	38,068	59,424	28,021	31,403	14,301	7,636	6,665
Appenzell A.Rh. AR	53,816	26,661	27,155	46,240	22,663	23,577	7,576	3,998	3,578
Appenzell I.Rh. AI	14,873	7,570	7,303	13,350	6,794	6,556	1,523	776	747
St. Gallen SG	444,891	219,405	225,486	359,936	173,882	186,054	84,955	45,523	39,432
Graubünden GR	186,118	91,879	94,239	161,142	78,065	83,077	24,976	13,814	11,162
Aargau AG	536,462	266,272	270,190	437,705	213,285	224,420	98,757	52,987	45,770
Thurgau TG	226,479	112,346	114,133	183,484	89,192	94,292	42,995	23,154	19,841
Ticino TI	306,179	146,298	159,881	225,780	103,479	122,301	80,399	42,819	37,580
Vaud VD	611,613	294,909	316,704	452,159	210,457	241,702	159,454	84,452	75,002
Valais VS	274,458	134,894	139,564	228,847	110,895	117,952	45,611	23,999	21,612
Neuchâtel NE	165,594	79,933	85,661	128,753	59,906	68,847	36,841	20,027	16,814
Genève GE	398,910	189,992	208,918	248,987	112,629	136,358	149,923	77,363	72,560
Jura JU	68,995	33,948	35,047	60,714	29,390	31,324	8,281	4,558	3,723
Switzerland	7,123,537	3,478,689	3,644,848	5,739,892	2,739,097	3,000,795	1,383,645	739,592	644,053

The three players in Swiss federalism – the federal government, the cantons and the communes – are interwoven in the *full line supply* of a welfare state. Armingeon analyses how the Swiss welfare state has step-by-step become increasingly comprehensive, but also more costly. It could be argued that the Swiss welfare state is the most interesting one in the whole OECD world today. It is large, as in Scandinavia, but it also contains clear status distinctions, as in the German model. When it comes to measuring the size of the welfare state and the public sector in general, then it is vital to employ Swiss data, taken from the data bases that are employed for the excellent and well-informed statistical yearbook of the country. This is also the information that is transmitted to, for instance, the OECD statistics, but there have been problems of comparability between these data and those of other countries at the OECD level.

Today Switzerland has a mixed economy where the Tax State takes half the GDP in the form of taxes and social security charges, not counting the user fees for the many public enterprises. This places Switzerland, as Armingeon underlines, well within the continental European welfare-state approach, which is far higher than the so-called liberal welfare regimes in the US, Japan and Australia. More research is needed in order to understand fully the mechanisms that have pushed up public expenditures in Switzerland in the post-war period.

Now, one could be tempted to play the corporatist card when accounting for the growth of government. Somewhat surprisingly, much research has been undertaken on organised interests in Switzerland without arriving at a definitive conclusion whether the country is corporatist or not, or more precisely to measure exactly how much corporatism there actually is. There is a full carpet of economic organisations dating back to the beginning of the century and they receive moderate support from members, but do they really engage in corporatist practices? Trade union density is not as high in Switzerland as in truly corporatist countries such as Scandinavia and Austria. And social partnership interaction is much less frequent. Wages tend increasingly to be set in decentralised forms at the enterprise level. But organised interests within agriculture have been influential in obtaining considerable benefits in the form of public policies of various kinds. When examining the Swiss political economy it is not a Keynsian regime, typical of corporatism, one should look for.

The key player has been the Swiss National Bank, conducting monetarist policies and underlining price stability ahead of full employment. It employs its independence from the federal government to attempt a rule-based monetary policy that is displayed and made credible through consistent actions over time. There is a very close connection in the Swiss data between the expansion of M1 and the growth in total output. Switzerland may have had a low rate of economic growth since the oil crises, but the country has not experienced stagflation or high inflation. Perhaps the Swiss political economy is an example of successful monetarism.

According to the 1999 constitution, the federal government rules the country. This is no normal government, as it rests upon an institution transplanted into Switzerland by no less than Napoleon, when he took the country and created 'La République Helvétique' in 1798. Klöti examines the meaning of directorate government in Switzerland today, the model institution itself dating back to Le Directoire between 1794 and 1799 in France. The Swiss federal government is an example of successful *collegiado*, or executive government. This seven-headed presidency should in theory concentrate upon administration, effectuating the decisions of Parliament and the people. In reality, we have institutional bending as the threat of the optional referendum forces the government to engage in very lengthy procedures for arriving at a unanimous decision that groups cannot then veto or change in a referendum.

However, what has made the directorate model of an executive serve the general Swiss spirit of amicable agreement is one special institution that very much guides the federal government, namely *la formule magique*. This is an implicit institution and not a constitutional one. It operates as follows today: two seats for the Radicals, Christian Democrats and Social Democrats each and one seat for the Swiss People's Party. The Swiss grand coalition has been considered the most typical expression of the system's orientation towards *Konkordanz* and not competition. Why has this permanent grand coalition made Switzerland the country with the most stable government in the world?

Two interpretations come to one mind. Either one points at the social fragmentation of the country in the form of ethnic and religious cleavages as in traditional consociational theory. But are they really manifest today as they were in the past? Or one resorts to the Neidhart argument again. In the former approach the grand coalition is an *institutional response* to the structure of society. From the latter perspective it is an *offsetting institution* against the referendum, especially the optional part and the peoples' initiative.

It should be pointed that the legitimacy of the grand coalition should not be taken for granted. It is far from considered a *sacred institution*. The rising

power of Blocher's Swiss Populist Party, SVP, may result in the termination
of the grand coalition, as the other parties may not wish to render the SVP
two government seats. What maintains the grand coalition is more the weak
party system, where no clear government alternatives can been seen in the
form of natural coalition partners.

In Swiss public debate a third explanation has frequently occurred,
namely that the grand coalitions prevent minorities from engaging in so-
called rent-seeking against the public purse. Thus, bringing almost all on
board makes it impossible for minorities to form temporary coalitions in
order to benefit themselves and their electorates. Unanimity promotes
efficiency, economists state. However, Klöti emphasises that the federal
government is 'big government', spending 50 billion CHF on its 30,000
employees, not including social security. This is about 13 per cent of
GDP. The Swiss political institutions may promote concord, if not
overthrown by the referendum, but they have not contained the strong
forces of modernity and post-modernity that result in the growth of
government.

Much effort has been devoted to making the central government operate
more efficiently and transparently. Thus, the structure of the federal
bureaucracy has been changed and a number of public enterprises have been
partially privatised or incorporated. The ambition to arrive at agreement
bordering on unanimity still hampers the federal government, as it calls for
extremely long processes of decision-making where all players are involved
somehow. Perhaps the time is right for Switzerland to sample competitive
democracy, for instance by abandoning the magic formula which enchants
fewer and fewer.

Kriesi draws the full implications of the main Swiss institutions for the
parliament in Bern. Here we have an example of *institutional deficit*, as the
Swiss Parliament is seriously weakened especially by the referendum but
also by the grand coalition. The parliament in Bern is made up of semi-
professional politicians without access to the resources that would make
them comparable to the federal government and its bureaucracy.
Organisations may be the outcome of their rule. They would then constitute
an *institutional reflex* of their rules. The Swiss Parliament operates in a way
that is 50 per cent decided by its rules. Thus, its federal chamber has a
centre-to-right majority because of the majoritarian elections to the Senate.
It gets its work done through a system of some 230 committees in both
chambers. When the two chambers deliver different opinions, then an
arbitration committee including the relevant chamber committees is set up.
This method of negotiation in successive rounds works well, as a common

standpoint is often arrived at. The Swiss parliament creates laws when it is instructed to do so, but it is the federal government that runs the show, although not quite completely.

Organisations may behave in such a way that they avoid their rules. They would then establish an *institutional lacuna*. The Swiss Parliament elects the seven-headed Swiss president, and it cannot fire this hydra during the normal four-year term in office. But it does not have to support all the proposals of the federal government, even when they come from a *Parteigenosse*. When there is little scope for manoeuvre for an organisation according to its formal institution, then it may decide to create space by its *own fiat*. Politics is not only institutions but also the will to hold power.

Furthermore, the centre players in Swiss politics, the Radicals (or Free Democrats) and the Christian Democrats, seek to control parliament. And they certainly succeed most of the time, because the left flank of the Social Democrats and the right wing of the Swiss People's Party have nothing in common except being Swiss. Thus, they cannot combine to challenge the centre parties. In addition, the small remaining parties do not succeed in becoming *pivot* parties. The median player in both chambers is located somewhere among the Radicals and the Christian Democrats – the old established parties of Switzerland with which one may now also count the Social Democrats. Despite its low degree of professionalisation, the Swiss Parliament has asserted its independence *vis-à-vis* the government in recent years, perhaps because of the strong links between parliamentarians and organised interests in Switzerland. It could do even better if its resources were reinforced or should a parliamentary regime be introduced at the same time as the magic formula is given up.

We need to say something about the players in the Swiss game, and not simply examine rules and their consequences. The political parties handle much of Swiss politics despite the optional referendum, although they are not as strong as parties in other West European democracies. Ladner here presents an insightful analysis of the Swiss party system with its peculiar bifurcation between the national and the provincial levels. One would be inclined to believe that Swiss political institutions shape the party system completely. They do exert influence, but there is more happening, changing the party system.

The federalist system, the referendum and the grand coalition are all institutions that weaken the party system. The magic formula concentrates national political power in the four parties, which receive about 80 per cent of the votes. The remaining parties are hardly players at the national level to be taken into account from one election to another, with the possible exception of the Green Party. However, the four parties in the grand coalition do not rule the country, because national politics is one thing and cantonal politics another. There are many more parties active on the cantonal scene, and the four parties have different election results in the various cantons. In addition, the referendum on the national and the cantonal scenes puts real brakes upon any ambition to create party government.

Swiss political parties have been looked upon as belonging to a type called '*milizsystem*', meaning that politicians tend to be non-professional politicians. Evidently, Swiss politicians are not American entrepreneur politicians, and Swiss political parties are not European down-to-earth disciplined parties. Yet they are not merely amateurs. The expansion of the public sector has one outcome that benefits the parties, namely an abundance of positions in committees and on boards. The parties manage to pay for their activities without any substantial state allocation – no mean achievement.

Much of what affects the Swiss political parties apparently derives from changes in their relationships with the electorate – changes which are occurring in any post-modern advanced society. Thus, the link between party and social group is slowly but surely weakening. Social heterogeneity is no longer the only or main reason for party choice. Thus, volatility is increasing and the populist SVP can achieve gains among both the right and left wings of the electorate. Vatter shows that despite all variation between the cantons themselves as well as between the cantons and the national party system convergence is taking place. Thus, the politics of the regional and the national levels are becoming similar.

FROM DECENTRALISATION, DIRECT DEMOCRACY AND GRAND
COALITION TO WHAT?

It is obvious that Switzerland today is very much reflecting upon its special institutions in order to make institutional changes in the future. The analysis of the Swiss institutions and their consequences is interesting not only for those who have a special liking for this small but economically very important country in the centre of Europe. But an understanding of Swiss politics and its strong institutional structures is also vital for comparative institutional analysis in political science. The political institutions of Switzerland constitute a mix seen nowhere else. What is unique about them is not each and every element, because those can be found elsewhere. It is the *institutional constellation* that matters. And the key problem is interpreting which institutions prevail and, so to speak, 'bend' the others. It seems, in fact, to be the direct referendum and its many facets that has the upper hand, and, at least in principle, it is not a consensus institution.

Some regard Swiss political institutions as a peculiar atavism mirroring the splendid isolation of the country, being neither a member of the UN nor the EU. Others have attempted to distil just one and only one institutional logic out of them. Thus, the consociational scholars have regarded Switzerland as the most consensual of all the democracies despite the fact that its most characteristic institution is the referendum – a majoritarian mechanism of decision-making – and despite the fact it lacks strong judicial review – the Lijphart position. Another very influential interpretation states that the referendum in reality has the effect of reinforcing bargaining and compromise among the elites to avoid an optional referendum – the Neidhart position. Finally, the referendum is only one additional veto mechanism in a system of decision-making that is heavily orientated towards unanimity – the Abromeit position.

Perhaps a more promising theory of Swiss politics is that we should give up the idea of *one* uniformity or of a common core among the institutions. There is more in the nature of contradictions in the way these institutions interact and work themselves out in practice. They do not constitute a coherent ideal-type. Thus, institutional reform is possible.

Swiss political institutions have at least *three* basic features in dealing with the basic forces: (1) strong political decentralisation as an historical legacy; (2) the most vital direct democracy in the world; (3) grand coalition governments at both the federal and cantonal levels. How these forces – decentralisation, direct democracy and *Konkordanz* – function in practice depends upon how Swiss institutions interact: by mutual reinforcement, contradictions or independence:

The originality of Swiss political institutions reflects, on the one hand, their origins. There is strong *institutional path-dependency* in Swiss politics. The extreme petrification of power is mainly a feudal legacy. Here we have a classical example of the theory of Max Weber that one tends to forget about, namely the constitutional implications of West European feudalism. The constitutional state is historically linked with the distribution of power in the feudal system. Switzerland was merely a set of feudalities in the Holy Roman–German Empire, but these fiefs protected their feudal rights with such success that they made themselves independent 1648. The device used was the interfeudal federation. However, the originality of the political institutions is not just strong historical legacy. The referendum mechanism derives its power from the extremely consequential manner in which it is applied. Not only does it span all the possible variations of a referendum, but it is also applied consistently at both the federal and cantonal level in a driven, if not to say in an absurd manner. The rules that were devised to offer a check upon politics have fallen prey to the use of opportunism, hoping that a low turnout will make it possible for a minority to defeat any majority.

Thus, Switzerland combines real decentralisation (RD) – its feudal legacy – and direct democracy (DD) – its modern feature, as well as *Konkordanz* or the grand coalition (K). The combination of these – RD, DD and K – goes a long way to explain the logic of the institutions. One may wish to draw also upon a *political culture* of amicable agreements. The mix – RD, DD and K – is highly appropriate in recognising the differences among the cantons – the old fiefs. Remember that referendum democracy is most frequently used at the cantonal level. The culture of mutual understanding and ambition towards unanimity could be interpreted as the cement of society, which holds all the parts together, despite the social heterogeneity of society. When social cleavages lose much of their relevance, then has perhaps *Konkordanz* played out its unifying function?

Analysing how these institutions operate in the 1990s, this volume focuses on the political and social outcomes as well as discussing the possibility of institutional reform. This is the common element, but each author tackles these questions about institutional performance in the manner to which his or her own research has led. The key questions include: What have been the results of these institutions? Is political behaviour of elites and ordinary citizens - at the federal, cantonal and communal levels - an outcome of these institutions? Is the operation of these six institutions in the process of undergoing major change?

The institutional outcomes include a mixture of both blessings and drawbacks. Thus, we have the fragmented party system as well as the low participation in elections and referenda. Moreover, there are too many veto players, but still a rather low level of judicialisation of politics. The federal government is still more like an autonomous executive committee, seeking to achieve unanimity, rather than a cabinet of political parties responding to the competitive logic of representative democracy.

Discussing the possibility of institutional reform, one wonders whether these political institutions work well today. Do the institutions need to be changed: *institutional sclerosis* versus *institutional adaptation*? Which institutional reforms would be the most urgent? Less direct democracy and more judicial intervention or legal review – such as an Ombudsman? Are the cantons optimal units for service provision or do cantons have to be merged? Should there be a stronger and more political role for the federal government in Bern? A parliamentary system of government instead of the special form of Swiss presidentialism? No more grand coalitions, but instead more competitive democracy?

All the contributions in this volume focus upon how these political institutions have worked and how the impact they have had upon the political system and society. And each assesses the present trends towards change. Thus, the centrality of the referendum could wane in the future as judicial review increases and as Switzerland accepts more EU regulations. Federalism has already been caught in a process of centralisation, which is likely to continue. The federal government looks more like a cabinet than a trust, and the corporatist framework faces difficulties when Switzerland is coping more actively with globalisation, which entails a reconsideration of its 'splendid isolation' policy. The *formule magique* appears to be in need of change because of its negative consequences upon the level of political contestation and competition in the country.

Yet Switzerland remains essentially a real decentralised federation, a feature which the independent Central Bank reinforces with its successful monetarist policy. The frequent use of referenda is the second characteristic of the political system, which bends the operation of the other institutions. And it counterbalances the institutions like the grand coalition and quasi-corporatism, which are conducive to *Konkordanz*. A referendum is basically not a consensual mechanism, because it introduces democratic struggle into the amicable agreement: The referendum implies contestation, transparency and simple majority outcomes. However, it may be transformed into yet another veto mechanism by the institutional logic of the entire set-up of institutions. It cannot be emphasised enough that Swiss politics lacks one powerful veto player in democratic politics today, namely judges or powerful ombudsmen.

Together with direct democracy and federalism, the rule of neutrality belongs to the core of the institutional design. While only a traditional means of Swiss foreign policy, the neutrality rule has strongly contributed to the 'uniqueness' of the political system. It has no doubt been strictly implemented, as Switzerland remains outside not only Nato but also the United Nations. But this institution has not helped the country position itself in relation to West European integration. It remains here only to refer to the elegant analysis by Dupont and Sciarini which, using a rational choice framework, draws the implications of domestic politics for foreign policy-making. They analyse the entire process of interaction between the federal government and the EEC, EFTA and the EU, focusing on the preferences of the government as constrained by the domestic institutions. And they venture to suggest that any full-scale integration – economically and politically – of Switzerland into Western Europe may first have to await institutional change within the country.

Switzerland remains puzzling with respect to neo-corporatism. Thus, one may focus on the organisation (structure) of labour rather than business, or one may deal with the type of institutional arrangements between the state, the unions and business. This makes for a balanced view of corporatism in Switzerland, as business is strongly structured and centralised, whereas the union structure is fragmented. Corporatist interest organisation seems strongest in agriculture. The major organisation is still the Union suisse des paysans (USP, Schweizerischer Bauernverband). It was stronger up to the late 1980s, but there are now two dissident organisations: the VKMB (in the German-speaking cantons) and the Union des producteurs suisses (UPS, mostly in the French-speaking regions). Both defend small and medium-sized farms, including organic production, and both are still much weaker than the main organisation. At the end of the 1980s, Swiss agricultural policy was still much influenced by the experience of the Second World War, but the situation has changed dramatically since then. Under internal pressure (popular initiatives) and – especially – external pressure (Uruguay-Round, European integration) a reform was launched, which is still ongoing, mixing ecology and market.

The political economy of the Swiss National Bank is successful monetarism. Yet economists have argued that the tight monetary policy conducted by the Swiss National Bank has had negative side-effects. Thus, the priority granted to price stability is often said to be the cause of the low economic growth rate since the 1970s. The main reason why unemployment did not increase in the late 1970s and 1980s was that Swiss firms sent thousands of foreign workers home. Had Switzerland not had the option to 'export' unemployment, the negative consequences of tight monetary policy would have been much greater. In the early 1990s, the Swiss National Bank again acted myopically, this argument continues, focusing too strongly on price stability – but this time it was no longer possible to send foreign workers home. Hence the sharp increase in unemployment. However, the existence of a generous system of unemployment benefits also played a role in the increase in unemployment. Monetarist policy is only credible when it is adhered to strictly.

Consensual Government in a Heterogeneous Polity

ULRICH KLÖTI

At all times and in all countries, the art of government has been one of the most challenging and exciting. In Switzerland, an extremely heterogeneous and culturally diverse country, it is particularly difficult to exercise this function. Since 1848, when the modern Swiss federation was founded, this task has always been entrusted to the Federal Council, a committee consisting of seven members. According to article 174 of the constitution: 'The Federal Council is the supreme governing and executive authority of the Confederation', a formula that was, in fact, only introduced during the 1960s and reflects the growing importance of governments in democratic polities. In the classical tradition of continental European law, governments were seen mainly as executive authorities. In the second part of the twentieth century, however, this vision began to change: government functions henceforth included the anticipation of new developments, planning and policy making.

The following account assesses the extent to which the Federal Council is able to realise the aims of the constitution, and analyses the structures and procedures of Swiss government along three dimensions: first, the institutional distribution of powers and responsibilities, and, in particular, the relationships between government, parliament, and direct democracy; second, the great stability of the Federal Council in terms of the theory of consensual government; third, the most important principles of internal organisation: the departmental structure, 'collegial government', and lack of a head of government. Finally, the latest developments in an ongoing reform process are assessed.

INSTITUTIONAL APPROACH: PRESIDENTIAL OR PARLIAMENTARY SYSTEM?

At first sight, the position of the government in the political system is rather strong. The Federal Council is equipped with a wide range of formal

Ulrich Klöti, University of Zurich

powers. According to articles 180 to 187 of the constitution, it is responsible for a great deal more than just the direction of the federal administration and the implementation of federal legislation. While its main task is to formulate primary goals and means of governmental policy and to plan and co-ordinate the activities of the state, the Federal Council also has legislative responsibilities; it proposes federal laws and decrees. In addition, it administers external affairs, and signs and ratifies contracts which must subsequently be approved by the parliament. It also ensures both the external and internal security of the country, co-operates with the cantons, and ensures that they respect federal law. This list of powers – which is not exhaustive – is expressed in concrete terms through federal legislation.[1]

The position of the government is further strengthened by the fact that its members are elected for a full term of four years. Although the Federal Council is elected by the Federal Assembly (the two chambers of parliament, acting jointly) rather than directly by the people, there can be no motion of no confidence. That is to say, the Council need not resign when it is defeated in parliament, or in a referendum. Furthermore, re-election after four years takes place almost automatically and early retirement on political grounds is extremely rare. The average term of office is, thus, relatively long. It has been around nine years, that is, more than two full terms of office. These averages have declined only slightly during recent years, despite the great burden of responsibility that rests on the shoulders of the members of the federal government. One might, in conclusion, observe that the position of an individual member of the Federal Council is pretty safe. His or her popularity can, of course, be measured by the number of votes they receive at re-election and these numbers do vary considerably. Nonetheless, the bottom line is that no member faces a serious threat of not being re-elected.[2]

The relationship between government and parliament has changed considerably since the nineteenth century. At that time the distribution of powers was simple and clear: parliament was responsible for legislation, and the Federal Council was the executive. After World War II, however, this clear-cut separation of powers was no longer operational. Law experts now agree that in many respects government and parliament co-operate and share powers. There is still considerable discussion regarding the distribution of powers, but in recent years parliament has clearly strengthened its relative position. With the introduction of new public management, it has asked for the right to intervene in executive affairs. In addition, after the (negative) vote on the European Economic Area (EEA) in 1992, it has had more say in foreign policy.[3] In many ways, however, the

Federal Council still dominates parliament. As in other countries, government is more flexible and better informed thanks to the support of the highly specialised administration. This connection is further reinforced in Switzerland by the fact that members of parliament still work on a non-professional, honorary basis which prevents them from having a continuous and tight control over government and the administration.

The Federal Council has a wide range of powers and is in a comparatively strong position *vis-à-vis* parliament. Nevertheless, considering the wider institutional context, the Swiss federal government's scope of action is rather limited. First, the provisions of direct democracy affect all stages of the decision-making process.[4] Amendments to and revisions of the constitution, as well as multilateral international agreements, are subject to a mandatory referendum. Federal laws, generally binding federal decrees and important international treaties face the possibility of an optional referendum. For this reason, the federal government not only has to look for a majority in parliament, but it must also seek a consensus among major interest groups and regional governments in order to ensure popular support for a particular bill. It cannot, in other words, behave as a hierarchically superior power but, rather, must manage a long and complex bargaining process. In addition, once a consensus is reached, it can be overthrown by a popular initiative. This requires the signatures of 100,000 Swiss citizens, and may seek the introduction, repeal or modification of specified articles of the constitution; it gives the voter the possibility of asking new political questions and exerting pressure on established forces, especially the federal government.

Second, it must be kept in mind that Switzerland is a Federation.[5] Each of the three levels of government – federal, cantonal and communal authorities – can decide more or less autonomously on certain matters. According to the Swiss constitution, the 26 cantons exercise all rights not explicitly entrusted to the federal power. In addition, the cantons are responsible for most of the implementation of federal law. Thus, although the cantons participate in the policy-making process at the federal level (as we have shown), federal programmes are not implemented in the same way throughout the country, nor does the federal government have any means of sanctioning exceptional applications. In recent times, an important process of centralisation has become evident, and this has increased the steering capacities of the federal government. Nevertheless, it does not offer the Federal Council a hierarchically superior position. Its role, rather, might be better described as that of the central partner in a complex network of intergovernmental relations. Leadership comes to mean mediating between conflicting interests, not issuing orders.

All in all, the Swiss system of governance can be classified neither as presidential nor as parliamentary. The fixed term of four years without any possibility of a vote of no-confidence is clearly a presidential element. The same can be said of the different 'checks and balances' resulting from direct democracy, federal institutions and of the subtle distribution of powers.[6] Yet the fact that the government is elected by parliament can be considered as a parliamentary element. The idea that the government consists of seven equal members and that the parliament is not fully professionalised are typically Swiss features. The extent to which the political system is decentralised and the extensive use of the instruments of direct democracy make the Swiss model of governance unique.

THE POLITICAL PERSPECTIVE: CONSENSUS OR COMPETITION?

The Swiss government is characterised by high stability. Since 1959, the seven seats on the Federal Council have been distributed amongst the four major parties according to the so-called 'magic formula', an informal arrangement that could, somewhat paradoxically, be changed at any election of the Federal Council. The Radical Democrats, the Social Democrats and the Christian Democrats each have two seats, whilst the Swiss People's Party (the Democratic Union of the Centre in French and Italian) has one seat.

The idea of proportional representation was introduced in the Federal Council following a long historical process of integration. From 1848 to the end of the nineteenth century, all seven members of the government came from the same party, the Radical Democrats; they held a majority in parliament until 1919, when proportional representation was first introduced in national elections. It was not until 1891 that the first member of the Catholic Conservative Party (now Christian Democratic Party) joined the government. In 1919, the party received a second seat. In 1929, the first member of the Party of Farmers, Tradespeople and Citizens, renamed the Swiss People's Party in 1971, joined; there has always been one member of the Swiss People's Party in government since. The Social Democrats did not gain a share in governmental responsibility until 1943, under the distinct threat of World War II and following long negotiations.

In recent years, the 'magic formula' of 1959 has been called into question. Following two strongly disputed elections[7] to the Federal Council – when the members proposed by the group of Social Democrats were rejected by a bourgeois majority in the Federal Assembly – left-wing circles within the Social Democratic Party have been arguing in favour of a return to opposition. These demands, however, have not been successful within their own party. Similarly, in 1995, right-wing groups within the Radical Democratic Party tried to change the magic formula and throw the Social Democrats out of government, an attempt that was not successful either.

In the 1999 federal parliamentary election, the Swiss People's Party made large gains, becoming the strongest party in terms of the percentage of the votes in the process.[8] The party accordingly claimed a second seat in government. Initially, the idea was to gain that seat at the expense of the weakest governing party, the Christian Democrats,[9] a position that would have been justifiable along the lines of proportional representation. In a subsequent move, however, the party's leadership decided to enter into a competition with the Social Democrats, primarily because its most prominent member, national councillor Christoph Blocher, was standing for office against the socialist Minister of the Interior, Ruth Dreifuss. The acting minister was re-elected by a large margin, but the new distribution of power in parliament has clearly provoked a discussion on the party-political composition of the Swiss government.

A number of other claims to proportionality exist alongside that of the parties. For federalist reasons, the most important criteria relate to the cantons. Article 175 of the constitution states that not more than one member of the Federal Council may be elected from the same canton. This rule is frequently contested because in certain cases it has been difficult to find an individual who is capable of doing the job and who does not come from a canton that is already represented. In addition, there is an unwritten rule that at least two federal councillors should come from non-German-speaking cantons. Linguistic and regional representation remain an important element in government elections. Since 1848, the cantons of Vaud, Ticino, Neuchâtel, Thurgau and Zug have been overrepresented, while Zurich, Geneva and Basle have been under-represented. The three largest cantons, Zurich, Bern and Vaud have had virtually permanent representation. Until recently, religion also played an important role in the election of a federal councillor. This, however, is no longer the case.

Since the introduction of the women's vote at the federal level in 1971, gender has played an important role at election time. The first woman, Elisabeth Kopp, a Radical Democrat, was only elected in 1984. Since 1999, however, there have been two women in government, Ruth Dreifuss, a Social Democrat, and Ruth Metzler, a Christian Democrat.

Considering all the different criteria together – party, language, region, gender – it is difficult not to conclude that the possibility of real choice is small. If only one member of the government is to be elected, he or she must come from a particular party, and a specific region. Furthermore, he or she may not come from the same canton as a member who is already in office, must be of the right sex, and has to speak the appropriate language. To say nothing of the general characteristics that are required of anyone who undertakes responsibilities within the collegial system: leadership, negotiating skills, forcefulness and a readiness to compromise. Game theory predicts that a person who fulfils all these requirements simply does not exist. If this is true, then objective criteria prevail over personal characteristics.

One result of this complicated set of requirements is that the electors, that is, the members of the Federal Assembly, tend to concentrate their attention on personalities well known to them. In the last few years they have made their selections almost exclusively from within their own ranks. This has led, not surprisingly, to the fact that most federal councillors have reached the respectable age of about 50 to 55 by the time of their election. There has been only one significant exception to this rule: in 1999, Ruth Metzler was only 35 years old when she was elected and she was not a member of the federal parliament.[10]

The system of proportional representation in government did not come to Switzerland by accident. Rather, it is an expression of the consensual system of Swiss government. For a long time, Switzerland has been considered a paradigmatic case of consociationalism. The literature classifies Switzerland, alongside the Netherlands, Belgium and Austria as being amongst those countries that have systems of mutual accommodation.[11] The Swiss have coined a special term for this model: they call it 'concordance' (*Konkordanz* in German).

A consensual system is characterised by the fact that decisions are not made according to a rule of majority, but rather in terms of a long process of negotiation and deliberation, including all relevant actors. The idea of seeking a far-reaching consensus – instead of quickly finding a majority – is deeply embedded in the Swiss political culture. Historically, it goes back to the political structures of the cantons prior to the foundation of the federation in 1848, and, going back even further, to the peace treaties after the religious wars in the seventeenth century.[12]

A working consensual government presupposes at least three elements.[13] The parties in government should co-operate in good faith in a coalition based on a treaty. Minorities should be taken into consideration adequately in all instances, and proportionality should guarantee a full representation of all parts of society. The Swiss model of governance meets two out of the three conditions. Federalism is the institutional element that balances out the different regions in culturally and economically heterogeneous Switzerland. Proportional representation ensures that all major cantons send representatives of several parties to the National Council in Bern. The result is a multi-party system that does not allow for the formation of single-party majorities. It has become commonplace in Swiss political science that direct democracy enhances 'concordance' government. Groups that might subsequently initiate referenda capable of undermining policies approved by parliament have been gradually allowed access to the Federal Council. In this way, their interests have been factored into the early stages of the policy-making dialogue.[14]

However, one element is lacking in the list of prerequisites for successful consensual government: the Swiss 'grand coalition' has never been based on any treaty among the four parties involved. To be sure, there are regular talks between the members of the Federal Council and the presidents of the four parties. But the results of these discussions are not binding on anyone. The Federal Council continues to make fully autonomous decisions and the parties feel free to oppose government policies as they please. In recent years, the Social Democrats and the Swiss People's Party have become adept at playing the double game of being part of the government and the opposition at the same time. This strategy has offered dividends at election-time, when both have been strengthened at the expense of the two other parties; the latter were left alone to defend unpopular governmental actions.

Despite its lengthy evolution, the Swiss system of 'concordance' has come under pressure in recent years. Together with a highly decentralised federalism, it has been accused of being a hindrance to effective government. The system, in particular, seems to prevent executive authorities from rising to new challenges, acting immediately and adequately in the case of previously unencountered problems, and developing innovative policies. Several political scientists and economists have even favoured a change to a more competitive parliamentary system of government.[15] Recent empirical analyses have, however, disproved the thesis relating to the poor effectiveness of consensual democracies,[16] but the issue has remained at the forefront of discussion on the Swiss Federal Council.

The system of 'concordance' has also been called into question from a different perspective. Historically speaking, the Swiss consensual system has been particularly successful in accommodating different minority groups. Catholics, Socialists, linguistic communities, and small cantons have all been successfully integrated through representation in the Federal Council. During the last decade of the twentieth century, however, a new

cleavage seems to have been gaining importance. It emerged in the context
of the debate on the relationship between Switzerland and the European
Union – an issue which initially culminated in the vote on the European
Economic Area (EEA) in 1992 – and was embodied in a new national and
conservative movement. The focal point for this movement is the Swiss
People's Party, under the leadership of the president of Zurich's cantonal
party, Christoph Blocher. By the end of the 1990s, it had succeeded in
absorbing most of the traditional national forces, at least in the German-
speaking part of the country, and had become the strongest Swiss party.
Until the end of 2000, the party was represented in the Federal Council by
Adolph Ogi, but, significantly, he did not defend the ideas and policies of
the dominant national-conservative wing of his party. Thus, it is not an
exaggeration to say that a significant minority of Swiss citizens have not
been represented in government recently.

Will this situation lead to a turning away from 'concordance' and bring
about a classical, competitive parliamentary system to Switzerland? This is
improbable. Instead, the issue of nationalist-conservative tendencies versus
internationalist-modernist preferences will be decided in a series of votes on
individual initiatives and referenda. Following a lengthy period of
opposition, the conservative movement will itself be integrated by being
offered a seat of its own on the Federal Council. In this manner, the current
stresses on concordance will be reduced. The system will probably continue
to operate on a consensual basis even in the Federal Council. We assume, in
sum, that Switzerland's traditional political culture will most likely survive
this temporary upheaval.

A MANAGERIAL APPROACH: COLLEGIAL OR DEPARTMENTAL SYSTEM?

This section analyses the functioning of the Swiss government from a
managerial perspective. It asks what the guiding principles are for the
internal decision-making process and the management of the federal
bureaucracy.

The first institutional element which has to be emphasised in this context
is collegiality. According to the constitution, the Federal Council exercises
corporate authority. This means that it is collectively responsible for
governmental activities as well as the entire federal administration. Most of
the decisions are not made by a single minister but by the Federal Council
as a body. To be sure, unanimity cannot be reached in each case, but
intensive discussions and elaborate preliminary consultation procedures

generally guarantee a broad consensus of the seven members of government. Federal councillors occupy identical legal positions in this decision-making process. Even the President of the Confederation – one of the seven members of the council – carries no special power. He or she is elected by the Federal Assembly for one year only. His or her office, in turn, is limited primarily to functions of representation. The chairperson presides over the meetings of the government, but does not have the 'directive' power of a prime minister in a parliamentary system. The President can be considered a *primus inter pares* (first among equals) without leading or co-ordinating capacities. A government head with supreme powers who can make policy decisions does not exist in Switzerland.[17]

The principle of collegiality has evident advantages provided it works correctly. First, it prevents a concentration of power. In a highly heterogeneous society it is important that no single person (or any single group) stand at the top of the state for a lengthy period. The collegial system, in this sense, is an institutional guarantee for pluralism. It also increases the quality of decision-making as the experience and know-how of several persons are brought together in government. Finally, it offers a definitive forum for co-ordination. If long and cumbersome consultation processes do not result in a workable compromise, the collegial government can take decisions in a setting in which all aspects of a policy question are fairly represented.

In practice, the disadvantages of collegiality have become increasingly important over the past decade. The reciprocal control of power can result in mutual obstruction and blocked decision-making processes. Good solutions are more difficult to reach because the Federal Council no longer discusses the needs of different groups in society but, rather, narrow departmental and administrative positions. Negative co-ordination prevails and members of government value the interests of their departments more highly than joint solutions. Routine procedures and incrementalism dominate over innovation.[18] More and more often, members of the government do not observe the implicit rules of the game.

The negative effects of collegiality increase the importance of the second guiding principle of organisation of the Swiss government: departmentalism. The constitution states in Article 175 that the functions of the Federal Council should be distributed amongst its individual members. As the Federal Council consists of precisely seven members, seven departments have been set up (see Appendix for organisation chart). These departments prepare and implement all of the Federal Council's business, and also carry out any other tasks that may be legally delegated to them. The practical effect of this arrangement is that the whole spectrum of government operations must be undertaken by the seven ministries. One member of the government may be responsible for communications as well as energy, transport and environmental protection, whilst another attends to foreign trade, industrial and labour matters, agriculture and housing. Meanwhile, one of their colleagues is responsible for culture, education and research, as well as health and social insurance.

The structure of government described above has two major organisational consequences. First, departmentalisation makes a delegation of competences to lower levels of the administration inevitable. Together with the considerable growth of federal tasks this has lead to an increasing differentiation within the federal bureaucracy.[19] As we have shown, the horizontal subdivision is limited to seven departments. Therefore a vertical structure with no fewer than seven different levels has been set up. At the top, we find the department, directed by a member of the Federal Council. So-called groups – including, for example, the Group for Science and Research in the Department of the Interior – may be directly subordinated to an individual member of government. The most important organisational unit, the office, follows at the third level. Important offices are further subdivided into major and minor divisions. In large offices, the classical section constitutes the sixth level, whereas in small units the hierarchy is limited to the department, the offices and the sections. Finally, large sections are even subdivided into smaller units at the seventh level. Given structures of this nature, the official channels to the top become extraordinarily long; the system does not correspond to the principle of 'flat hierarchies' propagated in most modern business administrations and New Public Management textbooks.

Second, the Swiss federal administration has developed time-consuming decision-making procedures.[20] Decisions of the Federal Council are always preceded by long preparatory processes in which all those interested in an issue can participate. Most decisions have to pass at least two procedural stages. In the initial step an inter-departmental consultation at the level of the offices takes place. The office having overall responsibility for a business has to submit its proposal to all of the other offices concerned, giving them a chance to make a statement on the matter. The second step, another consultation known as 'co-reporting', is organised at the level of the departments. Each department head proposing a motion must concurrently open a written consultation with his six colleagues. This lengthy process can last for several months; it is designed to allow for a clarification of the positions of the members of government and relieves some of the strain in the meetings of the Federal Council. In this way, the government can concentrate on any remaining disagreements in controversial matters. Only a small proportion of the roughly 3,000 decisions taken by the Federal Council every year is not resolved in the two preparatory consultation procedures.

The organisational structure and the decision-making procedures partly compensate for the problems caused by the collegial system of government. Nevertheless, a basic tension between the principles of collegiality and of departmentalism remains. From a strictly managerial perspective one could suggest that the head of the government co-ordinates the different departmental interests and makes final decisions. For political reasons relating to proportional representation, however, the collegial system must be maintained. As we have shown in the previous section, political considerations prevail in Switzerland.

REFORM

In light of the difficulties discussed above, it is not surprising that the structures of the Swiss system of government have come under pressure. Criticisms from academics came as early as the 1960s.[21] Since that time, three major developments have aggravated the situation: first, the government's scope of action has grown dramatically. Federal outlays have risen from 1.5 billion in 1950 to almost 50 billion Swiss francs in 2000, and the number of employees in the core administration has doubled, now reaching nearly 30,000. Increases of a comparable scale can be seen in the number of pages of federal laws and regulations with which the government must contend. Second, and more important, the government is responsible for numerous new policy fields and is confronted with more complex and interrelated problems. Co-operation and co-ordination have become a more demanding task. Finally, almost all Swiss problems have an international dimension. International relations are by no means limited to the Department of Foreign Affairs or to the Defence Department. Bilateral and multilateral negotiations have become important in most policy areas. This trend cannot be reversed even though Switzerland continues to stay outside the European Union.

In the last 30 years two major attempts at government reform have been undertaken. The first reform initiative was undertaken in the early 1970s. The goals of that 'reform of government and administration' were twofold: (1) to relieve the Federal Council from its heavy workload, and (2) to provide it with more time for inter-departmental and collegial aspects of government.[22] The results of the reform process were modest. The secretary-generals of the departments were charged with some new staff functions and the Federal Chancery was transformed from a simple typing, recording, and translating office into a modern staff for the Federal Council. Basic changes in the structure of the federal government, however, were not agreed upon.

At the beginning of the 1990s, the disadvantages of the existing system became more evident and yet another reform process was launched. Several initiatives from members of all major parties in parliament asked that the Federal Council analyse and review all aspects of the structure, organisation and leadership of government. The Federal Council charged a small but prominent working-group with a mandate 'to evaluate the federal system of government and to develop scenarios for reform'.[23] In sum, the reform processes initiated in the 1990s are distinguished by two characteristics: reform of the system of government in the first place and, secondly, reform of public administration.

The reform of public administration has proved to be far-reaching and quite successful. First, in line with the international mood, managerialism has been implemented in parts of the federal public administration. Second, the organisation of offices and departments of the federal administration has become more flexible. Some offices have been merged or grouped in larger units, and others have been assigned to different departments. This has reduced the control span of the department heads. It has not, however, changed the scope of the Federal Council's task as a whole. Third, and most important in the long run, the large state enterprises (including the post office, telecommunications and federal railways) have been partially privatised. This has reduced the workload of the federal government at the operational level.

At the same time, the process of governmental reform has not produced any substantial results, despite the fact that a prominent working-group presented several alternative models of government.[24] Two of them were nothing but a brief description of existing systems of government: one summarised the essentials of a parliamentary democracy wherein a prime minister heads a non-fixed number of cabinet members, and a parliamentary opposition controls government. The second one simply depicted the presidential democracy of the USA with its separation of powers and system of 'checks and balances'. These two models were rejected almost immediately by the Federal Council and later by the Federal Assembly; they seemed to contradict the basic elements of Swiss democracy, concordance and the principle of collegial government. The main reason was that neither an office of prime minister nor that of a president could be proportionalised.

In a second step, an alternative model that proposed increasing the number of federal councillors and thus the number of departments to nine or 11 was eliminated. It would have solved several structural problems and would have made room for some specialisation of the ministers. However, the directorial function of a president would have had to be strengthened in order to provide for some leadership in a larger government. This would have interfered with the principle of collegiality that could not be given up for the political reasons already mentioned.

A model of government at two levels is all that currently remains in the political debate. A small collegial body of five (or seven) would be responsible for the functions of government *per se*. It would have to deal with political questions at a strategic level. At a lower operational and tactical level, 11 to 18 junior ministers would have to take care of the administrative units, organised along purely functional considerations. The junior ministers would be nominated by the Federal Council.

After 150 years of the Swiss Federation, a reform of the structure of government seems to be inevitable. Innovations need not be revolutionary. The requirements for election concerning language, region, gender and career could be relaxed without any revision of the constitution. Even the 'magic formula' could be changed without giving up the advantages of a consensual political culture of concordance. For these types of reform, the only thing needed is the necessary political will of the parties and parliament.

A basic reform of the constitutional provisions for the Swiss government will be far more difficult to achieve. Those who profit from the existing structures will, of course, defend them. Nobody can guarantee that new institutions bring better solutions to the policy problems of the future. As Switzerland is not really a country in a deep economic crisis, one would expect a majority of citizens to prefer the status quo. And finally, as long as the acting Federal Council does not really favour structural reform, nothing will happen. Therefore, we can expect that the structures and procedures of government and administration depicted here will persist – with all their contradictions – well into the twenty-first century.

APPENDIX

ORGANISATION OF THE FEDERAL ADMINISTRATION

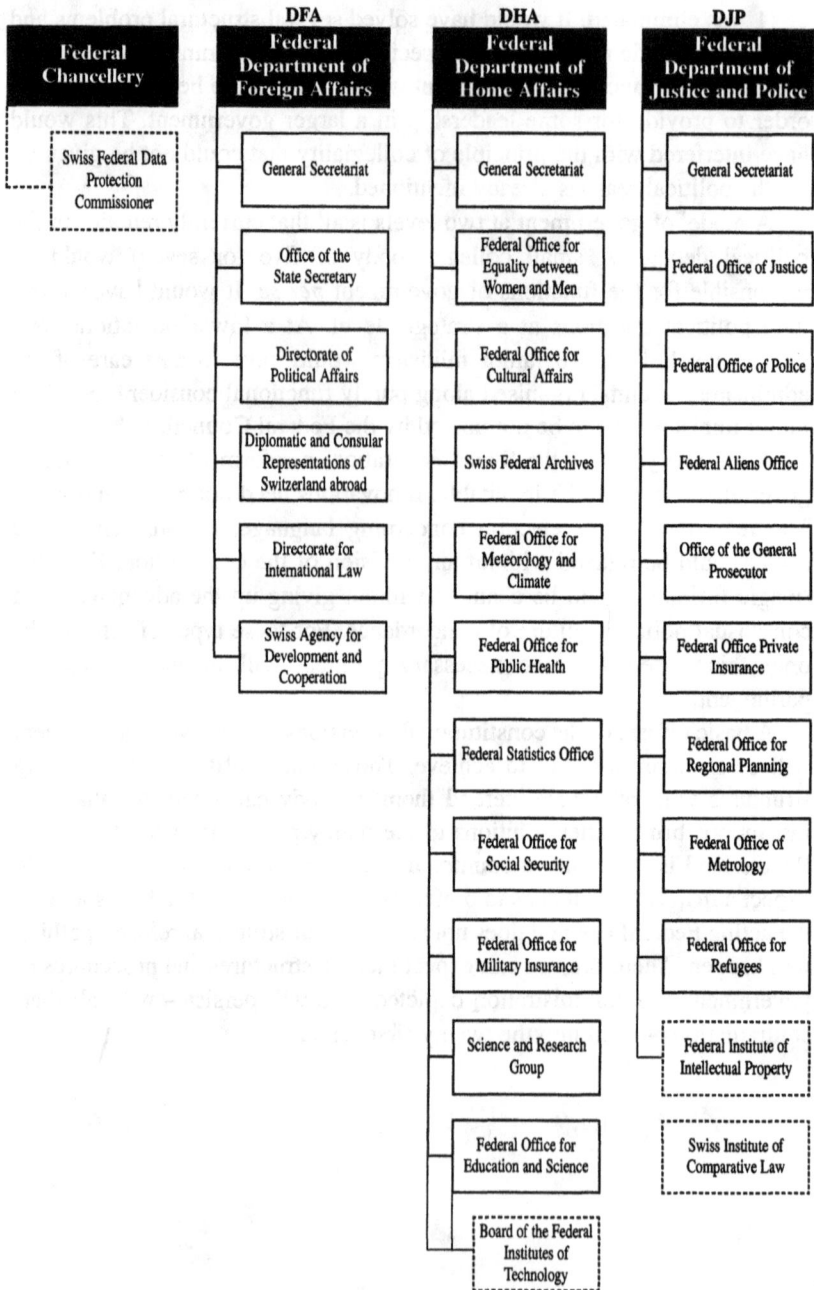

	DFA	**DHA**	**DJP**
Federal Chancellery	**Federal Department of Foreign Affairs**	**Federal Department of Home Affairs**	**Federal Department of Justice and Police**
Swiss Federal Data Protection Commissioner	General Secretariat	General Secretariat	General Secretariat
	Office of the State Secretary	Federal Office for Equality between Women and Men	Federal Office of Justice
	Directorate of Political Affairs	Federal Office for Cultural Affairs	Federal Office of Police
	Diplomatic and Consular Representations of Switzerland abroad	Swiss Federal Archives	Federal Aliens Office
	Directorate for International Law	Federal Office for Meteorology and Climate	Office of the General Prosecutor
	Swiss Agency for Development and Cooperation	Federal Office for Public Health	Federal Office Private Insurance
		Federal Statistics Office	Federal Office for Regional Planning
		Federal Office for Social Security	Federal Office of Metrology
		Federal Office for Military Insurance	Federal Office for Refugees
		Science and Research Group	Federal Institute of Intellectual Property
		Federal Office for Education and Science	Swiss Institute of Comparative Law
		Board of the Federal Institutes of Technology	

APPENDIX (Continued)

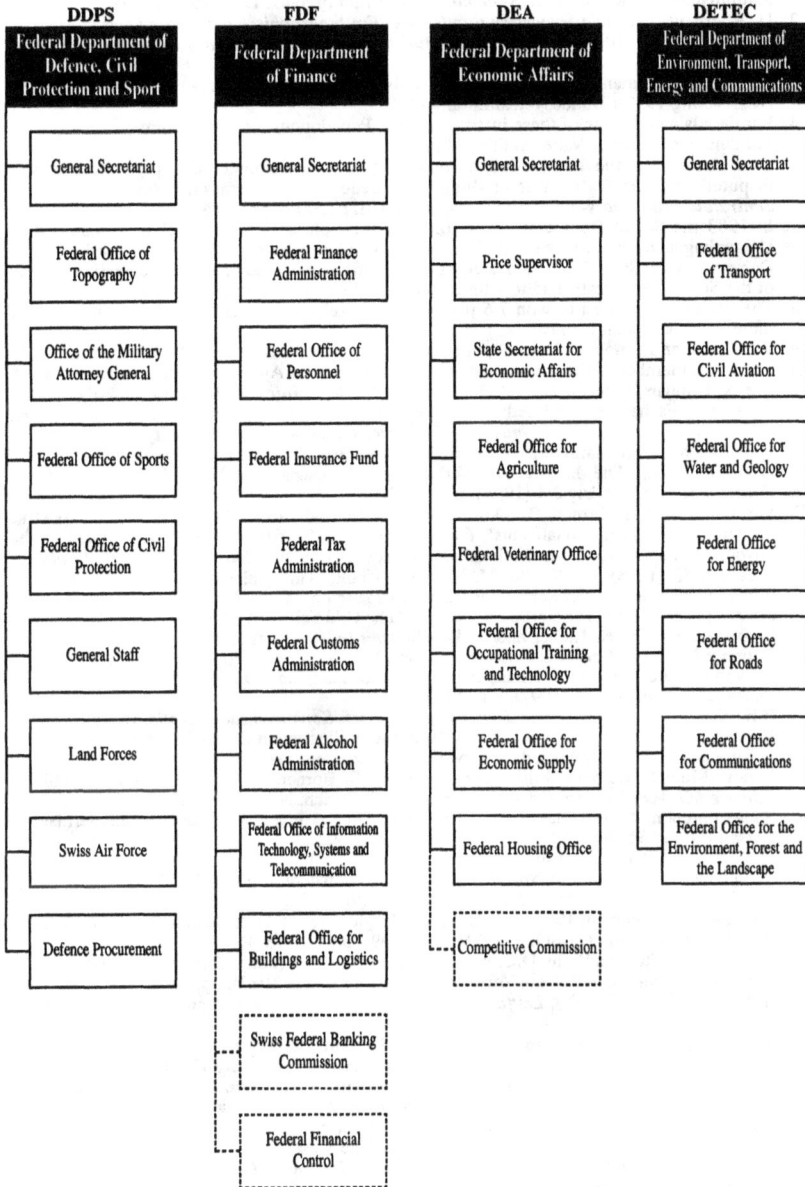

DDPS	FDF	DEA	DETEC
Federal Department of Defence, Civil Protection and Sport	**Federal Department of Finance**	**Federal Department of Economic Affairs**	**Federal Department of Environment, Transport, Energy and Communications**
General Secretariat	General Secretariat	General Secretariat	General Secretariat
Federal Office of Topography	Federal Finance Administration	Price Supervisor	Federal Office of Transport
Office of the Military Attorney General	Federal Office of Personnel	State Secretariat for Economic Affairs	Federal Office for Civil Aviation
Federal Office of Sports	Federal Insurance Fund	Federal Office for Agriculture	Federal Office for Water and Geology
Federal Office of Civil Protection	Federal Tax Administration	Federal Veterinary Office	Federal Office for Energy
General Staff	Federal Customs Administration	Federal Office for Occupational Training and Technology	Federal Office for Roads
Land Forces	Federal Alcohol Administration	Federal Office for Economic Supply	Federal Office for Communications
Swiss Air Force	Federal Office of Information Technology, Systems and Telecommunication	Federal Housing Office	Federal Office for the Environment, Forest and the Landscape
Defence Procurement	Federal Office for Buildings and Logistics	Competitive Commission	
	Swiss Federal Banking Commission		
	Federal Financial Control		

NOTES

1. The most important points are regulated in the 'Law on the Organisation of Government and Administration' (RVOG), see *Systematic Collection of Swiss Law*, SR 172.010.
2. U. Altermatt (ed.), *Die Schweizer Bundesräte. Ein biographisches Lexikon* (Zurich/Munich: Artemis 1991); J. Blondel, *Government Ministers in the Contemporary World* (London: Sage 1995).
3. R. Lüthi, 'Parlament', in U. Klöti *et al.* (eds.), *Handbuch der Schweizer Politik* (Zurich: NZZ-Verlag 1997); Bundesversammlung (1997).
4. For details and the use of these instruments see Papadopoulos in this volume.
5. For details see Linder/Vatter in this volume.
6. Graf shows that the distribution of powers among government and parliament is still disputed. M. Graf, 'Gewaltenteilung und neue Bundesverfassung', *Schweizerisches Zentralblatt für Staats- und Verwaltungsrecht* 101/1 (2000), pp.1–15.
7. In 1983 the Social Democrats were foiled in their plans to have the first woman, Lilian Uchtenhagen, elected to the Federal Council. The other three parties voted for another Social Democrat, Otto Stich. Ten years later, Francis Matthey who had been elected against the will of the Social Democrats, had to withdraw and make room for Ruth Dreifuss.
8. The Swiss People's Party won 7.6 per cent and reached 22.5 per cent of the vote, slightly more than the Social Democrats.
9. The Christian Democrats lost 0.9 per cent and fell to an all-time low of 15.9 per cent.
10. She was a member of the government of the tiny canton of Appenzell Innerrhoden, however.
11. See A. Lijphart, 'Consociational Democracy', *World Politics* 21/2 (1969), pp.207–25. The early analysis has been refined: A. Lijphart, *Democracies. Patterns of Majoritarian and Consensus Government in Twenty-One Countries* (London: Yale University Press 1984).
12. Lehmbruch used the latin term of '*amicabilis compositio*' for the peace of Westfalia in 1648. G. Lehmbruch, 'Die korporative Verhandlungsdemokratie in Westmitteleuropa', *Swiss Political Science Review* 2/4 (1996), pp.19–41.
13. We follow here H. Keman, 'Konkordanzdemokratie und Korporatismus aus der Perspektive eines rationalen Institutionalismus', *PVS* 3 (1996), pp.494–516. See also M. Bogaards, 'The Favourable Factors for Consociational Democracy: A Review', *European Journal of Political Research* 33 (1998), pp.475–96; M. Brändle, 'Konkordanz gleich Konvergenz? Die Links-Rechts-Positionierung der Schweizer Bundesratsparteien', *Swiss Political Science Review* 5/1 (1999), pp.11–30; and P. Sciarini and S. Hug, 'The Odd Fellow: Parties and Consociationalism in Switzerland', in K. Luther and K. Deschouwer (eds.), *Party Elites in Divided Societeies. Political Parties in Consociationalism* (London/New York: Routledge 1999), pp.134–62.
14. A. Vatter, 'Die Wechselbeziehungen von Konkordanz- und Direktdemokratie', *Politische Vierteljahresschrift* 38/4 (1997), pp.743–70.
15. R.E. Germann, *Staatsreform: Der Übergang zur Konkurrenzdemokratie* (Bern/Stuttgart/Vienna: Haupt 1994); Y. Papadopoulos, 'Défense et illustration du système parlementaire', in P. Knoepfel and W. Linder (eds.), *Verwaltung, Regierung und Verfassung im Wandel* (Basel/Geneva/Munich: Helbing & Lichtenhahn 1999); S. Borner, A. Brunetti and T. Straubhaar, *Schweiz AG. Vom Sonderfall zum Sanierungsfall?* (Zurich: NZZ-Verlag 1990).
16. K. Armingeon, 'Konkordanzzwänge und Nebenregierungen als Handlungshindernisse?', *Swiss Political Science Review* 2/5 (1996), pp.277–303.
17. See Articles 176 to 178 of the constitution.
18. For a detailed discussion of collegiality see M. Breitenstein, *Reform der Kollegialregierung: Bundesrat und Staatssekretäre in einem zweistufigen Regierungsmodell* (Basel/Frankfurt: Helbing & Lichtenhahn 1993), and U. Klöti, 'Regierung', in U. Klöti *et al.* (eds.), *Handbuch der Schweizer Politik* (Zurich: NZZ-Verlag 1999), pp.170–75.
19. U. Klöti, 'Switzerland', in D.C. Rowat and C. Donald (eds.), *Public Administration in Developed Democracies* (New York/Basel: Marcel Dekker 1987), pp.189–204.
20. Bundesamt für Justiz (ed.), *Leitfaden für die Ausarbeitung von Erlassen des Bundes* (Bern: EDMZ 1995).
21. The problems were summarised in two official reports. See Hongler, *Expertenbericht über Verbesserungen in der Regierungstätigkeit und Verwaltungsführung des Bundesrates* (Bern: Mimeo 1967), and Huber, *Bericht und Gesetzesentwurf der Expertenkommission für die Totalrevision des Bundesgesetzes über die Organisation der Bundesverwaltung* (Bern: EDMZ 1971).
22. See Botschaft zur Reorganisation der Bundesverwaltung, in BBl 1975 I 1453; and U. Klöti, 'Entrenching New Instruments for Goverment: The Case of Switzerland', in C. Campbell and B.G. Peters (eds.), *Organizing Governance, Governing Organizations* (University of Pittsburgh Press 1988), and 'Political Executives and the Struggle to Lead Strategically in Small Federal Systems: Switzerland', *Governance* 3/3 (1990), pp.279–98.
23. See AGFB, *Arbeitspapier zu konkretisierten Reformvorschlägen für das Regierungssystem. Arbeitsgruppe Führungsstrukturen des Bundes* (June 1992).
24. Ibid

How Does Direct Democracy Matter? The Impact of Referendum Votes on Politics and Policy-Making

YANNIS PAPADOPOULOS

DIRECT DEMOCRACY IN THE FEDERAL POLITICAL SYSTEM

Throughout the world, referendum procedures display a wide variety of forms. A majority of European countries and more than one-third of UN members have had some form of referendum in their history. In Switzerland – the country with the largest number of referendums held at the nation level[1] – this variety is highly codified. The referendum has been mandatory for any constitutional change since the beginnings of the federal state in 1848. The domain of mandatory referendums has subsequently been extended to the ratification of major international treaties and for membership in supranational organisations. In addition, constitutional referendums have been held increasingly frequently owing to the constraints of federalism. In federal Switzerland, the growth of central state activities – a typical feature of most modern welfare societies – systematically requires formal approval by a double majority of voters *and* cantons.

The focus of this account is not, however, the consequences of mandatory referendums. Instead it is concerned with referendum mechanisms that result from pressure 'from below', which differentiate Switzerland, Italy at the national level (to a lesser extent), plus several American states from the many other countries with referendum institutions.[2] As a rule, the countries where referendums are used most frequently are those where referendums can be initiated from below. In Switzerland, notwithstanding the increase in mandatory votes (206 since 1848),[3] referendums generated by a petition from below are more than half of the total: 132 optional referendums since the constitutional reform of 1874, and 127 popular initiatives since the reform of 1891.[4]

These referendums share the property of *not* being under the control of the political system.[5] By way of petition, a number of citizens (be it an

Yannis Papadopoulos, University of Lausanne

absolute number or a proportion of the electorate, of voters in a previous election, or suchlike) can, as a rule at any time, decide that an issue should be submitted to a vote. The outcome of this vote is not merely consultative but binding. What matters here is that the initiative for the vote originates in part of the electorate, not in a political institution – the presidency, the government, the majority or even a minority in parliament. Hence, as viewed by those 'above', these referendums cause more uncertainty than referendums which can be anticipated because of constitutional provisions, or those decided in a discretionary way by political bodies: '[t]ypes of popular votes in this category probably raise the most questions and problems regarding the compatibility and integration of the referendum phenomenon with constitutional representative government'.[6] Significantly, Swiss citizens were not granted these referendums by the governing elites. The referendums were introduced into the constitution under pressure from reform movements in the second half of the nineteenth century, after a number of cantons had accumulated some experience with them.

There are two types of referendum 'from below' in Switzerland at the federal level (and others at the cantonal level):[7]

1. the optional referendum (henceforth 'referendum'): if 50,000 voters sign a petition opposing a bill 90 days after its passage in the bicameral Parliament, the bill must then be approved by a majority in a referendum vote in order for the bill to be enforced;

2. the popular initiative (henceforth 'initiative', equivalent to 'propositions' in the United States): if 100,000 signatures are collected within 18 months to propose a constitutional amendment,[8] then a referendum must be held. The outcome will be binding, provided a majority of voters *and* of cantons supports the proposal.

Thus, it appears that referendums and initiatives serve different functions in Switzerland.[9] The optional referendum allows a group of citizens to attempt to overrule an existing decision, whereas the right of initiative enables citizens to put radically new proposals on the agenda. Optional referendums close the legislative process and thus seek to correct 'sins of commission', whereas initiatives open the process, attempting to correct the parliamentary majority's 'sins of omission'.[10] Referendums result in 'votes of control', and initiatives result in 'votes of promotion'.[11] It can be argued that the latter are even less under the control of the system, for their impulse is not conditioned by any prior decision of parliament. Hence, initiatives more strongly constrain the margin left to representatives.

There is little doubt then that '(semi-) direct democracy matters'.[12] It matters when the outcomes of referendum votes are not those desired by the federal government or by a majority of parliamentarians. It matters even when these outcomes are congruent with their wishes, for the voice of the people confers additional legitimacy on policy choices. However, here we should scrutinise the more subtle *indirect* effects of direct democracy and their overall impact on the Swiss political system. On one hand, direct democracy mechanisms that remain uncontrolled are expected to block the choices of the ruling elites (referendum) or to upset their priorities (initiative). These mechanisms can engender governability problems, because they may cause 'irritation' to the political system, as sources of 'noise' impeding its ordinary operation. On the other hand, as viewed 'from below', they are a useful resource likely to modify the power balance in favour of outsiders confined to a marginal position in the official decision-making process.[13] Consequently, established elites and organisations will also, in all likelihood, do their best to influence the outcome of uncontrolled referendums: by making recommendations to the rank-and-file and their sympathisers, by campaigning in the media, and so forth. Yet, the attitudes and behaviour of the populace can always surprise the rulers, making referendums more than a simple reproduction of the balance of forces in parliament. For example, approximately one in four bills rejected by the voters were supported by *all* parties in the federal grand coalition as well as most interest groups, and were opposed solely by very marginal national-populist parties.[14] As a result, those in power often try to erect protective barriers and defensive mechanisms, as a form of risk management, to cope with the uncertainty caused by referendums emanating from below. Thus, individual referendum votes are not only decisive for policy outputs, but also direct democracy as an institution requires that the political system as a whole adjusts to the pressure caused by it.

Political actors do modify their behaviour in response to the challenge of direct democracy. This is by no means a simple, deterministic 'iron law' of direct democracy. There is no mechanistic process, whereby the universal constraints of direct democracy dictate a single appropriate response by political actors: political systems are not 'trivial' mechanisms.[15] Strategies and choices in politics are, more often than not, the outcome of reflection, calculus, routine, inheritance from the past, and so forth, as stated in the vast literature on rational choice, bounded rationality or path dependency. Consequently, similar pressures exerted from below, by virtue of direct-democracy mechanisms, can be interpreted very differently and can trigger diverse responses by actors socialised in different settings, as is shown by comparative research on the issue.[16]

Nevertheless, it can be argued that adaptive behaviour to the challenge of direct democracy has taken three forms in Switzerland. These are the major strategies pursued by elites in order to lessen risks arising from the referendum. The first two strategies aim to *prevent* recourse to direct democracy, the third to *steer* the processes it engenders:

1. Widening the executive formula, to encompass all parties likely to make efficient use of the referendum if not co-opted as partners in the governing coalition (it should be remembered here that inclusive grand coalition governments are typical power-sharing devices in consociational democracies).

2. Anticipating the veto risk by negotiating *ex ante* with opponents to the policy reforms that originate in government or parliament. Bills are amended as early as in a pre-parliamentary phase, to incorporate the claims of '*referendumsfähig*' actors (associations, parties and movements that enjoy a reputation of winning majorities in referendum votes). Alternatively, these bills are simply withdrawn if they encounter too much opposition.

3. Negotiating *ex post* when recourse to direct democracy cannot be prevented. This occurs in the case of initiative promoters whose claims can be partially met in a formal counter-project (a more moderate constitutional amendment also requiring a double-majority referendum vote) or, more frequently, can be met in legislative amendments that will not necessitate a popular vote (unless challenged by an optional referendum).

One section is devoted to each of these strategies, before an examination of whether this institutionalist approach thoroughly captures the dynamics of the Swiss political system, and before conclusions on the validity of the traditional functions of direct democracy today.

THE GRAND COALITION AS A DISINCENTIVE TO USING DIRECT DEMOCRACY

In Switzerland, direct democracy contributed to the advent of consensual practices in spite of, or rather because of, its majoritarian characteristics as a decision mode. Consensual practices have been established to prevent or to moderate the use of direct democracy. This well-established thesis on the impact of the referendum originated with Leonhard Neidhart, in a pioneering work that was neo-institutionalist *avant l'heure*.[17] Following this line of thought, direct democracy is the most important *'Konkordanzwang'*:[18] a constraint that forces political elites to adopt a strategy of co-operation rather than confrontation. In his *Democracies*, Arend Lijphart may have been too hasty in concluding that direct democracy is specific neither to majoritarian nor consensual democracies, though he was right in considering the great variety of its forms that prevents almost all generalisation. Direct democracy is typically a majoritarian device. As a result, where direct democracy is well-established, it may in the long run trigger consensual responses to avoid it, although – as noted earlier – this is by no means necessary.[19]

The first group to make successful and extensive use of the referendum was the Catholic-Conservative Party in the second half of the nineteenth century. Although they managed to keep control over their cantonal strongholds thanks to federalism,[20] the Catholics had been excluded from the central government since their defeat in the *Sonderbund* war and the creation of the Swiss federation in 1848. Hence, the referendum proved to be a useful tool. It enabled them regularly to challenge important decisions of the incumbent Radical Party, which concerned the centralisation of competences and secularisation of society. In 1891, this result, together with the rise of the socialist movement that forced the bourgeoisie to silence its internal contradictions, led the parliament to elect the first Catholic-Conservative member of the collegiate federal executive. Prior experience with coalition government in the cantons (which are frequently laboratories of institutional innovation) helped allay fears about what was an important novelty at the time.

Gradually, through a process of learning and imitation, other parties with a strong referendum power also joined the federal government, leading to the so-called 'magic formula' of seven members. The 'magic formula', unchanged since 1959, safeguards the representation of the four major parties in principle in proportion to their electoral strength: two federal councillors (ministers) for the Radicals (now a right-wing party, mostly representing business interests), the Christian Democrats (ex-Conservatives, mostly based in Catholic cantons), and the Socialists. In addition, there is one member for the Swiss People's Party (SVP, initially an agrarian splinter of the Protestant Radical milieu, but increasingly a nationalist-populist party, and today the strongest party in the country). Parties able to demonstrate a 'blackmailing power' through direct democracy thus managed to convert this into 'coalition power'.[21]

The case of the Socialists, however, shows the limits of this integrative process, and illustrates its non-mechanistic character: 'paths' are not always straightforward in path-dependency patterns. Their first member of the federal government was elected in the middle of World War II in 1943, in an atmosphere of 'holy alliance' between the major social and political forces of the country. Prior to this, the Socialist Party had had to water down its programme dramatically and had made considerable efforts for over a decade to be accepted as a partner in the governing coalition. By 1943, its representation in the Federal Council was similar to that of the People's Party, which was ideologically much closer to the Radical and Conservative incumbents, and had been accepted as a partner much earlier, although it only had half the electoral strength of the Socialists. It was not until 1959 that the Swiss Socialists obtained representation in government proportional to their electoral support. This suggests that, even if rulers 'learned' from their opponents' frequent use of direct democracy, this learning process took considerable time and was also influenced by the ideological profile of those who were to be co-opted.

Notwithstanding these qualifications, the magic formula in turn seems to have had some impact on the practice of direct democracy: since the 1960s, the proportion of bills challenged by referendum has fallen to just seven per cent. In addition, when referendum votes do take place, voters more frequently support government policies. Although only 54 per cent of parliamentary decisions submitted to the vote (mandatory and optional) between 1848 and 1960 survived the challenge, this proportion increased to 72 per cent between 1961 and 1999. This change is particularly striking in the case of bills submitted to referendum by petition. It was not only the proportion of bills challenged that decreased, while the increase in the total number of optional referendums was simply due to increased legislative activity by parliament. Prior to 1960, a majority of bills challenged were rejected by the people (41 out of 65). Subsequently, only a minority of them was rejected (26 out of 67).

What is more, we observe in Switzerland a differentiation between direct and representative democracy.[22] This created a 'fragmentation of political risks':[23] it is possible that the safety valve of direct democracy has prevented opposition parties from gaining more influence in the sphere of electoral competition and of parliamentary politics. This isolating cocoon prevents contagion from the referendum to the representative scene and could help explain the low volatility of the federal party system. To give but one example, the strong support for xenophobic popular initiatives contrasts with the weak electoral support for parties backing these initiatives.[24] The differentiation of the systems of direct and representative democracy has been a major ingredient for the overall integrative role of direct democracy in Swiss politics.

The effects of direct democracy on elite behaviour and on the mechanics of decision processes are not limited to impacts on the composition of the federal executive. 'Governmentalising' opponents to public policies is only the formal aspect of their co-optation, a way to neutralise their veto power by awarding them some influence. Other less formal aspects – albeit strongly consolidated now and no doubt equally, if not more, relevant[25] – accompany this facet of co-optation, and will be surveyed in the next section.

EX ANTE NEGOTIATION AS AN ANTICIPATION OF DIRECT DEMOCRACY

Not only have opposition parties gradually been co-opted into the federal government, but the views of any group considered to be a credible user of direct democracy are considered too. The decision process is long and complex,[26] with a high level of institutional redundancy. Several phases succeed one another, with actors playing 'nested games', seeking in each phase to anticipate the power balance in the next one, particularly in the most decisive referendum phase.

There are several moments when, in a direct or in an indirect manner, the Damoclean sword of the referendum shapes actors' behaviour:

- The decision process often begins with a pre-parliamentary phase, more frequently when decisions seem important. Sometimes, in addition, an expert committee will meet regularly to draft a preliminary version of the bill.[27] Despite the name, the members of these preparatory bodies are primarily representatives of social forces that count. Their activities thus combine the principles of 'intellectual cogitation' and of 'social interaction'.[28] Furthermore, according to interviews given by their members, their work takes place in the shadow of the referendum, whether mandatory (a majority must be obtained) or optional (the referendum would better be avoided).[29] This is not to say that these very respectable experts, who happen to defend particular interests quite openly, would overtly make threats. The experts internalise the 'second face' of power sketched by Peter Bachrach and Morton Baratz in their *Power and Poverty* in a much more subtle way. It leads them to self-censor with respect to actors having blackmail potential – even those not represented on the committee.

- In a substantial number of cases, the pre-parliamentary phase continues beyond the usual informal contacts between the federal bureaucracy and various groups. The process continues with the highly institutionalised 'Vernehmlassungsverfahren', whereby major groups are officially consulted on a first draft of a bill. The outcome of these consultations is then analysed and interpreted by the administration. Even in the absence of conclusive empirical findings, it can be reasonably argued that, the greater an actor's referendum power, the more consideration is given to its support or criticisms.[30] The federal executive must then choose between simply presenting the bill in parliament, amending it, or withdrawing it. The federal executive thereby remains an important filter in the decision process. But perhaps the real power lies in the hands of high bureaucrats who are better able to assess the life chances of a bill, or, ultimately, in the hands of actors with veto power, as a result of the referendum.

• There is another veto point: the federal parliament, where bills are debated before being submitted to a popular vote. The power of parliament is subject to some controversy in Switzerland, since the Federal Assembly makes few amendments to government bills, and only recently has its input into federal legislation grown.[31] But it cannot be said that the parliament merely ratifies decisions made informally in the pre-parliamentary phase. The pre-parliamentary phase cannot perfectly anticipate parliamentary behaviour. Some bills that proved to be very controversial in parliament had undergone intensive pre-parliamentary consultations. This suggests that, when conflict is acute at the outset, consociational procedures do not absorb conflict and that they have reached their limits.[32] More importantly, a simple parliamentary majority is not enough to avoid defeat in a subsequent referendum.[33]

The plurality of veto points makes it all the more necessary to form wide coalitions around reforms. The inevitable consequence is a bias toward incrementalism in policy-making.[34] Stripping Swiss consensual politics of the sacred aura that surrounds it, Franz Lehner and Benno Homann reduce it to attempts at securing parliamentary support *and* popular majorities. Yet this is not an easy task either. Even when a bill is widely supported in parliament, many actors – and sometimes governing parties too – may shift their position in the referendum campaign.[35] As a result, the level of parliamentary consensus has no impact *at all* on a bill's chances of success when challenged by the optional referendum.[36]

In sum, before addressing the systemic impacts of the initiative, we can conclude that the threat of the referendum was quickly perceived as a source of stress and uncertainty. The referendum is more frequently used for 'deterrence' rather than 'incapacitation'' (Jon Elster): preventing a bill from being voted on by parliament instead of vetoing a law already passed by parliament. Integrative devices are crafted to preclude recourse to the referendum by incorporating opponents into the political system in a number of ways. In order to limit the referendum risk, policy designers became very prudent about bold innovations and ambitious reforms. Preventive strategies, such as the '*Vernehmlassung*', which reduce the risk of a challenge by optional referendum, strengthen the influence of distributive coalitions that fear losing their rents. Once again, because the referendum is seldom used, it achieves its impact indirectly rather than directly. This weapon protects entrenched interests, inhibits the achievement of redistributive goals and engenders a pro-status quo bias. This includes not only social measures, but also any policies that entail some form of resource reallocation. Scholars frequently observe a link between consensual polities and conservatism, which they explain by the *de facto* contractual, and not vertical, nature of policy-making. The most commonly cited example is federal regimes that require the additional consent of territorial sub-units in policy-making.[37] However, the referendum imposes similar constraints that make it hard to bring about far-reaching innovations.

The pursuit of compromise was rewarding, however, as only seven per cent of parliamentary bills were challenged by referendum. The increased transaction costs caused by bargaining are thus the price to be paid for anticipating and neutralising the referendum risk. It must be added, however, that this form of consociational decision-making was adopted by the political elites as a reaction to the 'direct-majoritarian'[38] institutions that their predecessors had been forced to establish. Besides, this strategy of referendum avoidance is not always successful. When referendums cannot be avoided, the prospects for bills can be grim. It is also a sign that preventive remedies were not of much use. Alain Valéry Poitry came to the surprising conclusion that bills were more likely to achieve a popular majority when they had *not* been submitted to debate in the pre-parliamentary phase![39] This contention underlines the strong element of unpredictability inherent in the referendum.

EX POST NEGOTIATION AS MANAGEMENT OF DIRECT DEMOCRACY

Avoiding the referendum is clearly a preventative strategy *vis-à-vis* direct democracy. It is badly needed because when a referendum on a bill is requested, the vote takes place with no further possibility for bargaining. Yet the political system has some manoeuvring room with respect to popular initiatives as well. When popular initiatives appear on the agenda, it is proof positive that the government and parliament were unable to anticipate some social demands and thus prevent this occurrence. Initiative pressure is, however, less than is the case with the optional referendum. Experience has shown that initiatives rarely achieve the required double majority of citizens and cantons (only 12 of 127 votes since the end of the nineteenth century). Thus, initiative promoters have less blackmail potential than referendum promoters do. They are typically outsiders, such as environmental movements, trade unions or left-/right-wing militant groups.[40] Nevertheless, initiatives also cause indirect effects. They also trigger negotiations. These, however, occur *ex post*, after the initiative has been deposited with the required 100,000 signatures, not *ex ante*, as is true for attempts to pre-empt a referendum.

A central institutional technology gives rise to the indirect effects of initiatives. The parliamentary majority may to some extent endorse an initiative request,[41] and, in response, the initiative promoters may withdraw their text. Almost one-third of initiatives have been withdrawn by their promoters. It is estimated that the parliament responded in some way to more than half, at least until the end of the 1970s.[42] It is also estimated that one-third of initiatives led to an informal response: a law repealed or amended, or a vote for new regulations. In these cases, half of the initiatives were withdrawn.[43] The same applies to initiatives that resulted in formal counter-projects (constitutional amendments). In other words, most initiative withdrawals can be attributed to a direct or indirect response from parliament, which was acceptable to initiative promoters.[44] Besides, the voters have approved almost all formal counter-projects once the initiative was withdrawn.[45] The systemic effects of initiatives are not restricted to the very few that passed the referendum test.

Overall, we note substantial openness and receptivity to popular initiatives in the political system. There is room for bargaining and giving consideration to the claims formulated by the proponents. Thus, even when the use of direct democracy is not anticipated, the federal elites are not wholly inactive. They have often responded to the initiative pressure, and have reached agreement with initiative promoters. The consequences of managing direct democracy are not the same for initiatives and optional referendums, however. Through their indirect effects, initiatives strengthen the pluralist dimension of the political system. As a rule, they stimulate novel options that would otherwise be neglected or, worse yet, be deliberately ignored.[46] Unlike the referendum, the initiative is an accelerating mechanism. Although we have just noted that this can be the basis for compromise, the initiative originates with a proposal that has circumvented the filters (expert committees, 'Vernehmlassung', bicameralism and the like) of the standard decisional process, which usually water down innovations. Thus, initiatives may upset the priorities set by established elites and may create an arena where the power balance is more favourable to preferences marginally represented elsewhere. This is the mainstream view on the impact of the initiative, a view which has not gone unchallenged in the literature.

Indeed, there is a gloomier side to the integrative capacity of the political system: the initiative deradicalises social movements. Instead of focusing on the systemic effects of the initiative, Rudolf Epple-Gass[47] has adopted the view from the bottom. He holds that initiatives are a double-edged sword that should be considered a constraint upon rather than a resource for social movements. Initiatives fragment claims into single issues, at the expense of global alternatives. What is more, according to this author, it is not true that the content of initiatives is unnegotiated. Although this is formally true, in practice initiative promoters moderate their claims in advance, anticipating that only modest innovations will be sufficiently acceptable to trigger the positive responses referred to above.

Besides, direct democracy restricts the action repertoire of social movements. As a result of organisational bounded rationality and routine, movements find it harder to opt for less familiar, less institutional and less conventional strategies. They rule them out even when these are more profitable to the achievement of their targets.[48] To these negative effects we may add the high costs of signature collection and campaigning, which meet with varying degrees of success. Between 1979 and 1992, no more than 60 of 98 initiatives achieved the threshold of 100,000 signatures.[49] Furthermore, integrative behaviour is also selective in its impact. Right-wing established parties seldom have to resort to initiatives, but when they do they are more likely to withdraw them subsequently. This clearly indicates that insiders have other means of gaining influence and that their blackmail potential through the initiative is higher too.

Finally, not only do the high costs of initiative campaigns deter minor groups from using them, but they also seem to strengthen the oligarchic component of larger organisations. Efficiency requires professionalisation, resulting in the bureaucratisation and centralisation of organisations.[50] Briefly put, the integrative effect of the initiative has its own price in democratic losses: organisational selectivity and some degree of elitism. If we add these considerations to the blackmail potential of established groups capable of threatening an optional referendum, then we come to a view of direct democracy that seriously challenges its emancipatory potential.[51] But this is yet another story ...

THE LIMITATIONS OF THE INSTITUTIONALIST THESIS

In previous sections, it appeared that direct democracy – in the form of referendum or initiative – not only matters directly, but also matters more indirectly. This form of pressure from below led to considerable modifications in elites' behaviour, and, in that sense, Leonhard Neidhart's thesis remains relevant. Nevertheless, the impact of direct democracy on compromise politics ought to be qualified. There is a degree of 'helvetocentrism' in Neidhart's argument, which does not fully capture all the dynamics of compromise politics. As noted earlier, similar mechanisms of direct democracy from below did not result in similar integrative responses in other systems. In addition, a number of countries, including Switzerland, are subject to pressures for concertation that have nothing to do with direct democracy. For example, consociational democracies were characterised by acute cleavages, mainly religious or linguistic. These impose a cooperative ethos on leaders of the various subcultures, necessary to work out agreements to counteract the centrifugal effects of social heterogeneity in these countries.[52]

To be sure, several points still remain to be elucidated in the study of consociational decision-making. Some points require a return to the neo-institutional paradigm, such as the still unexplored role of institutional design in appropriately addressing crucial sources of conflict. Others require familiarity with the dimensions of deliberative democracy.[53] For example, which arguments had more resonance in debates among political leaders, and how did the leaders learn to coexist peacefully? The conceptual lens of consociationalism, however, remains relevant for understanding the origins of compromise-seeking.

In Switzerland, the first major concession by rulers was a constitutional compromise on centralisation in 1848. This compromise took place in the absence of any referendum pressure, because all mechanisms of direct democracy by petition were introduced into the constitution much later. After winning a short civil war against the Catholic-Conservative cantons, the Swiss Radicals (a liberal secular party mainly based in Protestant urban areas that recruited then from the rising bourgeois class) left much power to the cantons. This enabled the defeated Catholic Party to remain a dominant force locally. Although excluded from the federal executive until 1891, the

Catholic Party kept the upper hand in its strongholds: consociationalism appears then much as a strategy for preventing the repeat of past traumas.

It can be argued that the acceptance by radical elites a few decades later of reforms that introduced into the federal constitution provisions for direct democracy 'from below', or the subsequent co-optation of those who successfully resorted to them would have both been impossible without a prior experiential learning of consensual politics.[54] Hanspeter Kriesi and Dominique Wisler[55] attribute the willingness of the Radicals in power to make concessions with respect to direct democracy to yet another condition specific to the Swiss setting: the weakness of coercive resources under control of the central power, that made harder to defeat opponents.

Switzerland also belongs to the grouping (which partially overlaps with consociational democracies) of small states with very open economies that make them vulnerable to the fluctuations of the international environment.[56] Here, the aetiology of compromise-seeking differs considerably from the consociational model. Internal cultural factors no longer matter, but international market constraints do. Being vulnerable to the international economy is thought to force politicians, bureaucrats and representatives of major associations to set up co-operative mechanisms in social-economic policy. Domestic concertation is thought to result in a decisive comparative advantage against competitors.

Consociationalism and this version of corporatism are not mutually exclusive, however, although they are responses to different problems, in different areas of policy-making. Domestic concertation might be easier in countries where elites have learned from a consociational tradition. Arend Lijphart and Michael Crepaz pointed out the parallels between consociationalism and neo-corporatism. Frans Van Waarden went so far as to argue that, for the Netherlands (and this also holds true for Switzerland), there is a causal relation between these two modes of conflict-resolution, which is more than an isomorphism.[57] Thus, a Swiss exceptionalism that is attributed to the peculiarities of domestic institutions like direct democracy must then be qualified.

Moreover, a fair number of institutional arrangements are functionally equivalent to direct democracy by similarly encouraging self-restraint by decision-makers to avoid vetoes. To give one example, consider systems of checks and balances, where parliamentary majorities live under the threat from institutions with a dissuasive blackmail potential, like the presidency or a constitutional court. Ultimately, we do observe social-economic limitations on policy-making, with private business interests exerting their blackmailing power by threatening 'exit', in favour of more propitious national settings ('*Standortkonkurrenz*'). No government will readily ignore that risk.[58] If we take into account these constraints that act as incentives to pragmatism, moderation and compromise-building, then direct democracy is just one more constraint. It increases the deterrent power of actors outside the political system – associations, firms, social movements, and so on – actors who, strictly speaking, would have counted anyway. Switzerland can thus be depicted as a polity where constraints act cumulatively on decision-making, which enhances the pressure for co-operative behaviour.

To be sure, comparative studies also tend to confirm the validity of institutional theses *à la* Neidhart, other things being equal (for example, the standard explanatory variables used in the 'does politics matter?' debate on social-economic policies). According to Ellen Immergut's rigorous survey of health reforms in Switzerland, compared with those in France (during both 4th and 5th Republic) and Sweden,[59] the very liberal and pro-status quo orientation of Swiss health policy results less from an unfavourable balance of power between left and right, than from the cumulative effect of veto points. In this case, the optional referendum was the rescue for opponents defeated in both Chambers of Parliament. Yet this confirmation highlights anew the limits of the virtuous role of direct democracy. This proliferation of veto points can be conducive to policy stalemates, as opponents not incorporated in the decisional procedures are awarded additional chances to block reforms and to impair innovation.[60] It seems that these limits of the integrative potential of direct democracy are increasingly prevalent.

A CHANGING ROLE FOR DIRECT DEMOCRACY?

Unlike Italy or some American states, overall the structural coupling between representative and direct democracy has been harmonious in Switzerland. It is also thanks to the systemic responses to referendum and, to a lesser degree, to initiative pressure that this country can be portrayed as 'a paradigmatic case of political integration' (Karl Deutsch). However, almost all observers criticise the high price that has been paid: a lack of innovative capacity in the political system, slow decision-making, adjustment difficulties – European integration is a case in point[61] – or predominantly piecemeal policies, as demonstrated by health politics studied by Ellen Immergut. The trade-off for these costs has been the system's superior integrative capacities, which, in comparative terms, enjoyed very high levels of mass support until very recently.[62] But are things changing now?

Considering first the fate of direct democracy, we can expect a decline in integrative capacities to result in more bills being challenged by referendum. Yet the optional referendum remains a seldom-used weapon. Notwithstanding a slight increase since 1970 compared to the decade immediately following the advent of the 'magic formula', the proportion of bills challenged holds steady below a threshold of ten per cent. As shown in previous sections, it is true that the most efficient referendums are those that did not take place because government or parliament acceded to the demands of powerful veto groups. Opponents then achieve their aims by other means, as they can merely make threats to use the referendum, without having to carry them out. Although it is hard to say if important legislation was obstructed by such threats, quantitative data do not support the argument of non-decision power. The number of bills voted on in parliament regularly increased, nearly doubling between the 1950s and the 1990s. Stability in the use of the referendum weapon is all the more puzzling as survey data clearly demonstrate that the Swiss federal system underwent a decline of confidence in government and parties, and the emergence of widespread feelings of political alienation.[63] This loss of legitimacy is more severe in Switzerland than in other systems because popular support had dropped from very high levels.

By contrast, the system's integrative capacities *vis-à-vis* popular initiatives seem to have weakened considerably. Since the 1970s, the number of initiatives has doubled. This is due primarily to the increasing complexity and differentiation of Swiss society, which leads to an increase in particularistic demands. Nevertheless, it also illustrates the limits of systemic adaptiveness: fewer issues are being adequately addressed by public authorities. What is more, the proportion of initiatives withdrawn after successful bargaining also decreased: no less than half in the post-war period, but only slightly more than one-quarter since the 1970s (32 of 122). Thus we simultaneously observe more initiatives and fewer satisfactory results (from the promoters' standpoint). A similar polarisation can be observed in the debates on initiatives in parliament. While in the past initiatives were usually rejected by an overwhelming majority of MPs across the political spectrum, they are now accepted by left-wing MPs and rejected by right-wing MPs.[64]

The question remains: why does the left mostly support popular initiatives to promote demands ignored by the right-wing parliamentary majority, without *also* making use of the optional referendum to challenge decisions made by the same majority? The Left–Right conflict in direct democracy is confined to popular initiatives. Between 1987 and 1999, nearly two-thirds of referendum votes with a Left–Right divide in party recommendations were initiatives (23 of a total of 37), which represent less that one-third of the total number of referendums (37 of 111). Almost none of the mandatory referendums (two of a total of 34) were marked by Left–Right conflict. This is hardly surprising given their nature, for a popular vote must take place even in the absence of any opposition. What is more interesting is that less than one-third of optional referendums (12 out of 39) caused a Left–Right conflict.[65] It is hard to explain the Left restricting its action repertoire in this way. Nevertheless, we know that the optional referendum is typically a pro-status quo device. So, when the Left parties disagree with the content of some reforms – finding them too timid, for example – and decide to challenge them by referendum, their only hope is a return to the status quo ante, which may not be desirable.

According to Kriesi,[66] however, the Left has recently started to make more use of the optional referendum as well. The most plausible explanation could be that the late advent of neo-liberal beliefs in Switzerland, combined with influence from outside,[67] unleashed an unprecedented wave of criticism about Swiss inflexibility on the part of mainstream economists as well as strong pressures from business interests and right-wing politicians, in favour of deregulation and liberalisation. As a result, Switzerland has in the last decade embarked upon large-scale changes in federal social-economic policies.[68] The demand for reform comes then predominantly from bourgeois forces, with the Left seeking to defend the former level of welfare measures.[69] It is therefore reasonable to expect that the Left will tend to use the referendum weapon too.

Yet there does not appear to be any confirmation of stronger backing of optional referendums by the Socialist Party. Instead, there are cyclical tendencies. Only during the 1975–79 and 1991–95 legislatures were a significant portion of optional referendums structured around Left–Right conflict. But this portion is not very important (27.3 per cent in both periods). During all other legislatures since 1971, including the last one, the fraction did not exceed 13.6 per cent. What happens is that votes on some recent reforms have split the Left. Soft-liners – among them the Socialist Party – seek compromises. Hard-liners – usually minor parties and associations – are eager to fight reforms through the referendum. Interestingly, reforms that led to a Left opposition in the referendum (like the first attempt to amend labour legislation) failed. In contrast, reforms where compromises had been reached, by combining retrenchment with improvement measures, avoided or survived the referendum obstacle (for example, unemployment insurance reform).[70] Even though the direction of policy change has shifted recently, one thing persists: the optional referendum is likely to split ideological camps into those who are satisfied with the compromises they negotiated previously, and those that find the reforms too ambitious or want to stick with the status quo.[71]

What then is the overall assessment of the systemic role of direct democracy in Switzerland? As noted earlier, systemic responses to the optional referendum have been better able to maintain their integrative role than the responses to popular initiatives. On the whole, however, direct democracy did not prevent the advent of legitimacy problems. Other institutional technologies, like the grand coalition formula, did not perform better in preventing the impressive decline of diffuse support for political elites and parties among the mass public. In addition, the Socialists' participation in government is challenged by part of the Right, and the participation of the increasingly national-populist Schweizerische Volkspartei is disputed by supporters of European integration. Hence, Switzerland is facing a wider crisis in the integrative mechanisms at the centre of its institutional system.

Referendum votes on external relations[72] serve to highlight this crisis. To be sure, they are, in some ways, atypical. Switzerland is increasingly confronted by decisions negotiated abroad on a multilateral basis, and this leaves no further manoeuvring room at the domestic level. The only option is to say 'yes' or 'no' to their ratification. It is no longer possible to search for compromises that would reflect the domestic power balance. In these cases, people are more likely to reject parliamentary decisions and the gap between elite and mass preferences is wider. Opposition to internationalisation comes predominantly from the underdog strata of people who perceive themselves to be losers in the modernisation processes.[73] These referendums are, nevertheless, associated with lines of conflict that seriously undermine internal cohesion, either by weakening links between linguistic communities (the French-speaking Swiss are much less sceptical of European integration than the Swiss Germans) or by undermining prior compromises between economic sectors (namely domestic and export oriented).[74] These votes therefore mirror the decline in the integrative capacity of conflict resolution strategies which had been identified as the necessary cement of social integration in small, culturally divided countries that are open to international economic competition, by both consociational and neo-corporatist theory.

Hence it comes as no surprise that direct democracy is blamed today for isolation and lack of adjustment, not only by economists, but also by some media and politicians too. At the same time, the mass public widely supports direct democracy. This is also quite logical, for it enhances the public's opportunity to control political elites that are no longer trusted.

Direct democracy itself is becoming the object of controversy. People only support reforms of the referendum system that they expect will grant them more power. Interestingly, they believe that the increasing importance of foreign policy issues requires expanding citizens' participation.[75]

Yet elites increasingly believe that direct democracy threatens Switzerland's governability and adaptability to international factors. The government recently tried to increase the number of signatures required for petitioning initiatives and referendums. This measure was buried by a majority of parliamentarians, who knew it was doomed from the start.[76] To be sure, the plethora of veto points makes the system unreformable in practice,[77] but inflexibility has thus far been accepted as the price to be paid for enhanced legitimacy. This consensus is being eroded today. Switzerland is confronted not only by an institutional crisis, but also a 'crisis of crisis management'.[78] When adjustment problems are addressed, political elites find it difficult to overcome a nostalgic popular opposition, and legitimacy deficits thus come to the fore. Conversely, should the political establishment address the legitimacy deficit by, for example, giving a stronger voice to traditionalist opponents, then adjustment problems would no doubt become more acute.

This is indeed a gloomy picture. We note a weakening of the harmonious coupling between direct and representative democracy in Switzerland, and the decline of trade-offs between the outcomes of input- and output-oriented choices.[79] Yet this picture is based on a rather short-term view. A major lesson of Swiss political history is that the long-term virtues of direct democracy in terms of political integration should be kept distinct from its short-term vices. What is more, the former appears as an indirect consequence – a by-product of the learning processes – of the latter. It may be too soon to assess the present capacities of direct democracy and of the Swiss political system as a whole. However, there is also no guarantee that history will repeat itself.

NOTES

The author would like to thank Jan-Erik Lane and Margaret Canovan for their helpful comments.

1. Between 1848, when provisions for referendums were introduced into the federal constitution, and 1993, of the 799 national referendums held in the whole world, 414 national referendums had been held in Switzerland. Since the end of World War II, the Swiss share has increased even more to over two-thirds of the referendums held in the democratic polities studied in A. Lijphart's *Democracies* (New Haven: Yale University Press 1984). Data provided by Trechsel confirm this accelerating trend: approximately half of the votes held in Switzerland between 1848 and 1997 have taken place since the 1970s (see A. Trechsel, 'Volksabstimmungen', in U. Klöti *et al.* (eds.) *Handbuch der schweizerischen Politik* (Zurich: NZZ Verlag 1999), pp.557–88.

2. Provisions for referendums by petition can be found in the constitutions of some other countries, but this weapon is much less used elsewhere. See Y. Papadopoulos, *Démocratie directe* (Paris: Economica 1998), part I, chap. 2: 'Démocratie directe et systèmes politiques contemporains: une analyse comparée (Suisse, Italie, Californie)'.

3. This includes 'counter-projects' formulated by the Federal Assembly as a response to popular initiatives (see below).

4. Unless otherwise noted, data are taken from the web page of the Centre d'études et de documentation sur la démocratie directe (http://c2d.unige.ch/index.msql) at the University of Geneva. All data are accurate as of 6 July 1999, including information on all referendums held before the end of the 1995–99 legislature.

5. Control is one of the dimensions of Gordon Smith's typology of referendums: see his 'The Functional Properties of the Referendum', *European Journal of Political Research* 4/1 (March 1976), pp.1–23. Referendums are strongly controlled by the system when public authorities are able to determine the issues to be decided, the timing of the procedure and whether the vote is to be binding or not.

6. P.V. Uleri, 'Introduction', in M. Gallagher and P.V. Uleri (eds.), *The Referendum Experience in Europe* (London: Macmillan Press 1996), p.6.

7. See the very useful chapter on Switzerland by A. Trechsel and H. Kriesi, 'Switzerland: The Referendum and Initiative as a Centrepiece of the Political System', in Gallagher and Uleri (eds.), *The Referendum Experience in Europe*, pp.185–208. Provisions for direct democracy may vary considerably across cantons. On the whole, referendum practice is much more intensive in the German part of the country: see A. Trechsel and U. Serdült, *Kaleidoskop Volksrechte. Die Institutionen der direkten Demokratie in den schweizerischen Kantonen 1970–1996* (Basel: Helbing & Lichtenhahn 1999).

8. There is no right of initiative for ordinary laws at the federal level. This is mainly a formal limitation, however, which is frequently circumvented by initiative committees whose proposals for constitutional amendments, if accepted, imply to change the laws that are the real target of the initiative proponents.

9. This is not always the case. In California, for example, laws can be abrogated by legislative initiatives and in Italy, the 'referendum abrogativo' indirectly plays a propositional role as well.

10. A. Auer, *Le référendum et l'initiative populaire aux Etats-Unis* (Basel/Paris: Helbing & Lichtenhahn – Economica 1989), pp.14 and 35.

11. Uleri, 'Introduction', pp.10–11.

12. There is a substantial body of literature, and considerable controversy, about the factors that matter in policy-making. I adopt here a perspective that emphasises the impact of institutions, like direct democracy, which is a centrepiece of the political opportunity structure in Switzerland.

13. See Y. Papadopoulos, 'Analysis of Functions and Dysfunctions of Direct Democracy: Top-Down and Bottom-Up Perspectives', *Politics and Society* 23/4 (Dec. 1995), pp.421–48.

14. This depends, in turn, on a number of factors. In a study of all federal referendums held between 1970 and 1996, I found that people regularly follow elites' orientations in economic policy, but less frequently in the fields of foreign policy and immigration, both of which offer fertile soil to nationalists. See Y. Papadopoulos, 'Les mécanismes du vote référendaire en Suisse: l'impact de l'offre politique', *Revue française de sociologie* 37 (1996), pp.5–35. As a rule, many party sympathisers are not very familiar with the voting recommendations of 'their' party and tend to ignore them, not to mention the increasing numbers without any party identification whatsoever. See H. Kriesi, 'Le défi à la démocratie directe posé par les transformations de l'espace public', in Y. Papadopoulos (ed.), *Présent et avenir de la démocratie directe* (Geneva: Georg 1994), pp.31–72. Furthermore, for a number of reasons, ordinary citizens do not behave in the same way as political elites, being embedded in a different communication context and facing a different mix of incentives and threats. See the discussion in part II, chap. 2 ('Autour du débat contemporain entre élitistes et participationnistes') in Papadopoulos, *Démocratie directe*.

15. I refer here to the sociological theory of N. Luhmann: see in English his *The Differentiation of Society* (New York: Columbia University Press 1982).

16. See the chapter of my book on Switzerland, Italy, and California: Papadopoulos, *Démocratie directe*.

17. See his *Plebiszit und pluralitäre Demokratie* (Bern: Francke 1970), and also Carl J. Friedrich's law of anticipated reactions in his *Constitutional Government and Democracy* (Boston: Ginn 1950). Direct democracy also provoked the identification of wider social groups (the petty bourgeoisie, peasants, workers, etc.) to a common set of democratic values: see A. Tanner, 'Direkte Demokratie und soziopolitische Integration des Mittelstandes, der Arbeiterschaft und Bauern in der Schweiz 1830–1914', in Eckart Schremmer (ed.), *Wirtschaftliche und soziale Integration in historischer Sicht* (Stuttgart: Franz Steiner Verlag 1996), pp.184–212.
18. According to R.E. Germann's concept: see his *Staatsreform* (Bern: P. Haupt 1994).
19. In his book, Lijphart only counts the number of referendum votes. This quantitative approach neglects the study of their impact. A more recent article compensates for this shortcoming: 'Changement et continuité dans la théorie consociative', *Revue internationale de politique comparée* 4/3 (Dec. 1997: issue on 'Les démocraties consociatives'), pp.679–97. See especially pp.690–92, where he considers direct democracy in Switzerland as a consociative device. The link between type of political system and effective use of direct democracy came to the fore in an intercantonal comparison: Adrian Vatter concluded that referendums and initiatives are more frequently used as counter-powers by active minorities excluded from the representative system in the more centralised cantons (with a weak communal autonomy) and in the cantons where governments approximate the majoritarian model. See his 'Die Wechselbeziehungen von Konkordanz- und Direkt-demokratie', *Politische Vierteljahresschrift* 38/4 (1997), pp.743–70. These conclusions were, however, qualified in A. Trechsel's recent study of cantonal direct democracy: see his *Feuerwerk Volksrechte. Die Volksabstimmungen in den schweizerischen Kantonen 1970–1996* (Basel/Geneva: Helbing & Lichtenhahn 2000), pp.109–23, 160–63, 182.
20. For the same reason, they were particularly strong in the second Chamber of Parliament, the *Ständerat* (Council of States) where all cantons have equal representation – as in the American Senate – whatever their size.
21. 'Blackmailing' and 'coalition' power are contrasted in G. Sartori's analysis of the role of parties, theoretically inspired by A. Downs' *An Economic Theory of Democracy* (New York: Harper and Row 1957): see his *Parties and Party Systems. A Framework for Analysis* (Cambridge: Cambridge University Press 1976). The Swiss case, however, shows that blackmailing power can be a fungible resource convertible into coalition power. In the sociological literature, blackmailing power is the property of actors who – by virtue of their resources in the form of authority, finance, organisation, information, or whatever – control much uncertainty, and as a result cannot be circumvented. See the seminal work by M. Crozier and E. Friedberg, *L'acteur et le système* (Paris: Eds. du Seuil 1981). Finally, for this power to exist, it has to be acknowledged by decision-makers. In Switzerland, decision-makers were quite frequently unable to anticipate the mobilisational capacities of marginal national-populist movements in direct democracy.
22. Smith, 'The Functional Properties of the Referendum', p.16, uses the metaphor of the 'isolating cocoon'.
23. M. Dobry, *Sociologie des crises politiques* (Paris: Presses de la Fondation nationale des sciences politiques 1986), p.167.
24. The recent electoral successes of the SVP, however, may mark a radically new phenomenon. This electoral success was sustained by intensive use of the initiative and of the referendum to pass national-populist-inspired policies, to veto more generous measures in immigration policy, and to perpetuate Swiss isolationism.
25. Hanspeter Kriesi, for example, contrasts the formal co-optation of the Left – which lacks influence on decisions – with the dominance of an informal 'core': a network of right-wing party members and leaders of economic associations. See his *Le système politique suisse* (Paris: Economica 1998, 2nd edn), chap. 9.
26. The most recent accounts of this process are Y. Papadopoulos, *Les processus de décision fédéraux en Suisse* (Paris: L'Harmattan 1997), and P. Sciarini's chapter 'La formulation de la décision', in Klöti *et al.* (eds.), *Handbuch der schweizerischen Politik*. See also two major works on the overall political system, Kriesi, *Le système politique suisse*, and W. Linder, *Schweizerische Demokratie* (Bern: Haupt 1999), which is a revised and extended version of his *Swiss Democracy* (London: Macmillan Press 1994).

27. See Kriesi, *Le système politique suisse* p. 196, who reinterprets data from the 1970s – the only available so far – collected by A.V. Poitry and presented in his *La fonction d'ordre de l'Etat. Analyse des mécanismes et des déterminants sélectifs dans le processus législatif suisse* (Bern: Peter Lang 1989). Assessment of decisional importance in advance is of course problematic, especially in the Swiss system where ordinary citizens have the final say. According to an index elaborated by E. Gruner and H.P. Hertig in their *Der Stimmbürger und die 'neue' Politik* (Bern: Paul Haupt 1983), pp.409–10, people seem to place more value on a referendum making safety belts compulsory than on one extending the referendum right to international treaties!

28. I refer here to the well-known distinction made by A. Wildavsky in *Speaking Truth to Power. The Art and Craft of Policy Analysis* (Boston: Little Brown and Co. 1979).

29. See R.E. Germann *et al.*, *Experts et commissions de la Confédération* (Lausanne: Presses polytechniques Romandes 1985), again the only study available, with the same problem of data obsolescence.

30. It should be mentioned however that a big business union recently complained that in the '*Vernehmlassung*', the bureaucracy would not weigh positions in proportion to the importance of their advocates. I do not share this criticism. Waelti argues that a similar blackmailing power is awarded to cantons that, in exchange for their cooperation in implementing federal policies, manifest their claims in the consultation phase too. See S. Waelti, 'Institutional Reform of Federalism: Changing the Players rather than the Rules of the Game', *Swiss Political Science Review* 22/2 (Summer 1996), pp.113–41.

31. For a synthesis of recent – albeit fragmentary – findings, see Sciarini, 'La formulation de la décision'. For a discussion of Swiss parliamentary power considering institutional rules and parliamentary resources (for example the so-called '*Milizsystem*' of – at least on paper – non-professional parliamentarians), see Papadopoulos, *Les processus de décision fédéraux en Suisse*, chap. 6.1 ('Dans quelle mesure le Parlement s'acquitte-t-il de ses fonctions?'). R. Lüthi maintains that the Swiss Federal Assembly is comparatively strong in her chapter on 'Parlament', in Klöti *et al.* (eds.), *Handbuch der schweizerischen Politik*, pp.131–57. Annina Jegher reaches similar conclusions regarding recent parliamentary influence on decision-making: see her *Bundesversammlung und Gesetzgebung* (Bern: Haupt 1999).

32. See Sciarini, 'La formulation de la décision'.

33. Even though implementation is rather unpredictable too, especially as federal legislation is usually enforced by the cantons or by non-public bodies, the so-called *parastaatliche Verwaltung*: see the research results presented by W. Linder in *La décision politique en Suisse. Genèse et mise en œuvre de la législation* (Lausanne: Réalités sociales 1987). It is widely believed, however, that the referendum confers additional legitimacy to public policies, reducing thus the risk of implementation conflicts, or that even a negative outcome of a vote is better than taking the risk to trigger mass mobilisation against a law. On the other hand, federalism allows opponents who were defeated in a nation-wide referendum to seek to exploit a more favourable power balance at the cantonal level in the implementation phase.

34. This argument is also used by P. Pierson regarding welfare retrenchment: see his 'Irresistible Forces, Immovable Objects: Post-Industrial Welfare States Confront Permanent Austerity', *Journal of European Public Policy* 5/4 (Dec. 1998), pp.539–60.

35. F. Lehner and B. Homann, 'Consociational Decision-Making and Party Government in Switzerland', in R.S. Katz (ed.), *Party Governments: European and American Experiences* (Berlin: de Gruyter 1987), pp.243–69.

36. P. Sciarini and A. Trechsel, 'Democratie directe en Suisse: l'élite politique victime des droits populaires?', *Swiss Political Science Review* 2/2 (Summer 1996), pp.201–32.

37. See F.W. Scharpf, 'Political Institutions, Decision Styles, and Policy Choices', in R. Czada and A. Windhoff-Héritier (eds.), *Political Choice* (Frankfurt/Boulder: Campus/Westview 1991), pp.28–53.

38. J.S. Fishkin, *Democracy and Deliberation* (New Haven: Yale University Press 1991).

39. See Poitry, *La fonction d'ordre de l'Etat*, pp.328–30.

40. It has been calculated that for 87 initiatives registered between 1974 and 1992, 27 were backed by Green associations, 11 by the Socialist Party and by trade-unions, and eight by national-populist organisations: see K.W. Kobach, *The Referendum: Direct Democracy in Switzerland* (Aldershot: Dartmouth 1993), p.101.

41. See above for the modalities of this reaction.
42. H. Werder, 'Das Politische System der Schweiz – Eine Skizze seiner Funktionsweise', in W. Linder *et al.* (eds.), *Planung in der Schweizerischen Demokratie* (Bern: P. Haupt 1978), pp.31–51.
43. Kobach, *The Referendum*, p.94. Clearly initiative promoters prefer informal reactions that do not entail a mandatory vote with its inherent uncertainty and the campaigning that precedes it.
44. B. Hofer, 'Die Volksinitiative als Verhandlungspfand', *Schweizerisches Jahrbuch für politische Wissenschaft* 27 (1987), pp.207–35.
45. Kobach, *The Referendum*, p.107. In contrast to this success, initiative and counter-project most often failed when simultaneously submitted to the vote. As late as 1987, voters hostile to the status quo had to choose between the two options, dramatically reducing the chances of either winning a majority. Thus, formal counter-projects were not only compromise-oriented but also strategically designed to split the reformist camp. It is interesting that the propensity to withdraw initiatives has recently declined. Although this is probably due to a change in the overall political climate (see below), it can be argued that initiative promoters can now better anticipate their chances and thus have fewer incentives to withdraw their proposal.
46. See J.-D. Delley, *L'initiative populaire en Suisse. Mythes et réalités de la démocratie directe* (Lausanne: L'Age d'Homme 1978), and L. Neidhart, 'Regierbarkeitsfragen in der direkten Demokratie', *Schweizerisches Jahrbuch für politische Wissenschaft* 23 (1983), pp.13–43.
47. R. Epple-Gass, *Friedensbewegung und direkte Demokratie in der Schweiz* (Frankfurt: Haag+Herchen 1991). It ought to be noted however that the author's conclusions mostly rely on studies of the pacifist movement.
48. In a comparative study, Hanspeter Kriesi and Dominique Wisler also come to the conclusion that the repertoire of action of new social movements in Switzerland is more moderate than in other countries without direct democracy. See their 'Social Movements and Direct Democracy in Switzerland', *European Journal of Political Research* 30/1 (July 1996), pp.19–40.
49. Kobach, *The Referendum*, p.95.
50. Delley, *L'initiative populaire en Suisse*, maintains however that direct democracy confers more weight to the rank-and-file, whose co-operation is necessary for signature collection and voting campaigns.
51. For a more in-depth discussion of this argument, see Papadopoulos, *Démocratie directe*, part III, chap. 2 ('Référendum et citoyenneté: les promesses non tenues de la démocratie directe').
52. See the founding work by A. Lijphart, *Democracy in Plural Societies* (New Haven: Yale University Press 1974).
53. There is today a substantial literature on deliberative democracy and policy-making. For a good discussion on the current state of debate, see J. Elster (ed.) *Deliberative Democracy* (Cambridge: Cambridge University Press 1998).
54. This is the argument put forward by the path-dependency school. G. Lehmbruch, for example, goes back as far as the eighteenth century to find the roots of peaceful resolution in religious conflicts in Central Europe. See his 'Die korporative Verhandlungsdemokratie in Westmitteleuropa', *Swiss Political Science Review* 2/4 (Winter 1996), pp.19–41.
55. H. Kriesi and D. Wisler, 'The Impact of Social Movements on Political Institutions: A Comparison of the Introduction of Direct Legislation in Switzerland and the U.S.', Cornell University, Institute for European Studies Working Paper 96/6 (1996).
56. A whole school of thought has now emerged around the seminal book by P.J. Katzenstein, *Small States in World Markets* (Ithaca: Cornell University Press 1985).
57. A. Lijphart and M. Crepaz, 'Corporatism and Consensus Democracy in Eighteen Countries: Conceptual and Empirical Linkages', *British Journal of Political Science* 21 (1991), pp.235–56; F. Van Waarden, 'Consociationalism and Economic Performance in the Netherlands', paper presented to the Conference on 'The Fate of Consociationalism in Western Europe', 29–31 May 1998, Center for European Studies, Harvard University. The overlap between the two models is not perfect, however, as a multi-nation comparison shows: see J.-E. Lane and S. Ersson, 'The Institutions of Konkordanz and Corporatism: How

Closely Are They Connected?' *Swiss Political Science Review* 3/1 (Spring 1997), pp.5–29.

58. See the thesis on 'the structural dependency' of societies with respect to capitalism: C. Offe, *Contradictions of the Welfare State* (London: Hutchinson 1984).

59. E. Immergut, *Health Politics. Interests and Institutions in Western Europe* (Cambridge: Cambridge University Press 1992).

60. To veto points should be added the 'clearance points' previously identified in Pressman's and Wildavsky's seminal study of policy implementation. Swiss 'co-operative' federalism frequently leaves the implementation of federal decisions to cantonal administrations, where either political will or capacity may be missing. On the similarity between 'veto' and 'clearance' points, see B.G. Peters, *Institutional Theory in Political Science. The 'New Institutionalism'* (London/New York: Pinter 1999), pp.74–5.

61. The requirement for a double majority (people and cantons) would make EU membership very hard to attain.

62. High quality of democracy combined with good social-economic performance seem to be common features of the consensus type of democracies. See A. Lijphart, *Patterns of Democracy. Government Forms and Performance in Thirty-Six Countries* (New Haven/London: Yale University Press 1999).

63. See, *inter alia*, C. Longchamp *et al.*, *Unterstützung von Bundesrat und Verwaltung* (Bern: GfS-Forschungsinstitut 1994), or any of the above-mentioned reference books on the Swiss political system.

64. Sciarini and Trechsel, 'Democratie directe en Suisse: l'élite politique victime des droits populaires?'. Other studies conclude to a more general Left–Right polarisation in parliament, but Sciarini, 'La formulation de la décision' maintains that the votes taken into consideration cannot be considered representative.

65. Information from our data base at the University of Lausanne. I wish to thank Jeremias Blaser for regularly updating the database and providing analyses.

66. Kriesi, *Le système politique suisse*, pp.103–4.

67. For this aspect of internalisation of globalisation, see the editor's introductory and concluding chapters in A. Mach (ed.), *Globalisation, néo-libéralisme et politiques publiques dans la Suisse des années 90* (Zurich: Seismo 1999). It should, however, be remembered that some demands for policy reform in contemporary states arise from domestic structural problems, unrelated to globalisation (slow growth, ageing populations leading to greater government commitments that entail more fiscal pressures, etc.): see Pierson, 'Irresistible Forces, Immovable Objects'.

68. For the economists' view, see various essays by Silvio Borner, namely S. Borner *et al. Die Schweiz im Alleingang* (Zurich: NZZ Verlag 1994), where Swiss isolationism is attributed to the entrenched positions occupied by pro-status quo (welfare or protectionist) distributive coalitions. These coalitions are able to threaten recourse to the referendum in institutionalised concertation procedures, which are favourable to rent-seeking. For deregulatory manifestos that served as the basis for the reorientation of some major social-economic policies, see F. Leutwiler *et al. Schweizerische Wirtschaftspolitik im internationalen Wettbewerb. Ein ordnungspolitisches Programm* (Zurich: Orell Füssli 1991), and D. de Pury *et al., Ayons le courage d'un nouveau départ. Un programme pour la relance de la politique économique de la Suisse* (Zurich: Orell Füssli 1996).

69. There is also the protectionist-traditionalist coalition of the populist right fighting for the continued isolationism.

70. G. Bonoli, 'La réforme de l'Etat social suisse: contraintes institutionnelles et opportunités de changement', *Swiss Political Science Review* 5/3 (Autumn 1999), pp.57–77. Swiss direct democracy typically belongs to the category of veto points listed by Pierson, 'Irresistible Forces, Immovable Objects', which are likely to discourage attempts at dismantling welfare provisions.

71. In the 1970s, it was mostly the Right that split between its government faction willing to compromise with the Socialists to modernise the political system, and a more conservative and ultra-federalist 'preventive minority' also belonging to governing parties. See H. Kriesi, *Entscheidungsstrukturen und Entscheidungsprozesse in der Schweizer Politik* (Frankfurt: Campus 1980). Two decades later, the major division within the Right in government is between those who favour international opening and those of a more protectionist or even nationalist persuasion.

72. A generic category encompassing foreign policy issues, among them European integration, as well as relations with foreigners (immigration and asylum policy). On referendums on foreign policy issues see P. Sciarini and L. Marquis, 'Opinion publique et politique extérieure: le cas des votations populaires en Suisse', *International Political Science Review* 21/2 (2000), pp.149–71.

73. For Switzerland, see S. Kobi, *Des citoyens suisses contre l'élite politique. Le cas des votations fédérales, 1979–1995* (Paris: L'Harmattan 1999). On new cleavages related to the international dimension of politics, see H. Kriesi, 'The Transformation of Cleavage Politics', *European Journal of Political Research* 33/2 (1998), pp.165–185.

74. For an analysis of the cleavage between linguistic communities, see H. Kriesi *et al.*, *Le clivage linguistique: problèmes de compréhension entre les communautés linguistiques en Suisse* (Bern: Federal Office of statistics 1996). Conflicts between economic sectors have been emphasised by studies focusing on the reform of Swiss agricultural policy and of cartel legislation. See P. Sciarini, *Le système politique suisse face à la Communauté européenne et au GATT: le cas-test de la politique agricole* (Geneva: Georg 1994), and A. Mach, 'Quelles réponses politiques face à la globalisation et à la construction européenne? Illustration à partir de la révision de la loi suisse sur les cartels', *Swiss Political Science Review* 4/2 (Spring 1998), pp.25–49.

75. See Longchamp *et al.*, *Unterstützung von Bundesrat und Verwaltung*, and more recent *Univox* reports providing information on direct democracy.

76. Both those who have high expectations of reform and those who fear it probably overestimate its impact. A binary comparison of the cantons which differ most in the generosity of their direct democracy provisions (Geneva and Aargau) showed that institutional dissimilarities have only a limited and uneven influence on the practice of direct democracy and on voters' behaviour. See R. Lachat, 'Réforme des droits populaires: quel enseignement tirer de l'expérience cantonale?', Department of Political Science of the University of Geneva, 1998.

77. See the incisive remarks by Germann, *Staatsreform*.

78. A concept used by Offe, *Contradictions of the Welfare State*, to describe the strain caused by conflicting requirements of capitalist prosperity and social policy goals. I use it here in a different sense: for more details, see Y. Papadoulos, 'De Charybde en Scylla: le système politique suisse entre crise de représentation et crise d'adaptation', in C. Honegger *et al.* (eds.), *Sociétés en construction. Identités, conflits, différences* (Zurich: Seismo 1996), pp.135–48.

79. I refer here to the distinction between institutional orders by Powell and DiMaggio and to the antinomy between policy choices as depicted by Fritz W. Scharpf. See W.W. Powell and P.W. DiMaggio (eds.), *The New Institutionalism in Organizational Analysis* (Chicago: The University of Chicago Press 1991), pp.1–38, and F.W. Scharpf, *Demokratietheorie zwischen Utopie und Anpassung* (Konstanz: Universitätsverlag 1970).

The Federal Parliament:
The Limits of Institutional Reform

HANSPETER KRIESI

How does a parliament operate in a system of government which is the very opposite of the Westminster model? Looking at the Federal Assembly – the bicameral parliament at Berne – allows us to understand how parliaments at the same time reflect their institutional environment and adapt to it in their search for a meaningful role that may be quite different from the one intended by their constitutional design.

THE STRUCTURE OF THE SWISS SYSTEM OF GOVERNMENT AND THE POSITION OF THE FEDERAL ASSEMBLY

According to the new Federal Constitution (Art. 148, al. 1), which reiterates the formulation of the old text of 1848, the Federal Assembly, that is the parliament, constitutes the supreme authority of the Confederation, except for the rights of the people and the cantons. The designers of the constitution of 1848 wanted to institutionalise the superiority of the Federal Assembly over the Federal Council.[1] However, they failed to provide the Federal Assembly with an efficient mechanism for the control of government. The Swiss system of government is not a parliamentary system since it does not have the motion of censure which would allow parliament to dismiss the government; conversely, the government cannot dissolve the Federal Assembly either. Nor does the Swiss system of government correspond to a presidential regime, given that the Federal Council is not elected by the people, but by parliament. Arend Lijphart considers the Swiss system to be a hybrid case which combines elements of both types of regime.[2] According to Philippe Lauvaux and Thomas Fleiner-Gerster, it constitutes a genuine third type, distinct from both the presidential and the parliamentary systems – a type which they call the 'directorial system' and which follows the model of the Directoire of the French Revolution.[3] This type of regime is

Hanspeter Kriesi, University of Geneva

characterised by a collegial executive which (as in a parliamentary system) is elected by parliament, but which, once elected (as in a presidential system) is no longer responsible to the parliament until the following general elections. For the duration of a legislature, this type of regime introduces a separation of powers which resembles that of the presidential system.

All parliaments in liberal democracies are today confronted with conditions that limit their role in the legislative process and which impose restrictions on their control of the government and the public administration. If the decline of parliamentary power may be less dramatic than is usually maintained,[4] the weakness of the Swiss parliament appears to be particularly severe. In the Swiss system, parliament not only suffers from a structural lack of control over the government, the Federal Assembly's position is also weakened by its lack of resources as well as by the implications of the direct-democratic elements of the Swiss political system.

The Federal Assembly is still a 'militia' parliament, that is, a parliament composed of amateurs who combine their professional activities with their parliamentary duties and do not receive a salary for their parliamentary mandate, but only recompense for their expenses. Of course, the idea of a 'militia' parliament has since long become a fiction. The survey by Alois Riklin and Silvano Möckli has shown that, on average, members spend about half of their working time on their parliamentary activities, and roughly ten per cent on other political activities.[5] On average, they spend only about one-third of their time on non-political, professional work. This means, that, in fact, the Swiss parliament has become a 'semi-professional' institution. However, as Wolf Linder points out,[6] the fiction of the 'militia' parliament still prevents the development of professional working conditions for the members of the Federal Assembly. While most of the parliamentarians interviewed by Riklin and Möckli wished to have better parliamentary services, more secretarial support for the parliamentary groups and personal collaborators, by a very large majority they opposed becoming a professional parliament. A limited reform bill was attacked by a referendum launched by the conservative camp in 1992. This bill had proposed to increase the remuneration of the parliamentarians, to improve their infrastructure (among other things, each member of parliament would have obtained one part-time personal collaborator), and to introduce some organisational rationalisation. In the subsequent popular vote, a large majority of the citizens rejected 'the disguised introduction of a professional parliament'. They only approved of the organisational changes (most notably of a reform of the committee system), which did not cost anything.[7] The real costs of the 'militia' system are, however, important: not only does it introduce unequal working conditions among the individual members of parliament, some of whom can afford to pay personally for the necessary infrastructure, while others cannot. It also weakens parliament in general: as a consequence of its 'militia' status, the Federal Assembly as a whole lacks time, information and professional competence and is consistently disadvantaged compared with the government and the federal administration.

In addition, the direct-democratic opportunities of the Swiss political system reduce the role of parliament in the legislative process. As Leonhard Neidhart has argued, this direct alternative has transformed the 'plebiscitary democracy' into a 'negotiated democracy'.[8] Even if he has somewhat overdrawn his case, his thesis is still largely true: the existence of the institution of the referendum, in particular, has led to the institutionalisation of elaborate pre-parliamentary negotiation procedures (expert committees, consultation procedures, working groups, round tables, hearings, and so on). These procedures integrate all the interest associations into the political process, and they are capable of making a credible threat to use the referendum at the end of the legislative procedures if their demands are not met. Since the outcome of a referendum is always uncertain, such a threat puts enormous pressure on the government to take the different demands into account when drawing up legislative measures. As a consequence, the preparliamentary procedures result in compromise solutions which are usually only marginally modified by the deliberations in parliament. In other words, the menace of the referendum introduces an atmosphere of doubt into parliament and fundamentally limits its freedom of action. As a result, the Federal Assembly has traditionally been unenterprising and rather timid. If, in the final event, the weapon of the referendum is only rarely used to attack bills promulgated by parliament, this does not disconfirm Neidhart's point. On the contrary, it confirms that the elaborate preparliamentary negotiations typically result in a compromise which then passes through parliament without significant modifications and avoids the plebiscitary test.

However, the mutual independence of parliament and government in the directorial system serves to strengthen parliament, as it is less constrained by considerations of party discipline and loyalty to the government. If the parliament in a majoritarian system, with a minimal winning coalition and a high degree of party discipline, does not much more than rubber stamp the government's projects, the Swiss parliament has more autonomy. In the Swiss system, the government does not fall if it cannot find a majority for its measures in parliament. Given the internal heterogeneity of the Swiss parties and the heterogeneity of the parties constituting the grand coalition, it is possible that parliament will not adopt a governmental measure, even though the parliamentary majority of the four governing parties is very large indeed. In other words, as is pointed out by Yannis Papadopoulos,[9] parliament has the capacity to inject uncertainty into the decision-making process, thus representing a possible veto-point with respect to governmental proposals. However, if party discipline in Switzerland is a far cry from the discipline we find in the British case, it is also very far from the legendary lack of loyalty of the parties of the 4th Republic in France. Studies of party discipline based on roll-call data up to 1991 show that the party discipline in the National Council is relatively high, even if it does not reach the levels of other European parliaments.[10] Swiss parliamentarians do not attribute as much importance to party loyalty as do, for example, their Italian and Belgian colleagues.[11]

THE STRUCTURE OF THE FEDERAL ASSEMBLY

The Federal Assembly is an instance of a strong bicameralism with symmetrical and incongruent chambers.[12] The two chambers – the National Council and the Council of States – have exactly the same competences. They are equal, but incongruent, because they are elected in different ways: while the 200 members of the National Council are elected according to a proportional electoral system, the Council of States, as with the US Senate, has two representatives for each of the 23 cantons, who are, with one exception, elected according to a majoritarian formula.[13] The bulk of the work is done in the committees of the two chambers. Until 1992, for virtually every legislative project a special committee was created in an 'ad hoc' fashion to prepare the debates in the plenary session. Thus, in the 1971–75 legislature, there were no fewer than 225 such committees in the National Council and 239 in the Council of States. On average, a national councillor sat on 20 such committees, while a member of the Council of States had an average of 52 committee seats! The (very partial) organisational reform of 1992 introduced a committee system with 12 permanent committees in each council, replacing the ancient Byzantine structure. Analysing the role of these committees in parliamentary work,

Lüthi found that the members of the two Councils pass the bulk of their time in committee work and that the plenary sessions virtually always (in 96 per cent of cases) follow the majority view of their preparatory committees.[14] As a result of the reform, the committees are now taken more seriously by the government than in the old system.

A legislative proposal is first examined by the committee of the chamber to which it is assigned by a joint decision of the presidents of the two chambers. The following deliberations in the plenary sessions of the first chamber include a first reading, followed by a detailed discussion of the text and a final vote. Next, the text goes to the second chamber – first to the committee responsible for the measure in question, then to its plenary session. If the second chamber does not agree with the first chamber, the proposal is referred back to the first chamber. If there are still differences after three deliberations in each chamber, the members of the committees responsible for the measure in the two chambers constitute an arbitration committee. If this committee cannot find a solution or if its solution is rejected by one or both of the two chambers, the proposal is deleated from the agenda. The capacity of the two chambers to find a compromise is high: 90 per cent of most of the issuess are resolved after at most two deliberations in each chamber.[15] The introduction of a new tax on energy constitutes a recent measure that went all the way through three deliberations in each chamber and was, finally, resolved by an arbitration committee which met just before the end of the legislative period in October 1999.

Let us now look at the composition of the two chambers. Since the introduction of proportional representation in 1919, the National Council has always been dominated by the four major parties which since 1959 have formed the government according to the 'magic formula'. From the mid-1960s to the late 1980s, these four parties lost some of their electoral attraction and their share of the electorate fell from roughly 90 per cent to barely 70 per cent. Since then, they have regained some of their earlier strength, mainly because of the impressive rise of the Swiss People's Party in the 1980s. Presently, the four governing parties together hold 87 per cent of the seats in the National Council and all the seats in the Council of States. However, the distribution of seats among the four parties varies substantially between the two chambers (see Table 1).

TABLE 1
DISTRIBUTION OF SEATS IN THE TWO CHAMBERS (1999–2003)

Party	National Council	Council of States
Social Democrats	51	6
Free Democrats	43	18
Christian Democrats	35	15
Swiss People's Party	44	7
Others	27	–
Total	200	46

The two largest parties in the National Council – the Social Democrats and the Swiss People's Party, which constitute the polar opposites among the 'gang of four', are relatively insignificant in the Council of States. The majoritarian electoral system as well as the strategic behaviour of the parties and of the electorate in the elections to the Council of States imply that the candidates of the moderate right (Free Democrats and Christian Democrats) win most of the seats in the second chamber.[16] As a result, the stability of the partisan composition of the second chamber has been even more impressive than that of the National Council. However, the Council of States has largely lost its function of representing the states. Given the fact that the political positions of the most important adversaries in federal politics of the nineteenth century – the (liberal) Free Democrats and the (Catholic, conservative) Christian Democrats – have become quite similar, the Council of States is today dominated by a very large coalition of the moderate (liberal) Right.

PARLIAMENTARY COALITIONS

The manner of operations of the National Council can be systematically studied on the basis of roll-call data. Up to 1991, such roll-call votes in the National Council were rather exceptional. Since the 1990s, however, all votes are recorded in this way and can be used for the reconstruction of the political positioning of the different partisan groups. On the basis of the voting behaviour of the 200 members of the National Council in the 1995–99 legislature, Michael Hermann, Heiri Leuthold and Hanspeter Kriesi have done a factor analysis of those 517 of the 942 votes in the National Council during this period, which were controversial and had a participation rate of at least three-quarters of its members.[17] The resulting two-dimensional distribution of the members of the Council is shown in

Figure 1. The arrangement of the parliamentarians in this figure largely corresponds to the way they are seated in the hemicycle of the National Council: the arch begins on the left with the few members of the Communist Party, crosses the Social Democrats and the Greens, reaches its peak with the Christian Democrats and descends to the right across the Free Democrats and the two wings of the Swiss People's Party, down to the members representing the small parties of the radical right. This distribution has two particularities worth mentioning: the closely related positions of the two moderate parties of the right (Free Democrats and Christian Democrats); and the rather clear-cut division of the parliamentary group of the Swiss People's Party into a more moderate wing (dominated by deputies from the Canton of Bern) and a more conservative wing (dominated by the deputies from the Canton of Zurich).

The horizontal axis in this diagram corresponds to the Left–Right cleavage. More than 60 per cent of the votes selected for the analysis concern this axis. They deal with classic social and economic policies, as well as questions of law and order (army, police and justice). A second axis runs from the upper left-hand corner to the lower right-hand corner of the diagram. This axis relates to issues of a more cultural type (such as liberalisation of drugs) and above all with the relationship of Switzerland to the outside world (European integration and immigration policy), which constitute about a third of the votes in question. While the three bourgeois parties form a coalition with regard to issues relating to the Left–Right axis, they divide with regard to issues dealing with the 'cultural' axis. On cultural issues, the more moderate bourgeois camp forms a reform coalition with the Left against the conservative group on the Right, that is, against the conservative fraction in the Swiss People's Party and the radical right, which are from time to time supported by the small Liberal Party from the French-speaking part of the country.

This structural arrangement explains why the groups of the Christian Democrats and the Free Democrats are almost always on the winning side in the National Council. Hermann and his collaborators have calculated the percentages of votes won by a each member of the National Council and the corresponding averages per party. Figure 2 presents the same distribution as Figure 1, but this time with contour lines indicating the percentages of votes won by the different parties. At the top of the arch, we find the parliamentarians who are almost always in the majority – they essentially belong to the moderate (liberal) bourgeois camp – with the Christian Democrats winning somewhat more frequently than the Free Democrats. Depending on the issue in question, the losing opposition is either on the

FIGURE 1

THE STRUCTURE OF PARTISAN DISTRIBUTION IN THE NATIONAL COUNCIL
(1995–99 LEGISLATURE)

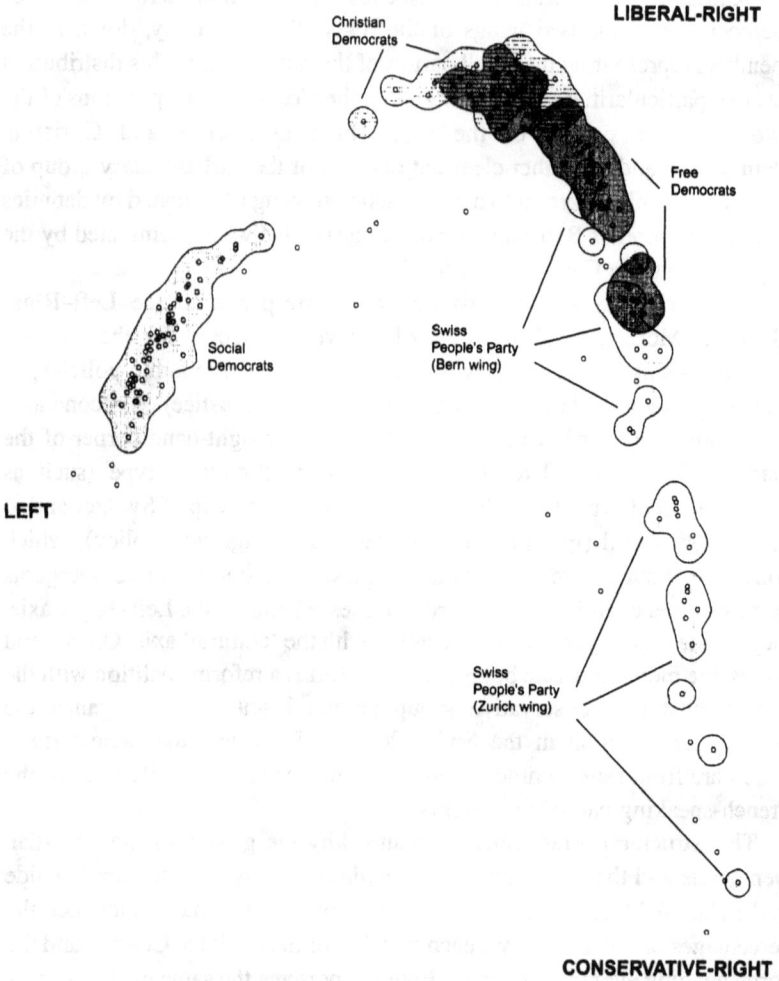

Source: M. Hermann, H. Leuthold and H. Kriesi, 'Die politische Landkarte der Schweiz', *Das
Magazin* 40/9, 15 Oct. 1999, Tages-Anzeiger, s.18–30. Michael Hermann has adapted
this figure for the present publication.

FIGURE 2

THE SUCCESS RATE OF THE DIFFERENT PARTISAN GROUPS IN THE VOTES
OF THE NATIONAL COUNCIL (1995–99 LEGISLATURE)

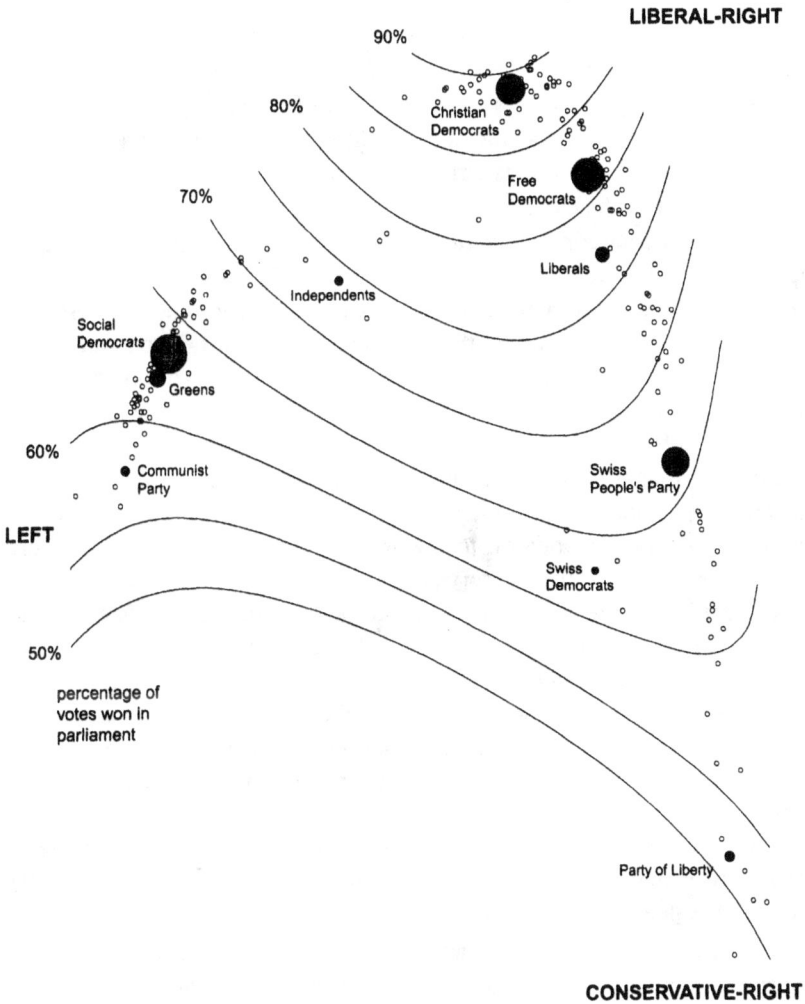

Source: as Figure 1.

Left or on the conservative Right. The bourgeois coalition which forms around the classic Left–Right issues wins most of the time (in 75 per cent of the votes). Sometimes the Christian Democrats and other bourgeois dissidents vote with the Left. The Centre–Left reform coalition which forms around 'cultural' issues wins virtually all the time (in 98 per cent of the votes), which is one reason why the conservative Right increases its populist appeals to the people by way of direct-democratic procedures. Very rarely, an 'unholy alliance' is formed between the two oppositional camps from the Left and the conservative Right. In the few instances where it takes shape, this kind of coalition is virtually always beaten by the moderate right (in 92 per cent of the cases).

Given this coalitional structure in the National Council, it is now also apparent why the number of conflicts between the two councils is much more limited than we might have expected, given the substantial differences in their partisan composition:[18] the same two parties of the moderate Right which dominate the Council of States are able to impose their point of view in the National Council, thanks to variable coalitions which they form either with the Left or with the conservative Right. Moreover, given this coalitional structure in the National Council, it now also becomes apparent how the opposition works in the grand coalition government: depending on the issue at stake, in addition to the small non-governmental parties, the Social Democrats or the conservative wing of the Swiss People's Party (augmented by some conservatives from the Christian Democrats and the Free Democrats) join the ranks of the opposition. Thanks to the governmental core support in the two parties of the moderate Right, which enter into variable coalitions with one or the other of their governmental allies and thanks to the (variable) support of some minor parties not belonging to the governmental coalition, the government usually gets its way.

To complete this account of the structural composition of the Federal Assembly, it should be added that its members have what Linder aptly calls 'double loyalties':[19] they not only represent their party, but also specific interest associations – either as part of their professional activities or simply as ordinary members. Moreover, the parliamentarians of the bourgeois camp are closely tied to the Swiss economy, as is documented by the average number of seats they occupy on administrative boards of private and public enterprises and the amount of capital they represent.[20] The parliamentarians' loyalty in nominal votes with regard to the interest associations they represent in parliament is virtually as high as it is with regard to their parties.[21] In other words, the farmers' representatives, or the trade unionists among the Social and Christian Democrats, or the business interests' representatives in the bourgeois parties or the ecologists from different parties vote loyally in favour of the interest groups which they represent. The colonisation of the Federal Assembly by these particularistic interests is especially pronounced because of the 'militia' character of the parliament. But, as Kerr has already observed and as Papadopoulos also suggests,[22] the professionalisation of parliament would not eliminate these ties to specific interests. Most likely, however, it would render the Federal Assembly more representative of the different sensibilities that exist in the population.

THE FUNCTIONING OF THE FEDERAL ASSEMBLY

Parliaments have several important functions; among them are the elective, the legislative and the control functions. As far as its elective function is concerned, at first sight the Swiss parliament seems to play an important role. It elects the government, the Chancellor of the Confederation, the federal judges, and the general in case of war. However, the elective function is subject to severe constraints – especially with regard to the members of the government. As Raimund Germann has observed:[23] 'In reality, the formation of a government in Switzerland is less the expression of a political will than the statement of a fact which the formal selection criteria rigidly impose.' Given these constraints, Germann speaks of the 'atrophy of the electoral function' of parliament. The selection criteria to be taken into account are all informal, but still quite established. They include the 'magic formula' of the government's partisan composition (two members each of the Free Democrats, Social Democrats and Christian Democrats, one member of the Swiss People's Party), the linguistic proportionality (at least two members from the linguistic minorities), the representation of the three largest cantons (Zurich, Berne and Vaud), and of women. The only formal criterion, the traditional 'cantonal clause', according to which only one member of the government could come from a given canton in the past, was abolished by a popular vote in 1999. Moreover, the number of vacancies to be filled is usually rather small (typically one or two), since the sitting members of the government are virtually always re-elected, if they wish to stay in power (as they often do). As a result of the combination of a large number of criteria that have to be met by a candidate and the limited number of vacancies to be filled, the number of possible candidates and the choice to be made by parliament is usually severely limited.

As far as the legislative function is concerned, it is important to consider the extent to which parliament initiates legislative processes. In this respect, Alain-Valéry Poitry, who has analysed the legislation of the period 1971–75 in detail, concludes that the initiating role of parliament is still very much alive.[24] Thus, parliament has launched almost half (46 per cent) of the legislative projects of the legislature in question, compared with 26 per cent which originated in the federal administration, 15 per cent which were launched by popular initiatives, and 13 per cent which had other sources. However, a more recent study of parliamentary motions and initiatives introduces a sceptical note in this regard. Martin Graf shows that the number of parliamentary initiatives and motions has in fact greatly increased since the 1960s.[25] But he also shows that parallel to the multiplication of the initiating activities by the parliamentarians their importance has considerably decreased. Thus, while the success rate of motions was still about a quarter in the early 1960s, it fell to just eight per cent in the 1987–91 legislative period. Most of the motions were not even discussed by parliament and simply dropped from the agenda for lack of time. With the instrument of the parliamentary initiative, parliament has the possibility to elaborate a project all by itself. As it turns out, however, parliament only rarely makes use of this possibility: 94 per cent of the proposals discussed in parliament originate in the Federal Council – to be more precise, from within the federal administration.[26]

Pre-parliamentary procedures tend to limit further the role of parliament in the legislative process. This is generally confirmed by the assessments of the political elite of the early 1970s, which indicated that the earlier, pre-parliamentary phases of the legislative process are much more important than the later, parliamentary ones.[27] Poitry's more detailed analyses, however, could not confirm Neidhart's view that pre-parliamentary negotiations limit conflict in parliament.[28] His empirical results rather suggest that it is particularly high where the pre-parliamentary negotiations were especially elaborate. Probably, this result depends on the fact that certain issues typically give rise to particularly high levels of conflict at all stages of the political process, and, as a consequence, particularly high levels of pre-parliamentary and parliamentary negotiations. Unfortunately, we do not have a measure for the overall level of contentiousness of a project. But if we control for the estimated importance of a project and the degree of its newness, the positive association between pre-parliamentary negotiations and parliamentary conflict becomes much weaker, which is an indication of its essentially spurious character. This empirical result also suggests that pre-parliamentary procedures do not always succeed in finding a stable compromise, and that for this reason parliament becomes a significant arena in some cases – especially for very important and controversial issues. Alois Riklin and Zehnder have examined the degree to which parliament has legislated autonomously in the period 1971–75.[29] Their study showed that it modified only roughly a third (37.3 per cent) of the 357 measures in question. Most of the modifications were either marginal (16.3 per cent) or moderate (14.6 per cent). In only 6.4 per cent of the cases parliament amended the government's proposal in important ways.

There are indications that the role of parliament in the legislative process has become more important in the recent past. On the one hand, the increasing polarisation of Swiss politics, the multiplication of the interest associations which are capable of launching a referendum and are, therefore, included in pre-parliamentary procedures, and the increasing competence of the federal administration, renders the pre-parliamentary search for a viable compromise more difficult. On the other hand, the rationalisation of parliamentary procedures has reinforced the working capacity of the parliamentary committees.[30] In some policy areas, such as energy policy, where a pre-parliamentary deadlock has prevented any kind of solution for a long time, parliament has become an important arena and some members of parliament have become key actors in the search for a viable compromise.[31]

As for its control function, the Federal Assembly, as already mentioned, does not have the possibility to sanction the government by a motion of censure. However, as Yves Mény points out,[32] even in parliamentary regimes, this measure is used less and less. Other instruments of control, which have been considered secondary, have become everywhere more important: questions and interpellations, the ordinary control committees, the special commissions of investigation, and hearings. In the Federal Assembly, questions and interpellations are numerous. The government has to respond to them in writing. In the parliamentary debate, however, these instruments are of lesser importance than in a parliamentary regime, where they are typically used by members of the opposition to check on the government's activities.[33] The committees of the Federal Assembly charged with the control of the administration have traditionally been weak, because of their lack of resources. In 1990, they were given a small administrative staff to increase their effectiveness, but that staff has already been scrapped. There were only four special commissions of investigation in the history of the Swiss parliament dealing with specific scandals: the scandal of the Mirages fighter planes (1964), the scandal of the secret services and the protection of the state, which gave rise to two commissions in 1989 and

1990, and the scandal of the federal pension fund (1996). Each of these scandals has uncovered enormous weaknesses with respect to the control exercised by parliament and the control process in general. Thus, the last case has shown that reciprocal control among the members of the Federal Council does not function, given that each one of them respects the domain of his or her colleagues. Moreover, the control organ of the federal pension fund, the 'Control of Finances', turned out to be hierarchically dependent on the federal councillor who was responsible for the problem of the pension fund in the first place. Finally, the party of the federal councillor in question immediately took up his defence, which politicised the issue and did not allow for a thorough debate about the responsibilities of the different individuals and instances.

More generally, we may conclude that, by trying to integrate a large number of interest associations into the political process and to share governmental power among all the large parties, the Swiss system of government systematically mixes up the responsibilities and thereby renders the parliamentary control process very difficult. The 'militia' system contributes to the intricate entanglement of the responsibilities, because the cumulation of roles which are typical in such a system allows for non-transparent operations of exchange between the different organs and interests. The lack of transparency of the political process in such a system implies, as Philippe Mastronardi has observed, that the responsibility for the results of this process can no longer be attributed to anybody.[34]

PROPOSED REFORMS

As we have seen, institutional reforms to strengthen the Federal Assembly were proposed in the early 1990s, but only a minority of them were adopted because of popular resistance led by the conservative camp. Proposals for a more fundamental reform of Swiss political institutions have been numerous in the recent past. The general objective of all these propositions has been to strengthen the Federal Assembly and the Federal Council as well as the relationship between the two. In addition to specialists of constitutional law, some political scientists have also contributed to this debate, among them most notably Raimund Germann, who proposed transforming the Swiss system of government into a bipolar system of the Westminster type, without, however, suggesting the outright introduction of a parliamentary regime.[35] With regard to the Federal Assembly, Germann proposed:

- to replace the proportional electoral system for the election of the National Council by a majoritarian system with single member districts;
- to abolish the Council of State, or, alternatively, to transform it into the equivalent of the German Bundesrat, that is, a real representation of the member states; and
- to professionalise the two councils.

He also proposed several measures – such as the introduction of a 'parliamentary referendum' and of the 'unified initiative' – to put the direct-democratic instruments under the control of parliament. More recently, he suggested a 'contractual' reform of government, given that institutional reform had not taken shape.[36] According to this idea, the members of a future coalitional government should draw up a contract allowing them to specify clearly the government's objectives and the basis of its actions. Such a contract should also include a 'peace clause', specifying that the members of government were no longer allowed to attack any government project by a referendum, and a 'responsibility clause', specifying that popular votes on crucial issues should be linked to the question of confidence. The intention of this proposition is to clarify the responsibilities in the system and to link the parliamentary majority more closely to the governmental programme, that is, to introduce elements of a parliamentary system.

Germann, however, never went all the way to advocate the introduction of a parliamentary regime for Switzerland. It is Papadopoulos who argues in favour of the introduction of a parliamentary system.[37] According to him, the parliamentary system is the one which introduces the largest number of constraints forcing the government and parliament to co-operate. In this context, it is important to add that the introduction of a parliamentary system would not necessarily imply the adoption of the model of a majoritarian democracy. As Lijphart shows,[38] there are parliamentary systems such as Belgium or the Netherlands which are, at the same time, consensus democracies. However, reinforcing the link between the government and parliament, the parliamentary regime strengthens the link between the elections, on the one hand, and the composition and policies of the government, on the other. In other words, the parliamentary system would give more weight to the elections and to the political parties, and it would, therefore, strengthen the elements of representative democracy in the Swiss political system.[39]

Moreover, and contrary to what is suggested by Wolf Linder,[40] there is no fundamental incompatibility between such a reinforcement of representative democracy and the existence of direct democratic elements in the political system. More specifically, as Papadopoulos points out,[41] if an important proposal of the authorities fails to be accepted in a popular vote, the government would not automatically be forced to step down. Given such a situation, parliament would have to decide whether or not it maintains its confidence in the government. In Switzerland, there is a tendency to confuse the parliamentary system with the majoritarian model of representative democracy. Papadopoulos is right to conclude that the Swiss debate on institutional reform should examine closely, 'without passion or blinkers', the advantages and inconveniences of different versions of the parliamentary system.[42]

The Swiss system of government which dates back to the nineteenth century is, indeed, an anachronism. But three considerations dampen the enthusiasm for institutional reform. For one, the system does not precisely function as designed by institutional engineering in the nineteenth century. It has adapted to the requirements of the time. If parliament is no longer the supreme authority in the system and if it is rather weak, it shares this predicament with other parliaments – even in parliamentary systems. Second, if put under great pressure, even with its present make-up, the system is capable of reforming substantive policies. As André Mach concludes a recent assessment of Swiss economic and social policy, Switzerland has never seen such a cumulation of reforms and innovations in these policy domains as in the course of the 1990s.[43] Finally, the popular myths of Swiss politics[44] tend to limit the possibilities of institutional reform, and even if institutional reforms were to come about, the 'helvetian cults' of compromise solutions and of popular sovereignty[45] will tend to limit the power of parliament, whatever its institutional structure.

NOTES

1. A. Kölz, *Neuere schweizerische Verfassungsgeschichte. Ihre Grundlinien vom Ende der Alten Eidgenossenschaft bis 1848* (Bern: Stämpfli 1992), p.570.
2. A. Lijphart, *Patterns of Democracy* (New Haven: Yale University Press 1999), pp.119ff.
3. P. Lauvaux *Les grandes démocraties contemporaines* (Paris: PUF 1990); T. Fleiner-Gerster, 'Le Conseil fédéral: Directoire de la Confédération', *Pouvoir* 43 (1987), pp.49–64.
4. Y. Mény, *Politique comparée. Les démocraties: Allemagne, Etats-Unis, France, Grande-Bretagne, Italie* (Paris: Montchrestien, 3rd edn 1991), pp.257ff.
5. A. Riklin and S. Möckli, 'Milizparlament?', in M. Bovey Lechner *et al.* (eds.), *Le Parlement – 'Autorité suprême de la Confédération'?* (Bern: Haupt 1991), pp.145–63.
6. W. Linder, *Schweizerische Demokratie. Institutionen, Prozesse, Perspektiven* (Bern: Haupt 1999), p.198.
7. S. Hardmeier, 'Analyse des votations fédérales du 27 septembre 1992', *Vox* 46 (Bern: GfS 1992).
8. L. Neidhart, *Plebiszit und pluralitäre Demokratie. Eine Analyse der Funktionen des schweizerischen Gesetzesreferendums* (Bern: Francke 1970).

9. Y. Papadopoulos, *Les processus de décision fédéraux en Suisse* (Paris: L'Harmattan 1997), p.101.
10. R. Lüthi, L. Meyer and H. Hirter, 'Fraktionsdisziplin und die Vertretung von Partikulärinteressen im Nationalrat', in M. Bovey-Lechner *et al.* (eds.), *Das Parlament – Oberste Gewalt des Bundes?* (Bern: Haupt 1991), pp.53–71.
11. G. Loewenberg and T.C. Mans, 'Individual and Structural Influences on the Perception of Legislative Norms in Three European Parliaments', *American Journal of Political Science* 32 (1988), pp.155–77.
12. See Lijphart, *Patterns of Democracy*, Chapter 11.
13. G. Lutz und D. Strohmann, *Wahl- und Abstimmungsrecht in den Kantonen* (Bern: Haupt 1998), pp.95–110.
14. R. Lüthi, 'Die Wirkung von institutionellen Reformen dargestellt am Beispiel der Reform des Kommissionensystems der Schweizerischen Bundesversammlung von 1991', *Revue suisse de science politique* 2 (1996), pp.81–111.
15. A. Riklin and A. Ochsner: 'Milizparlament?', in U. Klöti (ed.), *Manuel Système politique de la Suisse*, Vol.2 (Bern: Haupt), pp.77–116.
16. H. Kriesi, 'Wählen aus Überzeugung und strategisches Wählen bei den Ständeratswahlen 1995', in H. Kriesi *et al.* (eds.), *Schweizer Wahlen 1995* (Bern: Haupt 1998), pp.193–218.
17. M. Hermann, H. Leuthold and H. Kriesi, 'Die politische Landkarte der Schweiz', *Das Magazin* (Tages-Anzeiger), 40/9, 15 Oct. 1999, pp.18–30.
18. R. Lüthi, 'Parlament', in U. Klöti *et al.* (eds.), *Handbuch der Schweizer Politik* (Zürich: NZZ-Verlag 1999), p.140.
19. Linder, *Schweizerische Demokratie*, p.212.
20. H. Kriesi, *Le système politique suisse* (Paris: Economica 2nd edn 1998), p.214.
21. Lüthi *et al.*, 'Fraktionsdisziplin und die Vertretung von Partikulärinteressen im Nationalrat', p.67.
22. H.H. Kerr, *Parlement et société en Suisse* (Saint-Saphorin: Georg 1981), p.251, and Papadopoulos, *Les processus de décision fédéraux en Suisse*, p.112.
23. R.E. Germann, *Administration publique en Suisse, Volume 1: L'appareil étatique et le gouvernement* (Bern: Haupt 1996) p.228.
24. A.-V. Poitry, *La fonction d'ordre de l'Etat. Analyse des mécanismes et des déterminants sélectifs dans le processus législatif suisse* (Bern: Lang 1989), p.180.
25. M. Graf, 'Motion und parlamentarische Initiative. Untersuchungen zu ihrer Handhabung und politischen Funktion', in Bovey-Lechner *et al.* (eds.), *Das Parlament – Oberste Gewalt des Bundes?*, pp.203–21.
26. Lüthi, 'Parlament', pp.139f.
27. H. Kriesi, *Entscheidungsstrukturen und Entscheidungsprozesse in der Schweizer Politik* (Frankfurt: Campus 1980), p.589.
28. Poitry, *La fonction d'ordre de l'Etat*.
29. Cited in W. Linder, *La décision politique en Suisse Genèse et mise en oeuvre de la législation* (Lausanne: Réalité sociales 1987), pp.40f.
30. Linder, *Schweizerische Demokratie*, p.217.
31. See H. Kriesi and M. Jegen, 'The Swiss Energy Policy Elite', *European Journal of Political Science* (2001, forthcoming), and H. Kriesi and M. Jegen, 'Decision-making in the Swiss Energy Policy Elite', *Journal of Public Policy* 20 (2000), pp.21–53.
32. Mény, *Politique comparée*, pp.247ff.
33. Lüthi, 'Parlament', p.144.
34. Philippe Mastronardi, *Kriterien der demokratischen Verwaltungskontrolle. Analyse und Konzept der parlamentarischen Oberaufsicht im Bund* (Basel: Helbing und Lichtenhahn 1991) p.521.
35. Raimund E. Germann, *Staatsreform. Der Übergang zur Konkurrenzdemokratie* (Bern: Haupt 1994); Raimund E. Germann, *Politische Innovation und Verfassungsreform* (Bern: Haupt 1975).
36. Germann, *Administration publique*, pp.274ff.
37. Papadopoulos, *Les processus décision fédéraux en Suisse*, pp.117ff.
38. Lijphart, *Patterns of Democracy*.

39. Papadopoulos, *Les processus de décision féderaux en Suisse*, p.130.
40. Wolf Linder, *Swiss Democracy. Possible Solutions to Conflict in Multicultural Societies* (New York, St. Martin's Press 1994) p.133.
41. Papadopoulos, *Les processus de décision féderaux en Suisse*, p.123.
42. Ibid, p.131.
43. A. Mach, 'Présentation générale et contexte socio-économique des années 1990', in A. Mach (ed.) *Globalisation, néo-libéralisme et politiques publiques dans la Suisse des années 1990* (Zürich: Seismo 1999) pp.11–50.
44. Kriesi, *Le système politique Suisse*, p.9ff.
45. Papadopoulos, *Les processus de décision féderaux en Suisse*, p.115.

Towards the Judicialisation of Swiss Politics?

CHRISTINE ROTHMAYR

THE JUDICIALISATION OF POLITICS

The concept of judicialisation is often used to describe the process whereby courts have broadened their influence at the expense of parliament and government: 'the expansion of the province of the courts or the judges at the expense of the politicians and/or the administrators, that is, the transfer of decision-making rights from the legislature, the cabinet, or the civil service to the courts'.[1] Furthermore, depending on the author's normative position, the term judicialisation is either characterised as threatening the basic values of democratic decision-making or regarded as increasing the protection of rights. However, no single definition of judicialisation has, as yet, emerged out of the already broad variety of studies examining the phenomenon around the world. Two aspects of judicialisation are examined here in the context of the case of Switzerland: the current influence of the Federal Supreme Court with respect to policy-making, and the extent to which its jurisdiction has broadened and its influence increased over time.

In March 2000, changes to the constitution intending to reform the Swiss judicial system were accepted by popular vote.[2] The original draft of the reform included the introduction of the concrete[3] review of federal laws by the Swiss Federal Supreme Court. The introduction of concrete review of federal laws would have expanded the constitutional jurisdiction of the highest court, which is currently obliged by the constitution to apply federal laws, even if it considers them to be unconstitutional. However, parliament rejected the proposal to introduce concrete review, and thus the version of the reform that was voted on no longer included the planned extension of constitutional review. It is thus necessary to explain why the proposed extension did not pass in parliament.

There is also the question of the current degree of influence of the Federal Supreme Court with respect to policy-making. The analysis here presents

Christine Rothmayr, University of Geneva

evidence to reject the presumption that its limited constitutional jurisdiction results in a generally weak role in policy-making.

Finally, does the rejection of concrete review indicate that Switzerland is not following the global trend of judicialisation? The term judicialisation usually evokes a belief in the increasing influence of courts over time. Thus, we need to assess the extent to which institutional reforms, as well as a changing jurisprudence of the Swiss Federal Supreme Court, have contributed to the expansion of its jurisdiction and an increase in its influence. In this analysis it is argued that a moderate trend of judicialisation can be observed in Switzerland, but that the process began at a lower level and developed at a slower pace than in other countries, thus, making the rise of judicialisation less visible.

THE SWISS FEDERAL SUPREME COURT AND ITS LIMITED POWER OF CONSTITUTIONAL REVIEW[4]

The Swiss Federal Supreme Court is the highest court, almost always the court of last appeal, and is regulated by federal law. It is not solely a constitutional court, and its jurisdiction covers cases of public and private law. The Court decides complaints against the violation of federal law, international law, inter-cantonal law, of guarantees of autonomy to municipalities or other public bodies, and cantonal and federal law on political rights.[5] The Court also decides cases involving conflicts between cantons as well as between a canton, or several cantons, and the federal government.[6]

The constitutional jurisdiction of the Federal Supreme Court, in terms of the power to overturn federal laws, is considerably restricted. First of all, Art. 190 of the federal constitution[7] requires the Court, as well as all other cantonal and federal authorities, to apply federal laws and ratify international law.[8] All other norms or decisions issued by federal authorities, by the Federal Council in particular, as well as norms and decisions issued by cantonal authorities, are freely reviewable.[9] However, Art. 190 is not a comprehensive ban against the 'review' of federal laws, as legal scholars and the Federal Supreme Court itself have explicitly recognised since the beginning of the 1990s.[10] The Federal Supreme Court can interpret federal laws and define their meaning. Furthermore, the Federal Supreme Court can identify gaps in the legislation and will, on occasion, criticise certain regulations. Therefore, Art. 190 is now interpreted as not forbidding the Federal Supreme Court from issuing its opinion regarding the constitutionality of federal laws, but at the same time obliging the Federal

Supreme Court and other bodies to apply federal laws, even if they are considered to be unconstitutional.

In 1996, the Federal Council tried to introduce the concrete review of federal laws and other acts of general effect of the federal legislature, as part of the reform of the federal constitution. This concrete review would have allowed any individual to make a claim against the violation of rights guaranteed by the constitution, however, only in connection with a concrete case of applying a federal law. In addition, the cantons could also have made a claim against a violation of the division of jurisdiction between the cantons and federal authorities, as prescribed in the federal constitution. There are several good reasons for expanding the jurisdiction of the Federal Supreme Court in such a manner.[11] The most pertinent ones are that the lack of constitutional review of federal laws creates a gap in the system of legal protection and that the Court has changed its jurisprudence with respect to the European Convention of Human Rights.

At the time when the Federal Supreme Court was created, the federal government had very few areas of legislative and administrative competences and it was rather the position of the powerful cantons that was more likely to threaten citizens' rights. Constitutional review was, therefore, limited to cantonal norms. Because many tasks and responsibilities have been transferred to the federal level, it no longer makes sense to offer more protection against the violation of rights by the cantons rather than at the federal level. Furthermore, cantons have no possibility, under the current system, to claim a violation of their jurisdiction by federal laws, another gap of legal protection that needs to be closed.

The Federal Supreme Court has also begun to change the scope of its jurisprudence and is now willing to verify the harmony of federal law with the European Convention of Human Rights (ECHR).[12] In the case of a conflict between federal law and the ECHR, the Federal Supreme Court has refused to apply federal laws that violate the ECHR in some recent cases, on the condition that the legislation did not wilfully legislate against international law.[13] In cases where a claim of violating the ECHR is possible, the Court, therefore, might not implement the obligation to apply federal law, if its conclusion was based on a violation of the ECHR. However, in the case of fundamental rights guaranteed by the federal constitution, the Court always follows the rule of applying federal laws.[14]

However, these reasons for introducing concrete review failed to find a majority in parliament and, thus, the proposal to expand the jurisdiction of the Court, to include the concrete review of federal laws and acts having general effect on the federal assembly, was defeated. Therefore, limited constitutional jurisdiction, dating back to the total revision of the constitution in 1874, is still part of the Swiss constitution. In order to explain the origins as well as the persistence of the constrained power of the Court, we now examine doctrinal arguments as well as the power relations between the various political actors.

THE FEDERAL SUPREME COURT AND SWISS INSTITUTIONS

The limited constitutional jurisdiction of the Federal Supreme Court is understood to be rooted in the tradition of parliamentary supremacy and the sovereignty of the people, as part of the direct democratic instruments, and due to the ease with which the constitution can be changed. The reasons for introducing the limitation were thus seen as grounded in the doctrine of the separation of powers and the supremacy of parliament and, most importantly, in the institution of direct democracy with its popular referendum which was introduced on the occasion of the revision in 1874. It has been argued that the reformers did not want judges to decide upon laws that had been accepted by a majority of the people. It is therefore also argued that the restriction of constitutional review reflects the greater importance given to democratic over liberal values.[15] An alternative explanation is offered by Auer, who points towards the political homogeneity and the clear majority of the Radicals in all federal institutions at the time of revising the constitution in 1874.[16] This political homogeneity explains the absence of a real debate on the limited constitutional jurisdiction until the adaptation of the proportional election system in 1918, which caused huge losses to the Radical majority and led to a much more fragmented, but more representative composition of the federal assembly. Within this new political landscape, a debate emerged that challenged the limited constitutional jurisdiction of the Court, which continued until the 1950s, including a popular initiative defeated in 1939.[17] In the 1950s, the discussion ceased, which was probably due to the system of 'concordance'[18] that established a stronger integration of different societal interests.[19] The threat of a referendum, it has been argued, became a much more valuable instrument to secure the recognition of one's interests than a retrospective review of federal laws by the Federal Supreme Court.[20] The expansion of constitutional review was taken up once again by the first proposition in the 1970s for a total revision of the Federal Constitution. This reform, however, was never realised.

The doctrinal beliefs of the political actors as well as their strategic choices influenced by the direct-democratic institutions and the system of 'concordance' also help to explain the latest defeat of reforming the constitutional jurisdiction of the Court.

INTRODUCING CONCRETE REVIEW: ACTORS, MOTIVES AND INSTITUTIONS

Empirical findings show that the capacity to reach a consensus between the two chambers, the Council of States and the National Council, after two rounds of debating is high, and only a small number of projects have needed to be debated in each chamber more than twice (ten per cent).[21] However, this was not the case for the reform of the judicial system, which even required a 'conciliation committee' in order to reach an agreement between the two chambers. Two changes were highly controversial: the introduction of concrete review and the adoption of measures to limit access to the Federal Supreme Court. While a majority in the Council of States supported the proposal of the Federal Council to introduce concrete review, the National Council rejected that proposal in the first reading. In the second debate, the Council of States stuck to its former decision, maintaining the disagreement between the two chambers. The National Council then tried to offer a solution which included a compromise between the opponents of restricted access and the supporters of concrete review. In order to win the support of the Left for concrete review, the prepartory commission offered to abolish the measures limiting access to the Federal Supreme Court.

The concrete review as proposed by the commission would have only permitted review in a concrete case when fundamental rights were violated by federal law. The National Council and later the Council of States both accepted this proposition. But, before the final vote, the National Council decided, 105 to 55 votes, not to include concrete review in the package of judicial reforms, again creating disagreement with the Council of States, and thus making a 'conciliation committee' necessary. The 'conciliation committee' decided to remove concrete review from the set of judicial reforms and thus not to give the people the possibility of voting on this question separately from the rest of the judicial reforms. This decision was accepted by the two chambers and, therefore, the final reform no longer contained an extension of judicial review.

In parliament, among the governmental parties, it was mainly the People's Party (Conservatives) and a considerable section of the Social Democrats which were against the introduction of concrete review, whereas majorities of the Radicals and the Christian Democrats were in favour. The different party composition of the Council of States and the National

Council partly explains the differences in voting behaviour in the two chambers.[22] An examination of the arguments put forward in the parliamentary debate reveals that opponents of extension used the arguments of the supremacy of parliament and the people. An extension of judicial review was seen as going against the direct-democratic tradition and violating popular sovereignty. The differences in the positions of the governmental parties in parliament towards concrete review can partly be explained on the ground of different beliefs with respect to the importance of direct democracy in Switzerland or rather the myths celebrated around this institution. However, the differences in beliefs do not suffice to explain the different positions of the four governmental parties in parliament and the final defeat of the judicial expansion in parliament.

We can observe that the direct-democratic institutions influenced the strategic choices of the actors by removing the controversial proposition to increase judicial review from the reform package. It is important to realise that the Swiss voters have the ultimate say on the package of judicial reform. Given the strong opposition in parliament, including two out of four governmental parties, the chance of failing was considerable. The judicial reform included other measures which were considered to be important and urgent and which were much less controversial. Because of the fear that the other reforms would also not be realised if the voters rejected the entire package of judicial reform, based on the inclusion of expanded constitutional review, parliament chose to drop the proposal from the reform package. There were obviously strong doubts as to whether the voters would consider the introduction of concrete review the best way to strengthen the protection of their rights. A majority believed rather that the introduction of concrete review would be perceived by the voters as reducing the people's sovereignty. The threat of a defeat of the whole reform package and the necessity to form a winning coalition, including those actors with the power to bring about such a defeat in order to pass a popular vote, influenced the final decision of not proposing the introduction of concrete review to the people.

Furthermore, the differences in beliefs are probably not sufficient to explain the differing positions among the governmental parties in parliament. The two governmental parties who were more frequently not part of the winning coalition in parliament were the Social Democrats and the People's Party.[23] Given the rather deferential tradition of the Swiss Federal Supreme Court's jurisprudence and the composition of the Court (see below), it is also more likely that the Court does not share or promote their perspective. Thus, introducing another player in the decision-making process is less desirable for the Social Democrats and the People's Party than the other two governmental parties.

In sum, we can observe that the direct-democratic institutions and the patterns of coalition building in parliament influenced the strategic choices of the governmental parties in parliament, and led to a strong opposition against concrete review and to the eventual removal of the controversial proposition to expand judicial review from the reform package. Despite the introduction of some form of judicial reform, Switzerland, therefore, still has relatively limited constitutional review written into its constitution.

However, the analysis of the formal institutions which assign jurisdiction to a court is in and of itself not sufficient to understand the political role of a court. Within the context of an identical formal jurisdiction, courts can intervene more or less actively and play a more or less important role in policy-formulation and interpretation.[24] The two following sections argue that we can neither conclude that, because of its limited constitutional review and the unsuccessful reform, the Federal Supreme Court is generally a weak and negligible player, nor that Switzerland is not also following the international trend of judicialisation.

THE POLICY INFLUENCE OF THE SWISS FEDERAL SUPREME COURT

The influence of the Court on policy-making has to be assessed by taking into account the political institutions as well as the functioning of the Court and its jurisprudence. However, the analysis would not be complete if the results of analyses of judicial impact are not taken into account. As a broad range of studies has shown, the impact of court decisions does not just depend on the content of their decision. On the contrary, different contextual factors influence the impact of court decisions, such as the stage of intervention in the policy-making process and the reaction of political actors towards a decision and developments within a particular policy field.

The political process in general and the distribution of power in particular have been used in order to explain how often and how actively courts intervene in the policy-making process. It has been argued that federalism, a weak central state, and fragmentation of power in the national government lead to a decentralised, non-hierarchical and reactive governmental system. A decentralised, non-hierarchical and reactive governmental system results in legal complexity and encourages the use of courts to ensure governmental accountability.[25] It could be argued that Switzerland has a comparably weak central government and a comparably strong federalist structure, which would rather encourage court activism and involvement. However, the fragmentation of power in Switzerland is counter-balanced by a consensual style of decision-making, flowing from the referendum and initiative process. As the result of a political culture of 'concordance', a legal tradition of supremacy of parliament, and limited constitutional review, policy conflicts are more likely to be disputed and resolved within the traditional political forums and arenas rather than in court. Furthermore, the Swiss constitution can be changed with comparative ease, and can be characterised as containing a rather concrete formulation of norms. Court activism also seems to depend on how abstractly and openly constitutional norms are formulated and how frequently they get changed. The more concrete the formulations are and the more frequently the constitution is adapted, the less court activism is to be expected.[26] Switzerland has a relatively flexible constitution with rather concrete formulations of norms. Thus, the characteristics of Swiss political institutions point towards rather moderate involvement of the highest Swiss court in the policy-making process.

The decision-making process of the Court and the professional background of the judges help to assess further how strong is its activism. An important question is the composition of the Court, such as who the judges are and how they reach their decisions.[27] The judges of the Federal Supreme Court[28] are elected by the Federal Assembly for a six-year term. The 'concordance' rule also applies to the selection of the judges. The four parties holding seats in the Federal Council share the number of seats on the Federal Supreme Court according to their relative strength. One seat usually goes to a smaller party. Accordingly, there is political homogeneity between the judges and the governmental parties, an additional fact that is considered to reduce court activism. Given the circumstances of the appointment process, one would anticipate that the election of judges is highly politicised, but this is not the case in fact, because re-election is a widespread rule and, despite their party identification, the election of judges is not highly politicised. The selection of judges for highly active courts is usually much more controversial and debated. In addition, we might also consider the professional background of the judges, for example, cantonal courts are an important source of recruitment.[29] While there is no institutionalised career for judges as in other European countries, it is also not the case that lawyers at the end of their career become judges, as is the case in common law countries. The latter system is seen as enhancing court activism because judges do not perceive themselves as being 'civil servants' but 'controllers' of state authority.[30] The low politicisation of the election, the political homogeneity between the Court and the governmental coalition, as well as the professional background of the judges point to a rather moderate court activism.

The judicial decision-making style also points towards a lack of strong court activism. The Federal Supreme Court must hear all cases that fall in its jurisdiction, yet it can decline to hear substantive claims for procedural and formal reasons. A judge-reporter is assigned to every case. He supervises the preparation of the report and the opinion outline prepared by a clerk or a personal assistant, which is then circulated to the other judges of the respective chamber. If a debate seems necessary, the judges of the chamber sit together, usually in a session open to the public, to discuss the case. In such a debate the reporting judge usually gives his reasoning first, followed by a discussion in which the clerk writing the final opinion can also present his opinion. Otherwise, the judges of the respective chambers give their written consent. This type of decision-making process is not particularly adversarial. The final opinions are not written by the judges themselves but by a clerk (with legal training). Possible dissenting opinions are not included in the final decision, and only important decisions get published.[31]

Analysing the Court's jurisprudence and the impact of its decisions partly confirms and thus far partly contradicts the assessment of a moderate involvement in the policy-making process. On the one hand, the Court has promoted a rather apolitical image through its jurisprudence.[32] In contrast to courts in other countries, it does not issue detailed policies, but it concentrates on stating principles. It interprets its role in the light of parliamentary sovereignty and frequently does not give its opinion on the specific subject matter, on the ground that it is the task of the political authorities to formulate a solution. The remarks about the sovereignty of parliament indicate that the Court prefers to refrain from intervening into the policy-making domain. This impression is supported by the low success rate of constitutional and administrative cases: the average rate of success from 1987 to 1996 was 7.7 per cent of the cases decided in the field of constitutional and administrative law.[33]

On the other hand, the Court also defines its role in a more active way. It has been argued that the fact that the Court is only allowed to nullify cantonal laws gave it the freedom to develop a more creative jurisprudence.[34] First of all, the Court has broadened the legitimate grounds on which one can file a constitutional complaint and has, therefore, actively defined procedural rules.[35]

Second, with respect to issues of substantive law, the Federal Supreme Court has acknowledged several fundamental rights which were not yet written in the constitution and has, thus, broadened the scope of legal protection of fundamental rights. The jurisprudence of the Federal Supreme Court on fundamental rights has, together with the jurisprudence of the European Court of Human Rights, greatly influenced the list of basic rights in the reformed constitution. The revised constitution now contains the fundamental rights developed by the Federal Supreme Court which had not previously been written into the Federal Constitution.[36] The jurisprudence of the Court has therefore been characterised as being creative and not strictly following an interpretative model.[37] We might even speak of a small 'rights revolution', as it has been termed in several common law countries.[38]

Third, the Court has changed its interpretation of the obligation to apply federal and international law, as well as its jurisprudence with respect to the ECHR. Since the beginning of the 1990s, the Court has been willing to review federal laws, in the sense that it states its opinions on their constitutionality, without the consequence of not applying the law or even nullifying it. This has been perceived as a reinterpretation of the constitutional clause obliging the Court to apply federal and international law.[39] Furthermore, as mentioned earlier, the Court has changed its jurisprudence with respect to the ECHR and is now willing to verify the compliance of federal law with the ECHR. In the case of a conflict between federal law and the jurisprudence of the ECHR, and on the condition that the parliament did not deliberately legislate against international law, the Federal Supreme Court has in some recent cases even rejected the application of federal law which violated the ECHR.[40] Thus, we can say that the Court plays an active and creative role in the domain of fundamental rights, correcting the image of a low-profile actor.

Finally, the influence of the Swiss Federal Supreme Court has to be assessed in light of the results of impact analysis. So far, there has been only a small amount of empirical research on the impact of decisions of the Court in the fields of constitutional and administrative law on policy-making. The Court only publishes about ten per cent of the decided cases, the ones it considers to be important from a legal perspective, and does not provide a database of all its decisions, which makes it extremely difficult to gain an overview of the effective contribution of the Court. Empirical research indicates so far that the Court can be a major player given certain circumstances, but that generally its contribution to policy-making is an incrementalist[41] one and accordingly not very dramatic.

The analysis of six decisions of the Federal Supreme Court belonging to three different policy fields[42] led to the following conclusions: the analysis revealed a weak to a medium strong impact in five out of the six cases.[43]

However, the results also indicate that making a general conclusion from the restricted jurisdiction of the Court as having a weak influence through its decisions on policy-making is not valid, because in one case the study found a strong impact. This exceptional case belonged to the field of assisted reproductive technology policies.

The policy-making process concerning assisted reproductive technologies took place in a bottom-up, rather than in a top-down manner. As the cantons are mainly in charge of health policy, they started to issue regulations before any federal laws were adopted. The Federal Supreme Court ruled against the highly restrictive law of one canton right at the beginning of the policy-formulation process on the federal level.[44] Through this decision, which stated basically that general prohibitions of certain techniques violate the right to personal freedom, the Court strongly influenced the policy-making process on the cantonal level, by stopping at least three more cantons from adopting restrictive laws, as well as pushing policy-making in two cantons which had already adopted restrictive laws in a much more liberal direction. Therefore, the Court's decision influenced the initial situation for the debate on the federal level. At the same time, the arguments of the Federal Supreme Court found a strong resonance with the political actors on the federal level. In particular, the proponents for a more liberal solution referred to the Court's opinion that general prohibitions violate the right to personal freedom. Thus, the Court did influence the policy-making process not only by changing the initial legal situation in the cantons, but also by directly influencing the federal political debate.

The analysis of this case reveals that the Court's decision had a marked influence for several reasons: the Court strongly affected the policy outcome on the federal level, not only because the decision contained basic value statements with respect to the right to personal freedom, but also because the Court intervened at a very early stage of the policy-making process,[45] and then because the issue moved to the federal level from the cantons, which had issued regulations before the issue was actually debated on the federal level.

The case illustrates that the Federal Supreme Court can play a decisive role for policy-making on the federal level by influencing policy-making on the cantonal level. However, the circumstances of the assisted reproductive case imply that such a decisive influence is the exception rather than the rule. Walter Kälin and Andreas Rieder have analysed all 1,800 cases[46] involving concrete or abstract review of cantonal norms from 1968 to 1998. In only 102 cases did the Court conclude that a norm violated the federal constitution or the ECHR. In contrast to the case described above, the Court most often only nullified or did not apply a single clause of a law, as opposed to the entire or the greatest part of the single law regulating a policy field, as was the case in the field of assisted reproductive technology policies.[47]

The discussion of the influence of the Court has so far revealed that it played an active role in interpreting fundamental rights, generally broadening the access to the court and in reinterpreting the constitutional provision which obliges it to apply federal and international law. At the same time, the results of judicial impact analysis indicate that the Court can under certain circumstances strongly influence policy-making despite the limited constitutional review, but that its influence is primarily an incrementalist one. Unfortunately, empirical analyses reconstructing its contribution to policy making in different fields are lacking and therefore a comprehensive assessment grounded in empirical research has been only partly possible.

SWITZERLAND: NO EXCEPTION TO THE GENERAL TREND OF JUDICIALISATION

The description of the somewhat active and creative jurisprudence of the Federal Supreme Court in the previous section already indicates that Switzerland is not an exception to the general trend of expanding judicial power. However, the country probably started out at a lower degree of judicialisation than other countries, and the impact of European integration on the process of judicialisation has so far been absent in Switzerland, which contributes to a less visible process of judicialisation in comparison with other countries.

As mentioned in the introduction, the reform of the judicial system introduced the guarantee of access to an independent court. Constitutional and administrative judicial review became independent from the executive branch rather late in Switzerland.[48] The constitutional amendment adopted early in 2000 in a popular vote, as part of a judicial reform, guaranteeing every citizen the right to appeal to an independent court is a further step in this development. It was only in the second half of the twentieth century that the cantons created separate administrative courts, and only since 1997 have they been obliged to provide access to an administrative court at least in those domains where an administrative appeal to the Federal Supreme Court is possible.[49] As for the introduction of concrete review for the Federal Supreme Court, it has been argued that, at the cantonal level, the doctrine of the sovereignty of the people, as part of the doctrine of direct democracy inhibited the creation of independent courts with the power of review separate from the cantonal government and administration. For a large part of the twentieth century there was, accordingly, no available review of administrative decisions by an independent court in many cantons, whereas the cantonal executive was the last instance in charge of reviewing a case.[50]

In the beginning of the 1990s, specialised court instances were also introduced on the federal level in order to review complaints against administrative decisions within particular units of the administration. These courts cover a large part, but not all of the various substantive fields; the recent judicial reform package will close this gap. Furthermore, there are a small number of cases where the Federal Council[51] is still in charge of legal review with no possibility of appeal to the Federal Supreme Court. The implementation of the recent judicial reform will probably transfer the larger part of the judicial review carried out by the executive to court instances.[52] The term judicialisation also refers to the practice of creating court instances, separate from administrative bodies or the government, and thus transferring decisional power from the administration to a judicial instance. Switzerland engaged late in the process of creating court instances for administrative review, a process that will be completed with the implementation of the most recent judicial reform.

As described in the preceding section, the Federal Supreme Court expanded its jurisdiction despite the failure to introduce concrete review of federal laws. The Court has broadened the number of legitimate causes where it is possible to file a constitutional complaint and therefore actively defined procedural rules. It has acknowledged several fundamental rights previously absent from the constitution and broadened the legal protection concerning fundamental rights. Furthermore, it has changed its interpretation of the obligation to apply federal and international law, and is now willing to review federal laws, in the sense that it states its opinions on their constitutionality, without taking the further consequence of not applying laws or even nullifying them. In addition, it has recently begun to verify the compatibility of federal law with the ECHR and, in the case of a conflict between federal law and the ECHR, has refused to apply federal law.

These developments clearly indicate that Switzerland is also following the global trend of an expansion of the power of its highest court. Given that Switzerland is not a member of the EU or the ECC, the process of European integration has not had the effect of expanding judicial power that has taken place in EU member countries. Legal scholars mostly agree that Art. 190 of the Federal Constitution could no longer be applied in cases where federal laws would conflict with Community law if Switzerland became a member of the EU.[53] This possibility raises the question of how the partial introduction of constitutional review of federal laws on the grounds of the ECHR might be explained in Switzerland, if it is not due to the effects of European integration.

Martin Shapiro has argued that the success of constitutional review may be the result of a division of powers, either through a federalist structure or a division of power in national government, but that 'rights generated review now takes its place beside division of powers generated judicial review'.[54] For Switzerland, the federal structure helps to explain the introduction of abstract and concrete review for cantonal laws. The willingness of the Swiss Federal Supreme Court to review the compatibility of a federal law with the ECHR and not to apply the federal law given certain circumstances, is the result of an extended protection of rights – for instance, a rights-generated review – even though still a limited one.

There are probably three forces which have been driving the process of judicialisation. First of all, the jurisprudence of the European Court of Human Rights forced Switzerland to revise its judicial procedures, to improve the protection of the rights of the accused and prisoners, and contributed to the adoption of the right of everyone to have their case reviewed by an independent court.[55] Second, the ECHR gave the Swiss Federal Supreme Court the legitimacy to change its jurisprudence. Before the Court changed its jurisprudence and agreed to verify violations of the ECHR, there were cases where the Federal Supreme Court refused to review the constitutionality of a law because of the constitutional obligation to apply federal law, even though the complaint made to the European Court of Human Rights was successful. This resulted in a unacceptable situation with respect to the protection of rights and led the Federal Supreme Court to alter its jurisprudence. Third, the role of the legal community should not be underestimated. Charles Epp has argued that rights revolutions need a support structure for legal mobilisation, and in the case of the common law countries he has studied it was a pressure from below that initiated the changes in establishing and protecting fundamental rights. In the case of Switzerland, it might not have been rights advocates *per se*, but the debate within the legal community which has also contributed to the above-mentioned changes; for instance, the decisions of the Swiss Federal Supreme Court take into account the arguments by legal scholars, and the Court explicitly states its agreement or disagreement with them. In addition to the recent debate on the introduction of concrete review, legal scholars, as well as legal practitioners, have generally been strong advocates for a greater protection of rights.[56]

CONCLUSION: A MODERATE TREND OF JUDICIALISATION

Recent attempts to introduce a reform which included concrete review of federal laws by the Federal Supreme Court failed principally because of the resistance of two out of the four governmental parties. The introduction of concrete review was regarded as diminishing the sovereignty of the people because a federal law accepted by the people could then be reviewed by the Court. The doctrine of direct-democratic instruments is a rather delicate issue in Switzerland, and any measure that is successfully portrayed as possibly reducing or limiting direct-democratic participation will have a hard time to find a majority or to pass in a popular vote. However, only a small number of laws undergo a popular referendum, and the concrete review of federal laws would review the work of parliament and government rather than control the will of the people. Therefore, the argument here is that one of the motives for rejecting the introduction of concrete review was the fear of reducing the negotiating power of those forces strong enough to bring about a referendum or a defeat in a popular vote.

However, the evidence presented in this account indicates a trend of judicialisation in Switzerland, which seems to be largely based on improving and expanding the protection of fundamental rights. But the changes in the jurisprudence of the Swiss Federal Supreme Court are rather moderate, because it still respects the obligation to apply federal laws, although issuing its opinion on their constitutionality. Furthermore, it has only refused to apply federal laws in a few recent cases because they violated the ECHR and, therefore, is still adhering to its former doctrine of applying the law, despite a violation of the ECHR. This moderate trend might be partly explained by the lack of impulse from European integration, which has initiated or at least enforced judicialisation in some member states. Overall, the judicialisation process has so far strengthened the 'Rechtsstaat' in Switzerland without greatly extending judicial power.

Given the changes in the jurisprudence of the Swiss Federal Supreme Court and a possible participation in the EU or the ECC, it seems to be only a matter of time before concrete review is introduced. However, it appears to be more likely that concrete review will be realised through a formal change of the constitution, rather than by the Federal Supreme Court changing the direction of its jurisprudence of its own accord and thus no longer applying federal laws if they violate the federal constitution or international law.

NOTES

1. T. Vallinder, 'When the Courts Go Marching In', in N.C. Tate and T. Vallinder (eds.), *The Global Expansion of Judicial Power* (New York: New York University Press 1995), p.13.
2. Popular vote of 12 March 2000: 86.3 per cent yes to 13.7 per cent no. The reforms consist principally of three changes: (1) the constitution will now permit the standardisation of civil and penal law procedures, which have varied broadly from one canton to the other; (2) it newly guarantees citizens' access to an independent court; (3) it allows the introduction of new courts, below the Swiss Federal Supreme Court, in order to reduce the work load of the highest court. The reform will be concretised and implemented by a federal law.
3. Concrete review: the constitutionality of laws can only be reviewed in connection with a decision applying the respective law, e.g. by challenging the decision applying the law.
4. In March 2000 changes in the constitution concerning the legal system and the Federal Supreme Court were accepted by the people: the references in this article already refer to the constitutional articles as accepted in the popular vote (see BBl 1999: 8633–5). All citations of legal norms refer to the legal situation of June 2000.
5. Federal Constitution of 18 April 1999: Art. 189, Abs. 1, BBl 1999: 8634.
6. Ibid.
7. Ibid.; Art. 190: 'Bundesgesetze und Völkerrecht sind für das Bundesgericht und die anderen rechtsanwendenden Behörden massgebend', 'Ni le tribunal fédéral ni aucune autorité ne peuvent refuser d'appliquer une loi fédéral ou le droit international' (FF 1999: 7832); translation by the author: 'Neither the Swiss Federal Supreme Court nor any other authority must deny to apply a federal law or ratified international law'; Art. 190 corresponds to Art. 113 Abs. 3 and Art. 114bis Abs. 3 before its total revision in 1999.
8. The Federal Assembly statutes on legal norms in the form of 'federal laws' or 'ordinances', Federal Constitution of 18 April 1999: Art. 163.
9. Note that the cantonal constitutions are approved by the federal assembly, and can not be challenged in the Swiss Federal Supreme Court; Federal Constitution of 18 April 1999: Art. 172.
10. BGE 117 Ib 373 in connection with ECHR; Expertenkommission für die Totalrevision der Bundesrechtspflege. Schlussbericht 1997: 33; A. Auer, G. Malinverni and M. Hottelier, *Droit constitutionnel suisse, Vol. 1: L'Etat* (Bern: Stämpfli 2000), p.649; W. Kälin, 'Justiz', in U. Klöti *et al.* (eds.), *Handbuch der Schweizer Politik* (Zürich: NZZ Verlag 2000), pp.198–201.
11. Botschaft über eine neue Bundesverfassung vom 20. November 1996, BBl 1996 I: 505–14; Reform der Bundesverfassung: Erläuterungen zum Verfassungsentwurf: 255, 273–6; Expertenkommission für die Totalrevision der Bundesrechtspflege: Schlussbericht 1997: 31–5; Auer *et al.*, *Droit constitutionnel Suisse* Vol.1, p.655 n.10; Kälin, 'Justiz', pp.198–201.
12. Switzerland ratified the European Convention of Human Rights in 1972, protocols 6 and 7 were ratified in 1987 and 1988 respectively.
13. Auer *et al.*, *Droit constitutionnel suisse, Vol. 1*, pp.651ff; Kälin, 'Justiz', pp.204–5; Botschaft über eine neue Bundesverfassung vom 20. November 1996, BBl 1996 I: 513–4. BGE 122 II 485, BGE 1919 V 171; BGE 117 IIb 367, BGE 124 II 480.
14. Auer *et al.*, *Droit constitutionnel suisse, Vol. 1*, pp.654–5.
15. W. Kälin, *Verfassungsgerichtsbarkeit in der Demokratie. Funktionen der staatsrechtlichen Beschwerde* (Bern: Stämpfli 1987), pp.90–92; J.-F. Aubert, *Traité de droit constitutionnel suisse* (Neuchâtel: Ides et Calendes 1967), Vol.I, pp.173–5; A. Auer, *La juridiction constitutionnelle en Suisse* (Bâle: Helbing & Lichtenhahn 1983), p.62.
16. Auer, *La juridiction constitutionnelle en Suisse*, pp.60–61.
17. Popular vote 22 Jan. 1939: Popular initiative for extending the constitutional jurisdiction of the Swiss Federal Supreme Court; No: 71.1 per cent, Yes: 28.9 per cent.
18. See Papodopoulos in this volume.
19. Integration of the Social Democrats into the Federal Council, introduction of the pre-parliamentary consultation procedure.
20. Auer, *La juridiction constitutionnelle en Suisse*, pp.104–5.
21. R. Lüthi, L. Meier and H. Hirter, 'Fraktionsdisziplin und die Vertretung von Partikulärinteressen im Nationalrat', in Parlamentsdienste (ed.), *Das Parlament: Oberste Gewalt des Bundes?* (Bern: Haupt 1991), pp.53–72.

22. In addition, the introduction of concrete review would have strengthened the position of the cantons as they do not have the means to legally challenge a violation of the distribution of responsibilities and powers between the cantons and the federal level. This change might also have contributed to stronger support among the member of the Council of States, the representatives of the cantons.
23. See Kriesi in this volume.
24. K.M. Holland, *Judicial Activism in Comparative Perspective* (Houndsmill: Macmillan 1991), pp.1–11.
25. R.A. Kagan, 'Adversarial Legalism and American Government', in M. Landy and M.A. Levin (eds.), *The New Politics of Public Policy* (Maryland: Johns Hopkins 1995), pp.89–118; R.A. Kagan, 'Should Europe Worry About Adversarial Legalism?', *Oxford Journal of Legal Studies* 17/2 (1997), pp.165–83; C. Rothmayr, *Politik vor Gericht. Implementation und Wirkung von Entscheiden des Schweizerischen Bundesgerichts in den Bereichen Fortpflanzungsmedizin, Lohngleichheit von Frau und Mann und Sonntagsarbeit* (Bern: Haupt 1999), pp.9–21; R. Kiener and R. Lanz, 'Amerikanisierung des schweizerischen Rechts – und ihre Grenzen. "Adversarial Legalism" und schweizerische Rechtsordnung', *Zeitschrift für Schweizerisches Recht* 119/2 (2000), pp.155–74.
26. Kälin, *Verfassungsgerichtsbarkeit in der Demokratie*, p.172; M. Shapiro and A. Stone, 'The New Constitutional Politics of Europe', *Comparative Political Studies* 26 (1994), pp.397–420.
27. Holland, *Judicial Activism in Comparative Perspective*, pp.1–11.
28. See Bundesgesetz vom 16. Dezember 1943 über die Organisation der Bundesrechtspflege, and Reglement für das Schweizerische Bundesgericht vom 14.12.1978.
29. There is no administrative career within the judiciary in Switzerland, in contrast to France or Italy. At the same time, judges are not, as in the US, lawyers who become judges at the end of their career.
30. Holland, *Judicial Activism in Comparative Perspective*, p.8.
31. Less than ten per cent of the cases are getting published according to T. Probst, *Die Änderung der Rechtsprechung. Eine rechtsvergleichende, methodologische Untersuchung zum Phänomen der höchstrichterlichen Rechtsprechungsänderung in der Schweiz [civil law] und den Vereinigten Staaten [common law]* (Basel: Helbing & Lichtenhahn 1993), p.599; Reglement für das Schweizerische Bundesgericht vom 14.12. 1978, Art. 18.
32. Auer, *La juridiction constitutionnelle en Suisse*, pp.104–5.
33. Bericht des Schweizerischen Bundesgerichts über seine Amtstätigkeit, 1987–96.
34. Auer, *La juridiction constitutionnelle en Suisse*, pp.104–5; nullification only possible in the case of a constitutional complaint (*staatsrechtliche Beschwerde*).
35. Expertenkommission für die Totalrevision der Bundesrechtspflege. Schlussbericht 1997: 11.
36. Botschaft über eine neue Bundesverfassung vom 20. November 1996, BBl 1996 I: 44, 62, 138; Kommentar zum Verfassungsentwurf 1996: 34–67. Konkordanztabelle Neue–Alte Verfassung (June 2000).
37. Auer, *La juridiction constitutionnelle en Suisse*, pp.104–5; Kälin, *Verfassungsgerichtsbarkeit in der Demokratie*, p.192.
38. C.R. Epp, *The Rights Revolution. Lawyers, Activists, and Supreme Courts in Comparative Perspective* (Chicago: University of Chicago Press 1998).
39. Auer *et al.*, *Droit constitutionnel suisse, Vol. 1*, pp.649–50.
40. Ibid., pp.651ff; Kälin, 'Justiz', pp.204–5; Botschaft über eine neue Bundesverfassung vom 20. November 1996, BBl 1996 I: 513–14.
41. M. Shapiro, 'The Success of Judicial Review', in S.J. Kenney, W.M. Riesinger and J.C. Reitz (eds.), *Constitutional Dialogues in Comparative Perspective* (Houndsmill: Macmillan 1999), pp.193–219.
42. Policy Fields: Assisted Reproductive Technologies, Labour Law, Gender Equality; Rothmayr, *Politik vor Gericht*.
43. A combination of two dimensions was used in order to measure the strength of the influence, e.g. the importance of the changes to the policy (no changes, changes to secondary aspects, changes to policy core) and the broadness of the impacts within the federal system by taking into account the division of decisional power and implementation duties between the federal level and the cantons in each policy-field. See Rothmayr, *Politik vor Gericht*, pp.28–32.

44. BGE 115 Ia 234.
45. R.A. Dahl, 'Decision-Making in a Democracy: The Supreme Court as a National Policy-Maker', *Journal of Public Law* 6 (1957), pp.279–95.
46. These are just the cases that have been published by the Swiss Federal Supreme Court.
47. W. Kälin and A. Rieder, 'Im Spannungsfeld von Verfassungsgerichtsbarkeit und Demokratie. Im Interesse der Grundrechte', *Neue Züricher Zeitung* 216 (18 Sept. 1998), p.17.
48. Kälin, 'Justiz', pp.192–4.
49. Bundesgesetz vom 16. Dezember 1943 über die Organisation der Bundesrechtspflege: Art. 98a; Kälin, 'Justiz', pp.192–4.
50. Kälin, 'Justiz', pp.192–4; H. Geser, *Bevölkerungsgrösse und Staatsorganisation. Kleine Kantone im Lichte ihrer öffentlichen Budgetstruktur, Verwaltung und Rechtssetzung* (Bern: Lang 1991), p.188.
51. Bundesgesetz vom 16. Dezember 1943 über die Organisation der Bundesrechtspflege: Art. 99.
52. Botschaft über eine neue Bundesverfassung vom 20. November 1996, BBl 1996 I: 642, 539–40; Federal Constitution of 18 April 1999: Art. 29. In addition, it is also worth mentioning that the institution of an Ombudsman has never prevailed on the federal level. A few towns and cantons have introduced an Ombudsman which functions as a mediator between citizens and the administration.
53. A. Epiney *et al.*, 'Schweizerische Demokratie und Europäsiche Union. Zur demokratischen Legitimation in der EU und den Implikationen eines EU-Beitritts der Schweiz für die schweizerische Demokratie' (Bern: Stämpfli 1998), p.108.
54. Shapiro, 'The Success of Judicial Review', p.200.
55. ECHR Art. 6, Ziff. 1; Kälin, 'Justiz', p.199.
56. Given the strong federalist structure of Switzerland it would be equally necessary to discuss the process of judicialisation on the cantonal level. Due to the lack of comprehensive research on the cantonal courts, the discussion of judicialisation in this account has remained limited to the Swiss Federal Supreme Court. In addition, the state of research also did not permit an examination of the differences in the judicialisation across different policy fields.

Institutions and Outcomes
of Swiss Federalism:
The Role of the Cantons in Swiss Politics

WOLF LINDER and ADRIAN VATTER

BASIC CHARACTERISTICS OF THE FEDERAL FRAMEWORK

Together with the United States and Canada, Switzerland is one of the three classical federations in the world.[1] Historically speaking, the Swiss federation can be considered as a case of 'non-centralisation'. When founding the federation in 1848, the 25 cantons kept their own statehood, their own constitutions and most of their political autonomy. They transferred only a few competences to the federal government and assured themselves significant participation rights in the decision-making of the central authorities. Article 3 of the Swiss constitution still defines the division of powers between the Federation and the cantons. A general subsidiarity clause assigns all tasks to the cantons unless explicitly delegated to the central state. As to the representation of the member states in the federal parliamentary system, the Swiss solution resembles that of the US: full bicameralism consisting of two legislative chambers, in which the National Council represents the people and the Council of Cantons the member states. Each chamber has the same competences and deliberates all issues one after the other. To become valid, a parliamentary decision needs the majority in both chambers. The principle of a double majority applies also for certain decisions in the process of direct democracy: constitutional amendments, proposed either by the Federal Chambers or by a popular initiative, are subject to a mandatory vote by the people. To be accepted, such a proposition must win the approval of the people and of the cantons.[2] Thus, all popular initiatives and parliamentary decisions on constitutional amendments and on some international treaties need a double majority representing the democratic and the cantonal majority.

The prominent role of the cantons in federal decision-making is not only found in the formal elements of the constitution[3] but also in the pre-parliamentary process of federal legislation and in the implementation of

Wolf Linder and Adrian Vatter, University of Berne

federal policies. Decision-making and implementation of federal policies can be characterised as a multi-level governance in which the central government, the 26 cantons and the 3,000 communes are involved. This network of a co-operating federalism has led to the disappearance of the clear vertical separation of powers which was the original idea of Swiss federalism in the nineteenth century.

Historically speaking, the Swiss federation was a political compromise between a Radical Protestant majority, protagonist of a strong national government, and a Conservative Catholic minority refusing to give away cantonal sovereignty. The result of the constitution of 1848, a 'weak' federation with strong cantonal autonomy, was a vertical power-sharing structure from the beginning. It allowed for peaceful coexistence and conflict resolution and the integration of the Swiss society which until 1848 had barely existed. Indeed, the segmented peoples of the Cantons, after four religious wars, were divided by a deep cleavage between Catholics and Protestants and between rural regions and urban centres. Moreover, federalism protected French-, Italian- and Romanisch-speaking minorities against dictates of the German-speaking majority. In the twentieth century, the vertical power-sharing elements of federalism were completed by elements of horizontal power-sharing, realised mainly through proportional representation between the four largest political parties. This allowed the political Left (Social Democrats) to become integrated into the bourgeois state, once dominated by the Centre-Right parties of Radicals, Christian Democrats and the People's Party. Thus, in Arend Lijphart's[4] terms of 'Consensus Democracy', federalism represents the historically oldest part in the 'structural' dimension of the Swiss power-sharing system.

Our analysis of Swiss federalism focuses on the role of the cantons. The first part gives an account on the functioning and the political outcome of the most important institutions of Swiss federalism. In taking advantage of the growing empirical research on Swiss federalism, the second part examines comparative findings of the political-institutional variations in 26 cantons, both their systematic interaction and their impact on policy outcomes. The final part discusses the needs and possibilities of reforms of Swiss federalism.

THE INFLUENCE OF THE CANTONS ON FEDERAL POLITICS

Division of Power between the Federation and the Cantons

Switzerland, up to the present, has remained one of the most decentralised countries. Despite growing responsibilities over the last decades, the central government controls only about one-third of public revenue and expenditure. In contrast, the cantons and the communes control for about two-thirds of public financial and personnel resources, are the main responsible actors in a wide range of policy programmes, and play a prominent role in implementing most federal programmes.

One reason for this non-centralisation is obvious: according to the basic constitutional rule, every transfer of power to the federation requires a constitutional amendment which is, as already mentioned, subject to a popular vote. The double majority of the people and the cantons is a high hurdle to be surmounted. Indeed, from 1848 to 1997 almost one-third of the 140 constitutional amendments proposed by the federal chambers failed in the vote. The success rate of the 121 popular initiatives was less than ten per cent.[5] Moreover, parliament is conscious of the difficulty of winning a majority among the politically heterogeneous cantons and therefore is cautious in its proposals for new federal competences.

A comparative look at the United States tells us, however, that a similar constitutional rule on the federal division of power need not necessarily produce the same results. Like the Swiss, the US constitution needs to be amended for the extension of competences of the central government. Confronted with similar political difficulties of ratification by the Senate and the states, the US authorities chose another way to extend federal competences. Instead of seeking formal changes of the constitution, the US government found a way round: it appealed to the Supreme Court which, under legal concepts of 'implied powers' or the 'interstate commerce clause', acknowledged many new competences of the central government. Neither government nor parliament in Switzerland have chosen this way of by-passing formal amendment of the constitution. Instead, they extended central powers by many modest amending steps that had a chance of being approved by the heterogeneous cantons and by the people. Thus, if both federations in the last 150 years have considerably extended the powers of their central government, they have done so in different ways: the US through authoritative judicial review that produced 'new' competences from the same constitutional document; the Swiss authorities through the political way of formal amendments approved by the people and the cantons. This may be the second reason why the Swiss federal system has so greatly resisted centralisation.

The Double-Majority Rule in Popular Votations as a Veto Power Device of Small Cantons

The two different majority rules – democratic and federalist – can produce different results for the same decision. In bicameral law-making, this is not a particular problem. If the National Council and the Council of States end up with different propositions on the same bill, they engage in a common procedure to eliminate differences. This procedure cannot be applied in a popular vote, when a particular constitutional amendment may win a majority from the people, but is rejected by majority of the cantons, and vice versa. In this case, the status quo ante prevails. Between 1848 and 1999 there were ten collisions, six of which occurred only in the last 30 years. Evidently, the risk of a collision between the democratic principle of 'one person one vote' and the federalist principle of 'every canton an equal vote' is growing. There are two reasons for this development. The first, the number of propositions for constitutional amendments – stemming either from parliament or from popular initiatives – is growing. The second, the difference in population size between cantons is increasing because of migration from rural to urban cantons. Whereas in 1848 one vote from the small canton of Uri cancelled out 17 votes from the largest canton of Zurich when the majority of the cantons was counted, today it is 34 votes. When the 11.5 smallest cantons vote together, they constitute a blocking federalist majority representing a small democratic minority. Theoretically, the smallest federalist veto power (51 per cent of the votes in the smallest cantons against all the other votes) in 1880 was more than 11.5 per cent of the Swiss population; today, it represents just nine per cent. Raimund Germann[6] therefore speaks of a change of balance: the weight of the federal principle is increased, while the weight of the democratic principle is reduced.

An analysis of the collision cases is revealing. The votes concerned important and controversial issues in national economic policy, federal energy, immigration and cultural policy. In eight of the ten collision cases, it was the federalist side that overruled a democratic majority. Adrian Vatter and Fritz Sager[7] have analysed the winners and losers of the double-majority rule: it is the preferences of small and medium-sized, mainly conservative Catholic cantons in German-speaking parts of Switzerland which are protected through this rule, whereas the urban cantons with the largest populations, like the canton of Zurich, were on the losing side in all eight cases.

Today, the double-majority rule is of particular significance in issues of foreign policy. The Swiss people are deeply divided on the question whether or not Switzerland should join the European Union, become a member of the UN, and abandon its old neutrality or foreign policy stance of 'economical integration without political participation'. In this cleavage, the small, rural and German-speaking cantons are strongholds of the non-integrationist conservatives, whereas bigger, urban or French-speaking cantons are on the modernist side that wants to open up Swiss foreign relations. Even though this is not a case of direct collision, the double-majority rule gives the non-integrationist conservatives a systemic advantage: they profit from their strongholds in the small, rural German-speaking cantons.

In sum, the double-majority rule in direct democracy is an effective veto-power device. It has even more political impact than in 1847 when it was designed for the losers of the 'Sonderbund War', those who were against centralisation, state intervention and policy changes. But one can doubt whether this historically biased federalist overrepresentation is a wise institutional design in matters of foreign policy in the twenty-first century. Moreover, the growing risk of collision leads us to the fundamental question: to what degree can it be justified that a small minority of the electorate can overrule a democratic majority?

Bicameral Law-Making and Cantonal Interests

Law-making in the Swiss parliament reflects the equal importance of democratic and federal influence. Both chambers may initiate constitutional amendments, new bills and regulations, as well as propose the revision of existing laws and regulations. Every proposition or bill destined to become federal law has to be approved by a relative majority in both chambers. How does this strong element of federalism work out in law-making? On the one hand, public opinion still considers the Council of the States to be a stronghold of cantonal interests, as was the intention of the fathers of the Constitution. On the other hand, empirical research has sometimes found that the Council of the States is not at all a federalist institution because it defends mostly the same group interests as can be identified in the National Council.[8] Indeed, there is a strong theoretical argument for this second opinion: the Council of States, unlike the German Bundesrat, is not a representative of the executive of the member states and therefore is responsive to the cantonal constituencies rather than to government interests. And these constituencies are the same for the National Council and the Council of the States. From the point of view of representation, however, we can identify clear differences between the two chambers which are due to different modes of election:

- Whereas the number of representatives in the 200-member National Council depends on the population size of a canton, every full canton elects the same number of senators (two) to the smaller chamber (46 members). In the Council of States, the small cantons, which are more rural, are overrepresented. Theoretically, the 23 senators of the smallest cantons which represent only 20 per cent of the population have a veto power on any decision of the Swiss parliament.[9] According to Lijphart,[10] Switzerland, together with the US, ranks highest on a Gini index of inequality among nine federal chambers.

- The National Council is elected on a proportional base. This leads to a fairly 'true' representation of electoral forces (see the account by Kriesi in this volume). The Council of States, however, is elected on majority rule. As no political party today has the necessary electoral backing of 50 per cent to win seats alone, the results of elections mainly depend on electoral coalitions. The latter are mostly found among the three bourgeois parties which form tickets with highly successful alliances. The Social Democrats can rely only on the small Green Party, or else have difficulty in finding a ticket-partner at all. Therefore the political Left is highly underrepresented, and the political Centre and Right are overrepresented in the Council of States.

- Proportional representation is generally more favourable to women's electoral success. Indeed, the National Council, in all elections since 1971 when women's suffrage was introduced, showed a comparatively higher proportion of women (24 per cent against 15 per cent in 1999) than the Council of States.

From these differences of representation one could theoretically expect a systematic bias of the Council of States in favour of rural interests or those of the small cantons, and against the political Left and group interests of women. An empirical comparison of all parliamentary decisions in the period of 1995–97 on the conflict dimensions Left–Right, Federalism–Centralism, Interventionism–Liberalism and Materialism–Postmaterialism gives some surprising findings. Congruent with the expectations, the National Council is more on the postmaterial side. Yet for the rest, not only the Council of States but both chambers modify government proposals in the same direction: in favour of the Right, of liberalism and of federal solutions. Empirical evidence for a 'federalist' and 'party' effect of the Council of States is only found in the 60 per cent of the cases where deliberations of the two chambers produce different propositions which have to be reconciled through bargaining in a formal procedure. In these cases, the Council of States' proposals were more to the Right, more liberal, more federalist – and more successful.[11]

These findings only partially confirm the traditional image of the Council of the States as a stronghold of cantonal sovereignty. Indeed, the small chamber may have lived up to this image only in the nineteenth century when the strong Catholic-Conservative deputation of the Council of States prevented power shifting to the Radical and Protestant central government. In the twentieth century, the main division is between bourgeois forces – often uniting Catholics and Protestants on one side, and the Social Democrats, concentrated in industrial and urban regions, on the other. Under the dominant Left–Right cleavage, 'federalism versus centralism' is no longer a principal issue but has become a pragmatic question in which all political parties sometimes favour centralism or federalism. For several reasons, then, we cannot expect to get a clear-cut profile of decision-making differences from the viewpoint of representation alone. Firstly, political parties now mobilise on more than one cleavage. In the Left–Right dimension, the Radicals as well as Christian Democrats do not represent a single block but are open to different tendencies. This variation offers chances of compromise and log-rolling with shifting coalitions among the governmental parties. Secondly, the Swiss government cannot be forced to resign on a vote of confidence. This makes the members of the Swiss parliament somewhat independent from the instructions of their factions. Thirdly, different decisions made by the two chambers may also result from differences of size and decision-making conditions. So it is often said that the Council of the States, whose members are older and have more political experience, adds a different quality to law-making as a 'chambre de réflexion' or as the 'legal conscience of parliament' that has more distance from daily political concerns.

We might conclude that the Council of States has not primarily subscribed to the federal ideal of maintaining decentralisation or the prerogatives of the cantons. A more convincing perspective is that different political forces – the Catholics, the bourgeois coalition and the rural cantons – used their overrepresentation in the Council of States to their own advantage. Thus, the Council of States has often in the past played a conservative role, protecting the status quo against innovations proposed by the government and the other chamber. Yet this is an effect of the specific political composition of its majority, and not of the system itself. If the Council of States does not live up to its attributed function of representing the interests of its member states, this does not mean that it must lose its legitimacy: Conservative parties may praise bicameralism or the Council of States even more as it serves their interests. As George Tsebelis and Jeannette Money[12] found in their comparative study, the common effect of bicameralism is a bias towards the status quo. Or, in the formulation of Thomas Jefferson: if the tea is poured from a first into a second cup, it is less hot to drink. For the Swiss system, this could mean that important role of the Council of the States, as a second *'chambre de réflexion'*, is to strengthen political stability and the consensual mode of politics.[13]

The Influence of the Cantons on Federal Policy Formulation

If the specific federalist role of the Council of States is rather weak, this does not mean that cantonal interests are not articulated at all. Indeed, looking at the whole policy-cycle, we can find that in the two phases of policy formulation and implementation the influence of the cantons is quite strong. Let us turn to the policy formulation first. In the Swiss decision-making process, policy formulation is tied to an extensive 'pre-parliamentary' process of participation and consultation. It takes place before the government hands its project over to the federal chambers. The pre-parliamentary stage consists of two phases, the evaluation or even elaboration of a first draft of the bill by expert commissions, and the consultation procedures in which political parties, the cantons, as well as economic, professional and social organisations give their views on the draft of the bill. The function of this pre-parliamentary stage is to prepare a consensus for the bill and to reduce the risk of a future defeat in a popular vote by securing participation of all societal organisations affected by the issue. Thus, when the Federal Council nominates a committee of experts to evaluate the various options of a new bill, it is especially concerned to appoint members who represent the standpoints of the different interest groups, parties and cantons affected by the proposed legislation. As Germann[14] showed in his extensive study, the cantons, especially the representatives of urban regions, were called on to participate on average in more than three out of four extra-parliamentary commissions in the 1970s. A similar result can be found for the consultation procedure. On average, the cantons participate in no fewer than nine out of ten consultation procedures.[15] However, in contrast to this relatively advantageous picture of the cantons' participatory power, Gerhard Lehmbruch[16] concludes that:

> the cantons themselves, as institutionalized corporate actors, have no strong influence in federal policy making – contrary to some preconceived ideas. They certainly play a role in decentralized issue areas, such as education policy, and ... cantonal actors may exert some influence in specific fields, such as territorial planning, but their role is relatively marginal to the central domains of economic and social policy.[17]

In line with this somewhat apodictic argument, several studies conclude that not the cantons but other actors such as some of the economic interest groups and the federal agencies exert significant influence.[18] This is not surprising, as we know[19] that the most important criterion for being selected to participate, and to be heard, in the pre-parliamentary procedure is the capacity to mount a successful referendum challenge. This corresponds to the main function of the preparliamentary stage to find a broadly supported compromise against which well-organised interest groups and parties will not launch a referendum. But interest groups are not always powerful. The influence of private vested interests varies significantly from one policy field to another. Thus, from a theoretical point of view, the variing relative bargaining power of private organisations and the cantons depends as well on their political capacity to mobilise a common group interest and to withhold their support.[20] With such a perspective, we understand why, according to many empirical findings, cantonal influence varies despite high formal participation. Small and structurally weak cantons, on the one hand, often lack the necessary expertise to judge complex federal drafts and are in many cases restricted to expressing the opinions of cantonal interest groups. Larger cantons, on the other hand, which are equipped with sufficient administrative resources, in some cases come to play a crucial role in the pre-parliamentary process.[21] This is particularly the case in policy fields in which the central government depends on the implementation resources and experiences of the cantons.

Co-operative Federalism

The arena with the uncontestably highest influence over the cantons is to be found in the implementation of federal policies. Today, this process is characterised by a high degree of co-operation between the subnational units and the federal government. Most federal programmes are implemented by the cantons and the communes. With some exceptions, there is no parallel federal administration with its own regional services, agencies or even courts, and only very few federal services deal directly with the public. The complexities of modern infrastructure, economic intervention and social policies stimulated the development of a co-operative federalism. In many policy fields, one of its main characteristics is the shift of basic legislation competences to the centre while the cantons regulate the implementation process and its modalities. Institutionally, it involves different levels of government co-operation in the same policy programme. This has simultaneously led to a broad system of financial compensation between the federation, the cantons and the communes that comprises revenue-sharing as well as financial compensation by block grants and subsidies.[22] A further consequence of the strong position of the cantons during the implementation process is the absence or only very reluctant use of coercive means by the federal authorities which leads in many cases to a strong variation across the cantons in the way the processes of implementation are organised.[23] Sometimes, minimal legal standards in the application of federal law can only be ensured by review through the Federal Court: a prominent case was Appenzell I.Rh. When women's suffrage was introduced in 1971 on the federal level, Appenzell men refused to implement it in their canton. It was only in 1990 by decision of the Constitutional Court that the canton fulfilled its obligation.[24] While the highly decentralised implementation may strengthen innovation, the system's conflict-resolution capacity, as well as its flexibility and adaptability, it does not ensure consistent policy outcomes. It weakens the centre's governance capacity. Multi-level finance systems and compensation reduce the responsibility of one single actor. In this context academics emphasise the ambiguous function of the Swiss way of policy implementation:

> The trade-off between legislative powers attributed to the center and implementing powers assumed by the cantons assures a certain power balance without which the cantons would be expected to make persistent use of their veto-power. Possible deviations of the policy outcome from the federal norms are considered to be the price to pay for the maintenance of this equilibrium.[25]

Self-Coordination between the Cantons

Thus far, we have considered the 'vertical' instruments of Swiss federalism that concern the relations between the federation and the cantons. In this section, we give an account of instruments of self-coordination between the cantons, or of the 'horizontal instruments' of 'co-operative' federalism which allow the cantons to take collective action without the involvement of the federation. There are two types: inter-cantonal organisations and agencies, and 'concordats', a form of contractual co-operation.

The most important elements of horizontal co-operative federalism are the concordats, that is, inter-cantonal treaties functioning as instruments of regional co-operation.[26] The concordats allow the subnational units to regulate administrative, legislative and juridical matters among themselves. However, there are severe limits to this instrument. Concordats are most effective if all cantons subscribe but it is difficult to reach unanimity. So, the particularism of half of the cantons starting the school year in spring and the other half of the cantons in autumn could not be overcome by a concordat for a long time. Other concordats can work with only some of the cantons participating. Whereas the eastern cantons have signed a high number of concordats, the cantons of French- and Italian-speaking Switzerland are less interested in co-operation through concordats. Nevertheless, the growing importance of this form of inter-cantonal co-operation becomes increasingly evident. Besides geographic, economic and integration-political reasons, it is also related to the fact that the cantons adopt this strategy – for traditional as well as new issues – increasingly in order to defend their own competences and to prevent the imposition of a central state decree. On the whole, the effects of inter-cantonal treaties prove to be ambivalent. On the one hand, regional concordats, in particular, enable the creation of specific solutions adapted to local needs. On the other hand, inter-cantonal agreements are severely affected by their insufficient democratic legitimacy and their bureaucratic character and unwieldiness, since their success depends on the unanimity of all members involved.[27]

Inter-cantonal organisations play an important role as consultative institutions. They provide a forum to share experiences and to co-ordinate tasks between cantonal politicians and officials. In total there are more than 500 inter-cantonal organisations, with the Conference of Cantonal Ministers traditionally being the most influential.[28] In the process of European integration, the Conference of Cantonal Governments was established as yet another organisation. With the aid of this body, the cantons attempt to extend their direct influence on the federation especially in the field of foreign policy and to secure a co-ordinated definition of problems. In the 1990s, these direct negotiations between cantonal and federal executives have, especially in the issue of European integration, thrust other channels of influence into the background. To conclude, the horizontal instruments of federalism have to be judged critically. Especially in recent years it has become clear that they hardly serve as effective means to prevent new federal competences. At the same time, they impede co-ordination with the federation and are unlikely to produce viable solutions, mainly due to the increasing differences between the cantons' administrative structures and interests. Traditional weak points of horizontal federalism institutions such as their technocratic and unwieldy character further add to this problem. Nevertheless, new bodies such as the Conference of Cantonal Governments have gained importance under the pressure of European integration and have thus introduced alternative and extended forms of horizontal cooperation favouring a distinctly executive federalism.

Policy Outcomes of Swiss Federalism

General characteristics of federal policies. Comparative studies show that Switzerland has one of the lowest rates of state consumption of all OECD countries. The proportion of revenue and public expenditure between the federation, the cantons and the communes is about 30:40:30 per cent, which means the central government controls less of the public budget than all other federal countries. It may be difficult to attribute these characteristics to federalism only. Indeed, it is plausible to conceive them as a combined effect of federalism and direct democracy. This is in line with the perspective of the new institutionalism.[29] Representatives of this approach emphasise that counter-majoritarian institutions such as federalism and direct democracy function as particularly powerful institutional veto-points which set limits to the scope of actions of the central government. Subnational actors, on the one hand, use their veto power in order to block centralisation and policy changes which are not in their interest. On the other hand, subnational actors have their own interest in national policies – for instance to participate in the central budget, to promote their own preferences which have not yet found a majority on the national level, or even to hand over unpopular responsibilities to the central government. In both cases, federal and subnational actors have to engage in negotiation and co-ordination processes in which the lowest common denominator between many actors has to be sought. If subnational units have heterogeneous interests and resources of their own, federalism tends to favour decentralised policy solutions and sets limits to expenditures of the central government. In addition, heterogeneous preferences of subnational units imply a systemic bias for the status quo and for incremental politics. This leads to political stability but prohibits quick or major policy changes in the federal system.

Such effects can be demonstrated in particular by looking at the development of the Swiss welfare state. In his study, Herbert Obinger[30] comes to the conclusion that the close interplay between direct democracy and federalism generated three major effects on Swiss welfare state development, 'namely a lag effect, a structural effect and a restrictive impact on welfare state funding. Together, these three effects largely explain the liberal trajectory and the belated formation of the Swiss welfare state from a comparative viewpoint'. First, due to the fact that almost all competences in social policy were originally in the hands of the cantons, it took a long time to transfer the power in the field of social security to the central level, since all constitutional amendments required a double majority of the people and the cantons in mandatory referendums.

Secondly, the lack of comprehensive federal social policy induced by the defeat of several social policy projects was compensated by private welfare organisations. Since the federation's policies were vetoed, the central government, as well as the cantons, began to subsidise the social security programmes of these private carriers. This led to the emergence of a peculiar public-private mix in the field of social policy.[31]

Third, the federal government had only limited fiscal capacity and a narrow tax basis which reduced its ability to fund welfare state programmes in a generous and constant way over a longer period of time. Political scientists and economists generally agree that the institutional veto points of direct democracy and federalism were the decisive factors that set limits to the expansion of public policies, confined centralisation and hindered expansive public spending as well as high taxes in the federal system.[32]

Implementation of federal policies: the structural factor. High subnational autonomy implies numerous responsibilities of the cantons in the implementation of federal policies. These responsibilities are the same for all cantons. But the cantons differ in population size. The needs as well as the capacity to implement ecological standards are not the same in Uri with its 30,000 inhabitants as in Zurich with its population of more than one million. Thus, in many cases administrative federalism results in lax and inconsistent implementation of policy standards because small cantons in particular are not sufficiently equipped with financial, personnel and administrative resources to fulfil these tasks.[33] Moreover, we find considerable differences of socio-economic development between 'poor' and 'rich' cantons. To a certain extent, economic deficiencies as well as lack of cantonal capacities to implement federal policies are compensated for by a complex system of financial perequation. This explains why transfers to the cantons occupy a comparatively high proportion of the federal budget.

Implementation of federal policies: the political factor. Unequal capacities are not the only reason for inconsistent federal policy outcomes in the cantons. New case studies[34] have confirmed the earlier results of Wolf Linder[35] that the degree of political consensus on the federal and the cantonal level is the most important factor of policy implementation.

In the multilevel arrangement of 'co-operative federalism', the level of consensus can be different at the federal and the cantonal level. Innovations of federal programmes, even though supported by a high federal consensus, can be compromised through cantonal vetoes. But certain cantons may have

strong preferences for their own innovations which do not find a majority at
the federal level. This leads to different implementation chances of federal
policies that can be conceptualised in Figure 1.[36]

Field I is the least problematic: under the condition of high consensus on
the federal and cantonal level, policy programmes are implemented with a
high rate of success. There is ample empirical evidence that under this
constellation the system of 'co-operative federalism' can prove its qualities:
the cantons compensate for eventual weaknesses of federal legislation,
share implementation experiences and are willing to learn from each other.

Field II, however, is a more frequent case: federal policies are blocked
by vetoes from some cantons. The different political preferences of the
cantons are more decisive than all other factors: comparative studies have
shown that the implementation of federal housing programmes or
employment programmes for refugees depends less on the housing or job
market of a canton than on the strength of political parties for or against
these programmes.[37] One could say that this field shows the critical
weakness of a federal system in which even clear decisions of the central
government cannot overcome subnational veto positions – as in the above-
mentioned Appenzell case of women's political rights.

Field III is characterised by weak federal legislation, while the cantons
strongly support their own objectives in the same policy field. These
objectives can be in line with federal legislation, but in many cases the
cantons have other policies in mind. In this situation, the cantons use the
federal policy as an instrument to promote their own, deviating objectives.
On the one hand, this can be interpreted as the typical weakness of a federal
system in which the central government has insufficient power to overcome
subnational vetoes. On the other hand, one could argue that it is precisely
the strength of a federal system that subnational units develop their own
policies if decisions of central government lack a clear political consensus
and support. Indeed, when the federal policy was blocked in the 1980s in
the conflict over continuing or stopping nuclear energy, it was some cantons
that developed different pilot programmes of energy saving. This was a
highly innovative process in which pioneer cantons with similar preferences

FIGURE 1
CONSENSUS CONSTELLATIONS AND IMPLEMENTATION CHANCES

	Cantons: Strong consensus	Cantons: Weak consensus
Federation: Strong consensus	I Full implementation	II Partial implementation of federal programme
Federation: Weak consensus	III Deviation from federal programme	IV Poor or no implementation

were engaged in a co-operative learning process that prepared for a consensus on the federal level.

Field IV finally is characterised by weak consensus on both the federal and the cantonal levels. It is a rare case to find policies that are decided on a weak consensus base on both the national and the cantonal level. But occasionally these conditions are met, as with popular initiatives that are accepted against the political will of national and cantonal élites. This was the case of the popular initiative for the protection of high moors. Its protagonists were able to win the double majority in the popular vote in 1987 but not to raise enough support against vested interests of farmers and tourism in the implementation process. Thus, policy outcomes are poor or even absent.

Federalism and the Solution of Multicultural Conflicts

The constitution of 1848 replaced old historical treaties for mutual assistance between the cantons by a modern common government. Yet at that time the cantons were deeply divided by four different languages, two religions and ethnicity. A 'Swiss society' barely existed; the constitution of 1848 consequently speaks of the 'peoples of the cantons'. Federalism, therefore, has been the structural element of power-sharing that offered the societies of the cantons the utmost autonomy for keeping their own government, ample opportunities to live differently and to maintain their regional tradition and culture as well. In the last 150 years, the cleavages of religion and language have cooled. To a large extent, Swiss society is a product of its political institutions, which led Karl Deutsch[38] to speak of a 'paradigmatic case of political integration'.

Today, the peaceful solution of multicultural conflicts and the integration of fragmented societies is one of the most difficult problems in many countries world-wide. To an extent, conflicts between different ethnic or cultural segments of the same society have replaced war between nations. Faced with this problem, only few democracies perform well. Lijphart,[39] in his seminal work on power-sharing, insists that consensus democracy is superior to the majoritarian model when it comes to the solution of conflicts in culturally divided societies.

With regard to federalism – which can be seen as the structural part of power-sharing – other theorists are not so shure as to its good effects on the solution of multicultural or minority conflicts. They argue: (a) that federalism protects only geographically segmented minorities that are able to control a subnational unit, which can lead to a new minority problem in this unit; (b) that creating subnational units for cultural minorities can lead to the separation of this minority as in Bosnia, and to a discriminating control through the majority; and (c) that federal systems of segmented societies with few subnational units – such as Belgium or the former Czechoslovakia – are unstable.[40]

The first argument is valid also for the Swiss case. Many minorities – the Jews, the foreigners (which account for 20 per cent of the population), or gypsies were never protected by Swiss federalism. Moreover, federalism protects the Swiss linguistic minorities only on the national level, where the authorities accept the four languages of German, French, Italian and Romanisch as equal. A German speaker in Geneva, however, has no minority rights and therefore has to address the authorities in French. Thus, federalism is a rather incomplete instrument to protect minorities. But why has Swiss federalism escaped the risks mentionend in the other arguments? According to Jörg Steiner[41] and Wolf Linder,[42] we find three factors generally favourable to minority protection in federal systems. Firstly, linguistic, ethnic and religious segmentation, until recently, was characterised by not too many, and not too small minorities. Secondly, economic, religious and linguistic fragmentation of the cantonal societies did not coincide socially or geographically. Some German-speaking cantons are mainly Catholic, some Protestant. There was only one case, the region of the Jura, which was poor, French-speaking and Catholic, and which felt discriminated against by the mainly Protestant, German-speaking and rich canton of Bern. Here, three cleavages coincided socially and geographically. This explains why the Jura is the sole case of a secession in the Swiss federation: after long political struggles, the Jura became an autonomous canton in 1978. Thirdly, in many cantons, there was no clean geographical separation of religious or linguistic groups. We find four bi- or multi-lingual cantons and, with regard to religion, all of them are mixed. Under these circumstances, the federal structure was beneficial for coexistence and learning processes between different religious and cultural groups: A liberal French-speaking politician in the canton of Valais is in a minority position in questions of party politics but belongs to the linguistic majority in his canton. As a member of the National Council, however, he is in a linguistic minority position, but normally forms part of the bourgeois majority. Thus, the members of the political elite have to learn both the minority and the majority roles. Co-operative federalism implies a constant process of negotiation. As coalitions change from one question to the other, the different actors need each other and have to accept each other. This favours win–win situations, learning processes and coexistence.

Thus, we can conclude from the Swiss case that structural federalism can indeed be favourable to peaceful solutions of multicultural conflicts, but only under specific circumstances.

COMPARATIVE ANALYSES OF POLITICAL INSTITUTIONS AND
OUTCOMES AT THE CANTONAL LEVEL

Institutional Characteristics of the Cantons

Swiss cantonal systems, developed and refined over the past 170 years,
represent a mixture of different, sometimes opposing, elements of direct and
representative democracy. Strong cantonal executives, elected by the
people, are more independent from their parliaments than on the federal
level. Further characteristics of the cantonal institutions are the
decentralised organisation of the cantons that have a high degree of local
autonomy, well-developed popular rights with various kinds of initiatives
and referendums, all-party executives, non-professional and weak
parliaments compared with government and administration. The
combination of these elements allows Swiss cantonal political systems to be
described as power-sharing or consensus democracies with the features of a
strong direct democracy. However, important differences exist among the
language regions: both direct democracy and local autonomy are less
developed in the French-speaking region than in the German-speaking
one.[43]

At the federal level, the structure-building function of the optional
referendum has been described most convincingly by Leonhard Neidhart.[44]
This fundamental finding is even today generally regarded as one of the
most important, but not the only explanation, for the development of power-
sharing structures on all levels in the Swiss federation.[45] Little attention has
been given, however, to the compensatory power-sharing functions of
optional referendums and initiatives which take effect in established
consensus democracies. Under these conditions optional referendums and
initiatives function as substitute power-sharing instruments for
insufficiently integrated minorities. A comparative analysis of the Swiss
cantons[46] shows the following interdependence: the less 'perfectly' a
consensual system is organised, the sooner optional referendums and
initiatives will be used by underrepresented minorities as alternative
instruments to power-sharing. Or, in other words, the more inclusive the
government coalition and the greater the local autonomy of the population,
the less opposing popular rights are used. However, in cantons where the
parliament is elected by a majority rule and high electoral thresholds apply,
popular rights are not used more often than in cantons with purely
proportional representation and low electoral thresholds. This finding,
surprising at first, is actually quite plausible when given further
consideration. Moreover, it is even possible that such a result actually

complements the findings of comparative democracy research. According to Linder,[47] influence by means of referendum is maximised in consensual systems with direct democracy, while at the same time the importance of elections is minimised due to the impossibility of a transfer of power. The low salience of parliamentary elections in the semi-direct consensual democracies of the cantons helps to explain why the proportionality effect of the electoral system, a basic element of power-sharing in representative democracies, does not have any influence on the use of optional referendums and initiatives.

The 26 cantons also provide an excellent opportunity to test the impact of direct democracy on political parties. The often-cited thesis that direct democracy weakens political parties cannot be maintained after carrying out a comparative analysis of the 26 Swiss cantons.[48] In cantons with an extensive use of referendums and initiatives, political parties are not weaker than in cantons with a low record of popular people's participation. On the contrary, direct democracy seems to lead to more professional and formalised party organisations. It is true, however, that in cantons which favour direct democracy, party systems are more fragmented and volatile and small parties receive a larger share of the vote. An empirical examination of the causes of such party fractionalisation in the two dozen cantons shows that the number of parties at the sub-national level is on the one hand a function of the religious heterogeneity of the cantons, and on the other hand a function of the effective electoral threshold.[49] Furthermore, socio-structural characteristics, such as urbanisation and population density, are a predictor both for the number of parties and the use of the popular rights.[50]

Policy Output and Outcomes

Earlier studies indicate that the differing sizes of the cantons have a strong influence on the way in which policies are developed and implemented.[51] As the population size of the cantons varies from one million to 20–30 thousand, this finding is not surprising. Whereas large cantons with professional and sophisticated administrative structures have been able to handle new and complex tasks (such as environmental protection), small cantons with little technical, organisational, professional and financial resources, not to mention part-time elected officials, have been overwhelmed. For an effective implementation of policy, three strategies remain for small cantons. The first is co-operation with other cantons, which offers economies of scale. The second concerns outsourcing: small cantons buy complex public services from bigger cantons able to produce them in sufficient quality and quantity.

The third, more often used in the last decade of liberalisation, applies to the privatisation of public services. These three strategies helped to maintain a highly decentralised system of cantonal policies, for instance in education and public health. But large cantons set the standards and take on a pioneering role which leads to their political predominance and market strength, while the small cantons are forced to find external support and are thus less autonomous. In this way it becomes clear that the practical meaning of cantonal autonomy depends on resources and capacities.

In general, the price to pay for a decentralised political system is in inequality of public goods. Swiss federalism tries to compensate for this by setting federal minimal standards and by a broad system of financial compensation between the federal government, the cantons and the communes. Education is a good example. The cantons have the main responsibility for education, but, since the nineteenth century, the federal constitution has required that the cantons provide sufficient basic education. This obliges the cantons to offer a minimum number of years' schooling free of charge but compulsory for everybody. This particular federal standard greatly influenced the evolution of the Swiss educational system, and the provision of equal, basic education became the common concern of all cantons. In higher education, however, great inequalities existed. In the 1960s, the federal government begun to subsidise higher education in the cantons. The federal objective to give talented students from rural areas a better chance at higher education was only partly successful. While the development of a decentralised system of cantonal schools has facilitated access to higher education in peripheral regions, social inequalities still persist. An illustrative example of this is gender. While in urban cantons such as Geneva, Basel and Zurich the percentage of women getting degrees of higher education is sometimes higher than that of men, women's proportion in small rural cantons such as Nidwalden, Obwalden and Appenzell Innerrhoden is often less than half that of the men. As in every country, social differences in access to higher education are more difficult to overcome than barriers set up by geographical boundaries. For Swiss federalism, we have to add the fact that regional equality is considered politically to be a more salient issue than equality between the social strata.

The above example illustrates that the implementation process in the cantons depends not only on the various administrative capacities and social structures, but on political intentions as well. As shown earlier, the implementation of federal government programmes cannot be taken for granted and consensus is required at different levels of government (see Figure 1). Programmes almost unanimously welcomed by the Federal

Assembly may be controversial in certain cantons. For example, an analysis of federal housing-programme subsidies in the 1980s has shown that money was not spent where housing was most needed, but in cantons where political forces willing to protect tenants were the strongest.[52] Another example is the implementation of the federal regulation limiting the acquisition of land and real estate by foreigners. Whereas in some cantons the sale of land and houses to foreigners stabilised or even fell, it rose sharply in others.[53] In some cantons the objectives of the federal law coincided with the canton's own strategies, as in Lucerne, which wanted slow and gentle development of tourist sites. In other cantons, such as Valais, the objectives of the federal regulation were compromised because the Valaisans needed foreign capital to finance their plans for the development of new tourist sites. Today, similar observations can be made on the implementation of a federal law restricting access to the labour market for asylum seekers.[54] All these cases, illustrate that the federal government has only limited influence on the cantonal governments to comply with federal law. The cantons, making use of their powers of legislation and implementation, are able to adapt the federal law to their own political needs.

Effects of Direct Democracy

Let us turn finally to the effects of direct democracy on the social and economic performance of the cantons. Unfortunately, there has been little research done by political scientists on this issue. A few economic studies have examined whether direct democracy would have a positive or a negative impact on economic growth and fiscal performance in Swiss cantons and cities. Most of these empirical studies at the sub-national level find empirical evidence that the institutions of direct democracy lead to positive outcomes. Gebhard Kirchgässner, Lars Feld and Marcel Savioz[55] conclude that public expenditures have lower growth rates in Swiss cities that have a well-developed direct democracy. Werner Pommerehne and Hannelore Weck-Hannemann[56] demonstrated that the willingness to finance government is higher and tax evasion is lower in cantons with more rights of direct participation of the people. Feld and Savioz[57] recently presented empirical evidence that cantonal systems which favour direct democratic elements have better economic performance than cantons which are based on a more representative democracy. These empirical studies have certain shortcomings in the fact that the validity of measuring direct democracy is questionable and that they omit some important control factors, not to mention their use of simple theoretical assumptions. To a certain degree, these studies stand in strong contrast to other studies by Swiss economists which ascertain that direct democracy is the main reason behind Switzerland's slow economic growth.[58] However, they confirm the veto player thesis[59] that direct democracy is an effective counter-majoritarian institution against public spending, taxation and public debt.[60]

IS THERE A NEED FOR AN INSTITUTIONAL REFORM OF SWISS FEDERALISM?

For some scholars, the 150-year-old institutions of Swiss federalism and the unbalanced resources and sizes of the 26 cantons are at the roots of an inconsistency of policy outcomes, a weak centre's capacity for governance, a systematic bias for the status quo and a weak innovation record of Swiss politics. It is therefore not surprising that the call for reforms to Swiss federalism has grown louder in the last few years. There are four fundamental reform strategies that will be discussed here in brief.

The Territorial Reform Strategy

Reducing the number of cantons. As many problems of federalism are due to the fact of too many small units, the advantage of merging the cantons of fewer and more homogeneous units seems reasonable. In order to ensure that Swiss politics are democratic, effective and 'Europe-compatible', some critics call for, above all else, a fundamental change in the basic structures of Swiss federalism, namely the rearranging of the borders of the component units and creating larger functional regions. René Frey,[61] for example, proposed the replacement of the 26 cantons by six or seven regions, each with more or less the same population size and economic power. This proposition seems promising from an economic viewpoint in that it would allow for economies of scale, reduce unnecessary redundancy as well as improve the competitive position of the Swiss member states against other European regions. However, this reform of Swiss federalism could disturb the long-standing balance of power among the cantons and between the sub-national units and the central government. Their self-protection as a cultural and regional minority would suffer. Furthermore, there are also economic arguments against the reduction of the number of member states, such as the increased planning costs and a lower competition among cantons, which restrict organisational and political innovation.

Creating new political bodies for urban regions. The migration of people from rural regions to the cities significantly shifts the demographic structure of the cantons, regions and communes. Old cities have been transformed into urban regions or agglomerations in the last 50 years which cross traditional communal boundaries and are composed of central cities with around 30 or more peripheral communes. There is no political body for the common needs of their inhabitants. Agglomerations constitute, in some way, the 'lost dimension' in Swiss federalism. In some agglomerations, the administrative co-operation among big cities, the canton and peripheral communes works well, in others it fails. The shortcomings of merely administrative co-operation lie in the fact that political conflicts cannot be resolved because of too many veto positions. Moreover, there is no planning authority for the agglomeration as a whole. Should there be a metropolitan authority for all shared services and public goods in urban areas? There is a strong theoretical argument for it in the idea that electoral and fiscal responsibility for a public good should coincide with those who benefit from it. In Switzerland, the idea of a political statute for agglomerations runs counter to the tradition of local autonomy. One could argue that the country does not need a fourth tier in a federal system that is already too complex. But the problem remains. European urbanisation is transgressing national boundaries and pushing for larger dimensions. This pressure will probably help the Swiss in finding their own solution. Such institution-building could occur in one of two ways: either the cantons and communes will see a revitalisation of historical districts, with the advantage that the old geographical patterns will be able to be utilised. Or a consolidation of urban government will be achieved by the statutory creation of a special region as is the recent attempt in the Fribourg canton. Urban regions can be designed effectively to cover the common geographical range of public goods, yet they may be considered artificial because their boundaries do not represent patterns of common political culture or reflect a sense of political community. If both methods are unsatisfactory, a third option has been proposed for the agglomeration of Berne.[62] It consists of a flexible organisation in which only those communes that are willing to share part of their facilities and public services co-operate. Prices for common public services are higher for non-members than for members. Thus, the organisation helps to keep eventual benefits of co-operation among members and creates incentives for initial non-members to become members.

The Sisyphus of Functional Reforms: Clear Separation of Responsibilities and Powers

Since territorial reforms are politically difficult and otherwise not very feasible, theorists and politicians prefer another strategy: functional reform, which is currently sought in two different ways.

Separation of powers and responsibilities. The current networks of fiscal federalism and political co-operation between the cantons and the federal government are complicated, not transparent, have many dated incentives and weaken political responsibilities. These disadvantages of co-operative federalism are not recent. The federation and the cantons therefore sought ways and means to separate powers and responsibilities over the last 20 years. In theory, a clear separation of responsibilities offers considerable advantages. It allows for financial equivalence of public goods, which means a clear definition of identical groups of payers and users, and minimises externalities if responsibilities follow the classic principle of subsidiarity. In practice, however, all political reforms for a clear separation of responsibilities have failed. There are several reasons for this. In the small-scale geography of Swiss federalism, spillovers of most cantonal policy programmes are unavoidable. Factual interdependence between federal and cantonal responsibilities cannot be cut off.[63] Finally, every federal system has in-built incentives for shared financing of political programmes. Therefore, the separation of responsibilities is like the rock of Sisyphus which, after being pushed up, rolls down the hill again.

Intensifying co-operation. If one accepts the fact that territorial reforms are impossible and the success of the separation of responsibilities is limited, one can try to make the best of handling the interdependencies. This means trying to find better forms of co-operation between the federation and the cantons and among the cantons themselves as well.

Institutional Reforms: Finding a New Balance between Democracy and Federalism

The growing differences in population size between cantons due to migration from rural to urban cantons has led to the imbalance between federalist and democratic principles. A group of small cantons that represent less than a quarter of the people can block decisions of national importance both in all legislation taken by the Council of States or in cases of constitutional amendment, requiring the double majority of the cantons and the people in the popular vote. This double-majority requirement is especially in need of reform. While favouring small rural, more conservative and German-speaking cantons, the language minorities are not protected at all by this federal institution. Moreover, the double-majority requirement prevents important innovations and policy reforms at the federal level and makes the international integration of Switzerland very difficult. This can be illustrated by the referendum on Swiss membership in the

European Economic Area in 1992, where only 50.3 per cent of the voters but 19 cantons rejected the treaty: 30 per cent of all votes, coming from the small cantons, were enough to block the project. For the approval of the treaty, however, a very strong majority of 55–60 per cent of the people would have been necessary to reach a minimum majority of 12 cantons. It is therefore evident that future government proposals to join the European Union will encounter particular difficulty when it comes to the popular vote.

Evidently, one of the main reasons that the principle of federalism has an increased weight in comparison to the democratic majority rule is the migration among cantons. Then why not reassess the relative importance of federalism and democracy? Why not go back to the equilibrium of 1848 for instance? Solutions could be found by redistributing the votes of the cantons in referendums with the double-majority requirement. Given the increasing difference in the population size of cantons, one could give large cantons three votes, the medium-sized cantons two votes and the small cantons one vote. Another possibility consists of introducing new majority rules. One could propose that only a qualified majority of two-thirds of the cantons can block a democratic majority. While these propositions for reform appear efficient, their introduction will lead either to the *de facto* suppression of the double-majority rule or – by using weighted cantonal votes – to a violation of the federal principle of equal representation of cantons. Alternatively, one could argue for a 'qualified popular majority' rule: a strong popular 'yes' of 55 or 60 per cent, for instance, could wipe out a 'no' from the cantons.[64] Even simpler is the proposition that in cases of a collision between the democratic and federalist majority, the 'stronger majority' (that is, the majority with the larger share of 'yes' votes) would be decisive.[65] Furthermore, one could also imagine rules for a division of power that would allow the federation to undertake new activities without amending the constitution in every single case. Despite all these propositions, one should not forget that they all have a catch: changing the rules of the game has to be done under the existing rules of federalism, and there is no reason for minorities to renounce their long-held minority rights when asked to do so.

New Actor Strategies instead of Institutional Reforms: Changing the Players rather than the Rules of the Game

Many transformations of Swiss federalism in the last 100 years took place without institutional reforms. Sonja Wälti[66] especially points out that the cautious use of federal control over the cantons, and, conversely, the renunciation by the cantons of the use of potentially powerful institutions to exert influence over central decisions (cantonal referendum, summoning of parliament) are due to the dominant strategies of decision-makers rather than a change of the institutional framework. Therefore, she comes to the conclusion that:

> an institutional reform of the federal configuration in Switzerland does not appear to be very promising. On the contrary, institutional reforms of federalism do not seem necessary nor are they necessarily suitable in order to accomplish better policy outcomes and the desired increase in the centre's governance capacity. In other words, the game can be influenced by changing the players rather than the rules of the game.[67]

Promising alternatives to institutional reforms in her mind are, on the one hand, more central intervention in the implementation process as well as a more extensive use of instruments of surveillance. On the other hand, Wälti proposes direct payments and assistance in the policy implementation of the federal government for the cantons with less financial and bureaucratic resources. Finally, she calls for the better integration of cantons in the entire policy formulation process, including the pre-parliamentarian stage, in order to reduce the danger of a successful veto in the final decision.

CONCLUSION

Our short overview of four reform scenarios shows that improving federal governance can be made from very different approaches and perspectives. Most proposals signify a radical change of federal traditions. The political feasibility of reform projects such as reducing the number of cantons, making a clear separation of responsibilities and powers is low. Thus, federal reforms will most probably be limited to less incisive measures. Each approach makes specific contributions to the sensible further development of Swiss federalism and can lead to improved governance in Switzerland. However, the possibility of implementing such radical federalist reforms is low. While radical reform projects such as the rearranging of cantonal boarders, making a clear separation of responsibilities and powers or making institutional changes, in the end cannot fail due to strong federal powers, less considerable, such as the intensification of co-operation or improved utilisation of existing instruments, are more uncertain. As Ulrich Klöti[68] points out, this means pragmatic and punctual adaptations. Unfortunately, this also means that Swiss federalism has to live with shortcomings that can easier be identified in theory than in practice.

NOTES

1. D.J. Elazar (ed.), *Federal Systems of the World – A Handbook of Federal, Confederal and Autonomy Arrangements* (London, 1991), p.252.
2. The majority of the people is calculated from the votes of all Swiss people voting. The cantonal majority is calculated on the votes of the people of every canton. On this basis, each of the 20 'full' cantons counts for two votes, each of the 6 'half' cantons for 1 vote. Thus, a cantonal majority is reached with 12 votes.
3. One could mention some further constitutional elements which are of less importance or scarcely used: the obligation of the parliament to consider the representation of different cantons or linguistic regions in the election of the Federal Council, the cantonal initiative whereby each canton has the right to submit a proposal of a bill to the parliament, the cantonal referendum by which eight states may call for a referendum on a contested issue, and the extraordinary summoning of the federal parliament by at least five cantons.
4. A. Lijphart, *Patterns of Democracy. Government Forms and Performance in Thirty-Six Countries* (New Haven/London: Yale University Press 1999).
5. W. Linder, *Schweizerische Demokratie. Institutionen – Prozesse – Perspektiven* (Bern/Stuttgart/Wien: Verlag Paul Haupt 1999), p.244.
6. R.E. Germann, 'Die Europatauglichkeit der direkt-demokratischen Institutionen in der Schweiz', *Schweizerisches Jahrbuch für Politische Wissenschaft* 31 (1991), pp.257–70.
7. A. Vatter and F. Sager, 'Föderalismusreform am Beispiel des Ständemehrs', *Swiss Political Science Review* 2/2 (1996), p.174.
8. L. Neidhart, *Plebiszit und pluralitäre Demokratie: eine Analyse der Funktion des schweizerischen Gesetzesreferendums* (Bern: Francke 1970).
9. H. Kriesi, *Le système politique suisse* (Paris: Economica 1995), p.69.
10. Lijphart, *Patterns of Democracy*, p.208.
11. A. Jegher, *Der Einfluss von institutionellen, entscheidungspolitischen und inhaltlichen Faktoren auf die Gesetzgebungstätigkeit der Schweizerischen Bundesversammlung* (Bern/Stuttgart/Wien: Verlag Paul Haupt 1998).
12. G. Tsebelis and J. Money, *Bicameralism* (New York: Cambridge University Press 1997).
13. J. Grangé, 'Suisse: Le Conseil des Etats', in J. Mastias and J. Grangé (eds.), *Les secondes chambres du parlament en Europe occidentale* (Paris: Economica 1987), p.20.
14. R.E. Germann, *Ausserparlamentarische Kommissionen: Die Milizverwaltung des Bundes* (Bern/Stuttgart: Paul Haupt Verlag 1981), p.63.
15. R.E. Germann, 'Die Beziehungen zwischen Bund und Kantonen im Verwaltungsbereich', in R.E. Germann und E. Weibel (eds.), *Handbuch Politisches System der Schweiz. Föderalismus Bd. 3* (Bern/Stuttgart: Paul Haupt Verlag 1986), p.350.
16. G. Lehmbruch, 'Consociational Democracy and Corporatism in Switzerland', *Publius: The Journal of Federalism* 2/23 (1993), p.54.
17. See also S. Wälti, 'Institutional Reform of Federalism: Changing the Players rather than the Rules of the Game', *Swiss Political Science Review* 2/2 (1996), p.124.
18. F. Gerheuser, A. Vatter und F. Sager, *Die Berücksichtigung von Stellungnahmen der Kantone im Vernehmlassungsverfahren des Bundes* (Bern: EDMZ 1997); Y. Papadopoulos, *Les processus de décision fédéraux en Suisse* (Paris: L'Harmattan 1997).
19. Kriesi, *Le système politique suisse*; Linder, *Schweizerische Demokratie*; Neidhart, *Plebiszit und pluralitäre Demokratie*.
20. Linder, *Schweizerische Demokratie*, p.118.
21. Gerheuser *et al.*, *Die Berücksichtigung von Stellungnahmen*.
22. H.P. Fagagnini, *Föderalistischer Aufgabenverbund in der Schweiz* (Bern/Stuttgart: Paul Haupt Verlag 1991).
23. W. Linder, *Politische Entscheidung und Gesetzesvollzug* (Bern und Stuttgart: Paul Haupt Verlag 1987), p.79.
24. W. Linder, *Swiss Democracy. Possible Solutions to Conflict in Multicultural Societies*

(London: Macmillan 1994), p.71.

25. Wälti, 'Institutional Reform of Federalism', p.123.
26. M. Frenkel, 'Interkantonale Institutionen und Politikbereiche', in R.E. Germann and E. Weibel (eds.), *Handbuch Politisches System der Schweiz. Föderalismus Bd. 3* (Bern/ Stuttgart: Paul Haupt Verlag 1986), p.323.
27. Ibid., p.326.
28. Ibid., p.330.
29. E.M. Immergut, 'The Theoretical Core of The New Institutionalism', *Politics and Society* 26 (1998), p.5; K. Thelen, 'Historical Institutionalism in Comparative Politics', *Annual Review of Political Science* 2/1 (1999), p.369; K.R. Weaver and B.A. Rockman, *Do Institutions Matter? Government Capabilities in the United States and Abroad* (Washington, 1993).
30. H. Obinger, 'Federalism, Direct Democracy, and Welfare State Development in Switzerland', *Journal of Public Policy* 18/3 (1998), p.257.
31. Ibid., pp.258–9.
32. U. Wagschal, 'Direct Democracy and Public Policy Making', *Journal of Public Policy* 17/3 (1997), p.223.
33. Linder, *Politische Entscheidung und Gesetzesvollzug*; Wälti, 'Institutional Reform of Federalism', p.133.
34. M. Spörndli, T. Holzer and G. Schneider, 'Diener dreier Herren? Kantonalbehörden und die Vollzugsvielfalt der arbeitsmarktlichen Bestimmungen im schweizerischen Asylrecht', *Swiss Political Science Review* 4/3 (1998), p.53.
35. Linder, *Politische Entscheidung und Gesetzesvollzug*.
36. Linder, *Schweizerische Demokratie*, p.178.
37. M. Bassand, G. Chevalier and E. Zimmermann, *Politique et logement* (Lausanne: Presses polytechniques romandes 1984); Spörndli *et al.*, 'Diener dreier Herren?'.
38. K. Deutsch, *Die Schweiz als ein paradigmatischer Fall politischer Integration* (Bern: Francke 1976).
39. A. Lijphart, *Democracy in Plural Societies* (New Haven/London: Yale University Press 1977).
40. G. Bächler, *Federalism against Ethnicity?* (Chur/Zürich: Ruegger 1997).
41. J. Steiner, 'Power-Sharing: Another Swiss "Export Product"?' in J.V. Montville (ed.), *Conflict and Peacemaking in Multiethnic Societies* (Toronto: Lexington Books 1990), p.107.
42. Linder, *Schweizerische Demokratie*, p.352.
43. Ibid., p.267.
44. Neidhart, *Plebiszit und pluralitäre Demokratie*.
45. Kriesi, *Le système politique suisse*; Linder, *Schweizerische Demokratie*; Papadopoulos, *Les processus de décision fédéraux en Suisse*.
46. A. Vatter, 'Consensus and Direct Democracy: Conceptual and Empirical Linkages', *European Journal of Political Research* 38/2 (2000), pp.171–92.
47. Linder, *Swiss Democracy*.
48. A. Ladner and M. Brändle, 'Does Direct Democracy Matter for Political Parties? An Empirical Test in the Swiss Cantons', *Party Politics* 5/3 (1999), p.283.
49. A. Vatter, 'Politische Fragmentierung in den Schweizer Kantonen. Folge sozialer Heterogenität oder institutioneller Hürden?', *Kölner Zeitschrift für Soziologie und Sozialpsychologie* 50/4 (1998), p.666.
50. H. Kriesi and D. Wisler, 'Social Movements and Direct Democracy', *European Journal of Political Research* 30/2 (1996), p.19.
51. H. Geser, *Bevölkerungsgrösse und Staatsorganisation: kleine Kantone im Lichte ihrer öffentlichen Budgetstruktur, Verwaltung und Rechtssetzung* (Bern: P. Lang 1981).
52. Bassand *et al.*, *Politique et logement*; Linder, *Politische Entscheidung und Gesetzesvollzug*, p.160.
53. J.-D. Delley, *Une étude de mise en oeuvre de la loi Furgler* (St Saphorin: Georgi 1982); Linder, *Politische Entscheidung und Gesetzesvollzug*, p.97.
54. Spörndli *et al.*, 'Diener dreier Herren?'.
55. G. Kirchgässner, L.P. Feld and M.R. Savioz, *Die direkte Demokratie. Modern, erfolgreich, entwicklungs- und exportfähig* (Basel/Genf/München: Helbing & Lichtenhahn 1999).

56. W.W. Pommerehne and H. Weck-Hannemann, 'Tax Rates, Tax Administration and Income Tax Evasion in Switzerland', *Public Choice* 88 (1996), p.161.
57. L.P. Feld and M.R. Savioz, 'Direct Democracy Matters for Economic Performance: An Empirical Investigation', *Kyklos* 50 (1997), p.529.
58. S. Borner, A. Brunetti and T. Straubhaar, *Die Schweiz im Alleingang* (Zürich: Verlag NZZ 1994).
59. G. Tsebelis, 'Decision Making in Political Systems: Veto Players in Presidentialism, Parliamentarism, Multicameralism and Multipartyism', *British Journal of Political Science* 25 (1995), p.289.
60. Wagschal, 'Direct Democracy and Public Policy Making'.
61. R.L. Frey, 'Europäische Integration, Regionalstruktur und Föderalismus', *Aussenwirtschaft* 50/2 (1995), p.295.
62. W. Linder *et al.*, *Zusammenarbeit in den Agglomerationen* (Bern: FSP 1992).
63. U. Klöti, 'Regieren im verflochtenen dreistufigen Föderalismus', in P. Knoepfel and W. Linder (eds.), *Verwaltung, Regierung und Verfassung im Wandel. Gedächtnisschrift für Raimund E. Germann* (Basel/Genf/München: Helbing & Lichtenhahn 2000), p.21.
64. Vatter and Sager, 'Föderalismusreform am Beispiel des Ständemehrs', p.193.
65. Linder, *Schweizerische Demokratie*, p.183.
66. Wälti, 'Institutional Reform of Federalism'.
67. Ibid., p.134.
68. Klöti, 'Regieren im verflochtenen dreistufigen Föderalismus', p.28.

Swiss Political Parties:
Between Persistence and Change

ANDREAS LADNER

From a comparative perspective, two aspects of the Swiss party system are particularly salient: the large number of parties and the relative stability of the distribution of power. Apart from social and cultural cleavages, the electoral system (PR), the competitiveness encouraged by the federal state and direct democracy can be seen as responsible for party proliferation in Switzerland.[1] Political stability stems from the integrative force of consociationalism, which has its roots in the small size of the country, its political culture, and the system of direct democracy. In Switzerland the most important parties are continuously represented in government, and there is no change of power between the parties in government and the parties in opposition. The composition of the national, as well as almost all cantonal, governments quite often remains unchanged over a long period. Since 1959, the national government, for example, has consisted of two members of the Radical Democrats (FDP), the Christian Democrats (CVP) and the Social Democrats (SPS), and one of the Swiss People's Party (SVP). This composition is commonly referred to as the 'magic formula'.

The combination of a large number of parties and political stability is not without interest, since the literature on party research, influenced by the experience of the Weimar Republic, the French Fourth Republic, and post-war Italy, for long treated multi-party systems as inherently unstable compared with two-party systems, such as that of Great Britain.[2]

However, in the last few years the Swiss party system seems to have become less stable. The 1995 and 1999 national elections brought about remarkable shifts in voting. The question is: will Swiss politics enter a period of instability and will there be serious changes in the party system? To grasp the importance of these changes, analyses restricted to the national level might be too narrow. It is a commonly accepted characteristic of the

Andreas Ladner, University of Berne

Swiss party system that the subnational level is of great importance. The federal structure of the political system has not only hampered the creation of powerful centralised national parties and led to much stronger cantonal parties,[3] it has also brought about distinctive party systems with different power configurations. Moreover, cantonal organisations of the same party are not always backed by the same segments of the population. The Swiss party system has thus to be regarded as one composed of 26 different party systems.

Thus, it is of crucial importance to know to what extent changes on the national level correspond with cantonal trends and whether cantonal trends precede national trends or vice versa. The different size of the voting districts (cantons) for national elections, with a number of districts in which more than 30 per cent of the vote is needed to gain a seat, not only favours bigger parties, but might lead to an underestimation of the changes occurring. Yet the nationalisation of politics[4] might have led to the disappearance of the differences between cantonal and national party systems.

The Number of Parties: A Decrease on National Level and an Increase in some of the Cantons

In the 1999 national elections, members of 14 parties were elected to the National Council (Nationalrat). This high number, of course, reveals only part of the story. Not all of these parties are of equal importance, some of them exist only in one or a few of the 26 cantons, whereas others are represented in all cantons. Basically, two groups of parties can be distinguished: the four governmental parties FDP, CVP, SVP and SP and the smaller parties like GPS, LPS, EVP, SD and others.[5] On a national level, the former group shares between 70 and 90 per cent of the vote, while the latter parties, individually, hardly gained more than five per cent of the vote.[6]

To appreciate the degree of fragmentation of the Swiss party system and its cantonal party systems in a comparative perspective, we need to know more about the parties elected. Giovanni Sartori's[7] criteria for the parties that 'count' are not very helpful, because the Swiss system of direct democracy allows even smaller parties to play a relatively important role and some are quite dominant in some of the cantons.[8] Thus, the assessment of the parties that count on national level and in the 26 cantons remains a rather hazardous and arbitrary task. Instead, comparative studies frequently refer to the effective number of parties, a measure introduced by Markku Laasko and Rein Taggepera[9] based on the Rae Fragmentation Index. The effective number of parties index has the advantage that it not only takes into account the number of parties, but also their size. Furthermore, it can easily be computed from electoral statistics.

After the 1999 national elections, the effective number of parties on national level amounted to 5.9 parties. Figure 1 reveals that this number is considerably higher than it used to be before the 1960s, but is remarkably lower than in the late 1980s and early 1990s. Responsible for the two peaks since 1945 were – to the detriment of the four governmental parties – the right-wing anti-immigration parties SD (formerly NA) and Republicans in 1971, and the Green Party (GPS) and its counterpart, the anti-ecologist Automobile Party (FPS), in 1991. Nevertheless, the effective number of parties in Switzerland can be considered as high compared with other countries. In the last four-year period of the twentieth century, only Belgium, Italy and France had a higher effective number of parties; the European mean is much lower and shows astonishing stability until the 1980s followed by a slight increase.

At first glance, the cantonal party systems do not reveal a similarly dynamic pattern. The mean is considerably lower than in the figures on a national level and the general trend only shows a slight and steady increase, the short-term ups and downs can hardly be distinguished. This is not surprising since average numbers have the inconvenience that trends are levelled out.

FIGURE 1

THE EFFECTIVE NUMBER OF PARTIES

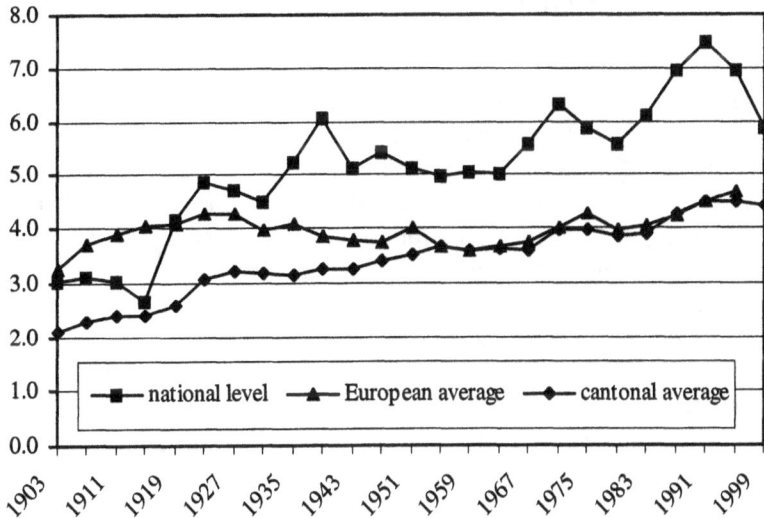

FIGURE 2

EFFECTIVE NUMBER OF PARTIES IN DIFFERENT GROUPS OF CANTONS

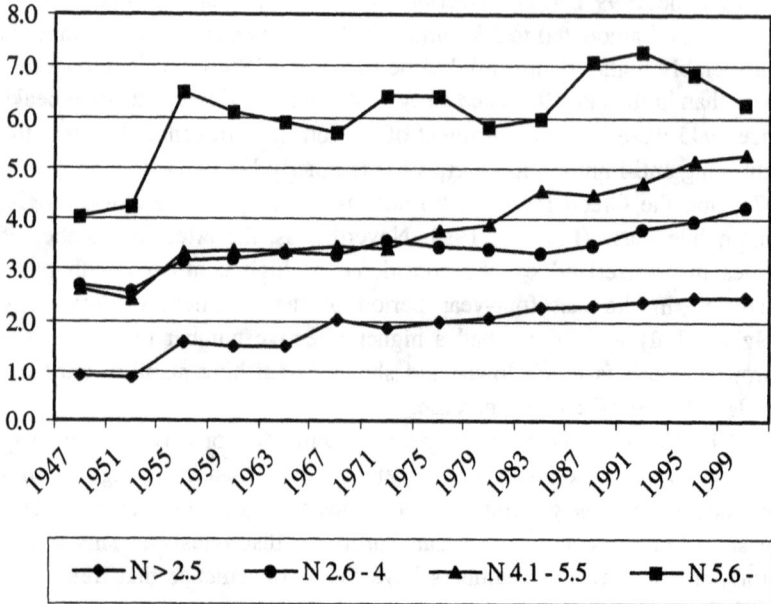

Notes: N= average effective number of parties in the two electoral periods 1980–83 and
1984–87.
< 2.5: UR, OW, NW, VS; 2.6 - 4: LU, SZ, GL, ZG, FR, SO, SG, TI, VD, NE; 4.1 - 5.5:
BE, SH, GR, AG, TG, JU; 5.6 -: ZH, BL, BS, GE.

Figure 2 shows the trends for four different groups of cantons, built
according to the average effective number of parties they had in the 1980s.
The cantons' effective numbers of parties at that time were between two and
well over 7.9. Figure 2 reveals significantly that the downward trend in the
1990s on national level also holds for cantons with a high number of parties
in the 1980s.[10] The average of those four cantons (ZH, BL, BS and GE)
which had more than 5.6 parties in the 1980s clearly decreases. For the
cantons with fewer parties the average number increases: only slightly for
those with less than 2.5 parties in the 1980s (UR, OW, NW, VS),
considerably for those with between 2.6 and 4 parties (LU, SZ, GL, ZG, FR,
SO, SG, TI, VD, NE) and for those with between 4.1 and 5.5 parties (BE,
SH, GR, AG, TG and JU).

Are there any characteristic differences between cantons with a different
number of parties and different trends in the 1990s? It is – apart from a few

exceptions (GE, JU) – in the confessionally mixed or dominantly Protestant cantons that the effective number of parties was high in the 1980s and decreased in the 1990s. Especially salient was the decrease in the cantons with important cities and universities like Zurich, Geneva and Basel. Cantons with a low, but slightly increasing, number of parties were – apart from GL, VD, NE – dominantly Catholic and of larger size. Almost no increase was found in smaller, off-centre, Catholic cantons dominated by the CVP.[11]

As far as the number of parties is concerned, there are thus quite important differences between the cantonal party systems and the national party system as it is depicted by national election results. The trend on the national level does not necessarily match all trends on the cantonal level. Nevertheless, the differences seem to disappear. The cantonal party systems become more alike, converging towards a medium effective number of parties between four and five, and the national party system is reduced to well below six parties. If there is anything like a nationalisation of cantonal politics, this should, in the long run, lead to similar party systems on all levels.

Volatility: Increase on a Low Level

Given the multitude of parties, the stability of the parties' vote and seat shares during the twentieth century is remarkable. This reveals, for example, the elasticity of voting strength, measured by the percentage difference between the largest and the least share of the vote which a party obtained at elections over a given time period.[12] The best and worst results of SVP and CVP since the introduction of the proportional system in 1919 and up to the 1995 election differ by less than seven per cent. For the FDP, this difference is less than nine per cent; only the SP passes the ten per cent mark. And the mean change, that is the average change in the percentage of the vote obtained by a party between each pair of elections during a period,[13] is very small. For the four governmental parties, it is 0.9 for the FDP, 0.7 for CVP, 1.3 for SVP and 1.4 for SP. All these parties would – according to the study by Maria Maguire[14] – belong to the group of parties with very little change.

Measured at the level of the whole Swiss party system, the volatility, that is half of the total change in percentage of votes between parties within a party system,[15] is also rather low compared with other countries. The average aggregated volatility in the time between 1919 and 1999 is five per cent. However, in the 1990s this varied. The average on national level in the three elections in the 1990s was up to 7.8 per cent, whereas in the years

before it was much lower (see Figure 3). Only in 1971 and before and after
World War II did Switzerland's party system witness similar volatility.
Especially salient is the low volatility in the 1950s and early 1960s, when
the magic formula was established in 1959.

The comparison with the developments in the cantonal party systems
reveals that there is a certain similarity between the two curves, but it cannot
be determined on which level new tendencies come out first. Again the
differences between the cantons are considerable. In the last electoral period
of the twentieth century, cantons like ZH, LU, OW, BS, SH and GE showed
aggregated volatility of over ten per cent. In cantons like SZ, NW, SG, GR,
TI and VS volatility was below four per cent.

The 24 cantonal party systems[16] offer a quite unique opportunity to test
the relation between the number of parties and the stability of a party system
under almost laboratory-like conditions. Figure 4 reveals that cantons with
a higher number of parties in the 1990s generally also have higher volatility.
The correlation between the two variables is significant. The term 'political
stability' has, of course, to be used cautiously. It can only be shown that the
more parties there are, the more election results tend to be subject to change.
Nothing can be said about the distribution of power and the stability of
policies.

FIGURE 3

VOLATILITY

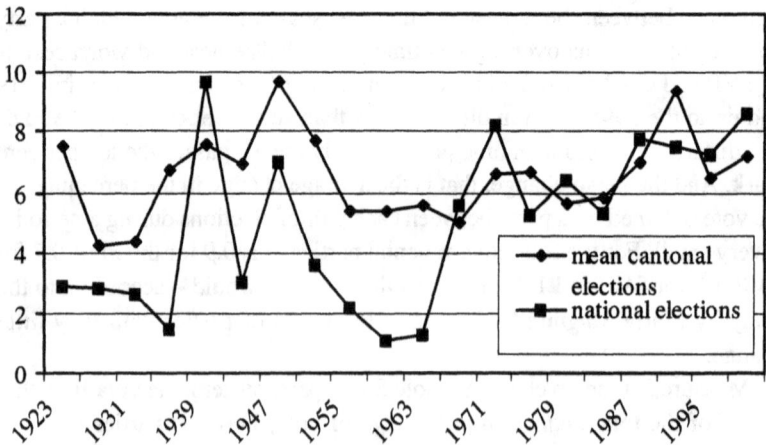

Note: y = per cent

FIGURE 4

EFFECTIVE NUMBER OF PARTIES (1990s) AND VOLATILITY (1990s)
IN 24 SWISS CANTONS

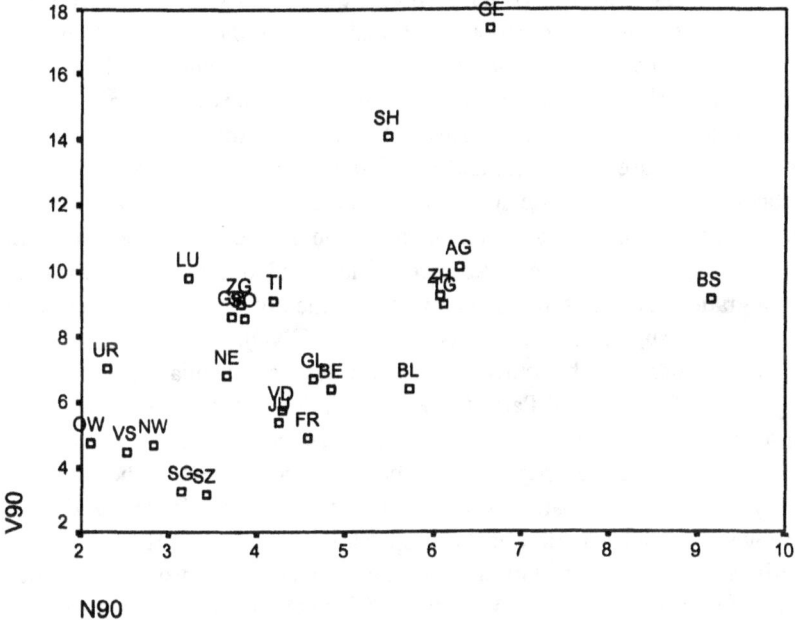

Note: Pearson corr: .548, sig.: .01; V90 and N90: average volatility and average effective
   number of parties in the three electoral periods 1988–91, 1992–95 and 1996–99.

Failure and Success of the Different Parties: The Ascent of the Swiss People's Party

The effective number of parties and aggregate volatility mirror quite accurately the changes in the Swiss party system in the 1990s, they remain, however, on an abstract level. The next step is to have a closer look at the most important parties.

The success of the Swiss People's Party (SVP) in the 1990s is probably the most striking in the whole electoral history of the Swiss party system (see Figure 5). Not more than 25 years ago, the SVP fell below ten per cent and was almost doomed to disappear. It was only with the 1991 elections that this downward trend stopped and, in the elections of 1995, the party reached an unexpected 15 per cent. The 1999 elections finally marked a real breakthrough. The SVP became the strongest party with 22.5 per cent of the vote (+ 7.6). It is the first time since the National Council (Nationalrat) was first elected by means of proportional representation in 1919 that such an important shift has occurred. In addition to its traditional strongholds, the party not only consolidated its position in cantons like LU, ZG, SO, AR, SG, where it entered the national political arena in the 1995 elections, but also gained votes in 'new' cantons like BS, AI, VS, GE and JU. The success of this formerly agrarian party is due to profound transformation, as it was forced to reorient itself because of the shrinking of its traditional membership base of farmers and merchants. It now favours a free-market economy and a reduction in state expenditure; however, its agricultural policy still tolerates massive state intervention. Domestically, the party puts great emphasis on the maintenance of law and order, is strongly anti-immigration, and in foreign policy it vehemently opposes Switzerland's accession to supranational organisations (EU, UNO).

The trends for the other parties are less spectacular, but not less significant. The Radical Party (FDP), which advocates a liberal economic order with a business-friendly framework, has been the biggest and most important party for a long time and has been considered as the founding party of the Swiss nation state; it had already experienced a decline following the introduction of the proportional system in 1919 and lasting until 1939. After a period of ups and downs, a new downward trend started after the elections of 1983. With the 1999 elections, the FDP for the first time lost its leading position among the three bourgeois parties.

FIGURE 5

ELECTORAL PERFORMANCE OF THE FOUR GOVERNMENTAL PARTIES IN
NATIONAL COUNCIL ELECTIONS

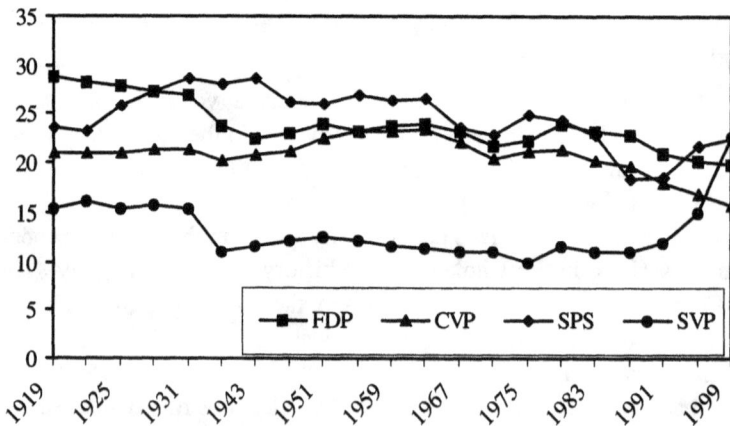

The Christian Democratic Party (CVP) professes the Christian social doctrine and advocates the establishment of a social market economy, allowing for state interventions in order to protect workers, craftsmen and agriculture. On ethical and moral issues, it adopts a conservative stance, and it attributes great importance to family values. The figures for the CVP show that there has been a marked drop since 1963, and more particularly since 1979. It is still suffering from the ongoing process of secularisation and is now the smallest of the four governmental parties.

Finally, the Social Democratic Party (SPS) stands for the protection of the socially weak and the environment. It is an advocate of subsidy programmes, active state intervention in the economy, and the creation of a strong social safety net that does not push the socially disadvantaged into the role of supplicants. The history of the Social Democrats is more agitated, which is partly due to the temporary success of other, more extreme left-wing and green parties. The SP fell below the 25 per cent mark before and immediately after the events of 1968, and below 20 per cent in the 1987 and 1991 elections, which were strongly influenced by environmental issues. In 1995 it recovered and even became the second strongest party in 1999 with little more than 22 per cent.

The smaller parties lost much of their attraction towards the end of the twentieth century. The LdU disappeared, the FPS is about to do the same, the Greens have been able to hold their share of the votes, but suffered a reduction of 1.1 per cent in the 1995 elections. The SD also suffered quite important losses and the LPS minor ones, whereas the shares of EVP and EDU remained unchanged. Thus, with the 1999 elections the four governmental parties again controlled more than 80 per cent of the vote; however, the clear winners in the last decade of the twentieth century were the parties at the poles of the left–right dimension, the SVP and the SP.

The 1999 elections also brought a new situation in regard to the composition of the national government. The success of the SVP was followed by the claim for a second seat in the Federal Council, which was refused by the other parties at the end of 1999 in the re-election of the government following the election of the National Council. However, the magic formula has lost much of its enchantment and changes are more probable than ever.

In the light of these developments, the question is whether the Swiss party system has lost its famous stability. There is obviously a reduction in the number of parties and an increase in volatility. This is not completely new. Long term analyses reveal that the Swiss party system has had ups and downs as far as volatility and the number of parties are concerned. But altogether the Swiss party system seems – apart from a few exceptions – to be moving towards a four-party system with the four governmental parties being even more dominant. At a first glance this supports Seymour Lipset and Stein Rokkan's thesis of the frozen party systems.[17] Their cleavage theory explains the emergence of the four parties quite well. However, the success of the SVP also threatens the very essence of the Swiss four-party coalition. Especially the two parties in the middle, FDP and CVP, are under enormous pressure and a reorganisation of the Swiss party system has become more probable than ever. And finally, the Lipset–Rokkan thesis only holds as long as the four parties still represent the same cleavages and stand for the same political ideologies. It is on the level of the parties and their organisations that the answer to this question of stability is to be found.

WEAK PARTY ORGANISATIONS, DEALIGNMENT AND REORIENTATION

The electoral records of the parties tell only part of the story. Without leaving any traces in electoral statistics, changes might take place within the parties, for example, in regard to the parties' organisations, their relationship to their adherents and members and their political orientation. It is, therefore, time to have a closer look at the parties themselves.

Swiss political parties are considered to be weak.[18] Most analysts point to the parties' handicap *vis-à-vis* interest groups and social movements. Further signs of their weakness are connected with the internal organisation of the parties, for instance, the small and largely voluntary party apparatus, limited financial resources, and the lack of centralisation and internal homogeneity.[19] These characteristics of the political parties can be largely explained with reference to special features of the Swiss political system.

Switzerland is a small country with a strong social and cultural diversity. Different language areas, confessions and degrees of urbanisation provide for all sorts of cleavages. Together with the very federalistic structure of the Swiss political system and the predominantly autonomous municipalities, the Swiss parties are, despite their large number, somewhat heterogeneous and stratarchically organised. Altogether there are about 180 cantonal parties and roughly 5,000 local parties.[20] As a consequence, the national parties have to make great efforts to solve their integration and co-ordination problems. At the same time, however, a decentralised party structure enhances flexibility in dealing with local and regional particularities[21] and offers more opportunities for voter identification. In cases where the cantonal party deviates from the national party, the party members can choose, according to their own preferences, which party to identify with more.

Even though the system of direct democracy contributed early on to the formation of the political parties in Switzerland,[22] most analysts argue that, at the end of the twentieth century, direct democracy weakens the position of the parties.[23] During voting campaigns, the financially strong interest groups and the social movements, which are easy to mobilise, far outpace the political parties. In addition, given the possibility of correcting unfavourable decisions by the popular vote, the elections themselves are relatively unimportant. Recent studies have shown, however, that in those cantons where initiatives and referenda are frequent, the parties tend to be better organised.[24] Either a large number of direct democratic ballots tends to force the parties to engage in continuous political activism, and this might lead them to professionalise their internal organisation, or having sufficient organisational capacity they tend to resort more often to direct-democratic instruments.

For small and heterogeneous states, a conflict regulation pattern based on consensus and power-sharing seems to be more appropriate.[25] The Swiss system of consensus democracy (consociationalism) allows the most important parties to participate in government. This provides much more integration than majoritarian systems with a strong division between the parties in government and parties in the opposition. In a consensus democracy, political problems are solved quietly. Representatives of the main interest groups take part in the decision-making process at an early stage and help to find a compromise to solve political problems. Such a conflict regulation pattern guarantees political stability, but blurs the borders between political interest groups and government actors. It remains unclear whose interests prevail in putting together a proposal.[26] Political parties tend to lose the possibility of showing their constituents a distinctive political profile.

Finally, the *Milizsystem*,[27] which is in part a consequence of the small size of the country, but which is also considered to be an element of Swiss political culture, weakens the position of the parties. Even though the *Milizsystem* has some advantages in that it favours the combination of roles across the social and political sub-systems,[28] it also implies that most political work is done by amateur politicians in a largely unprofessional manner. Finally, since the parties are able to offer their members only unpaid positions, this does not significantly enhance the attractiveness of the parties.

There seems to be a broad consensus among various authors[29] that political parties have passed through different stages of development during the twentieth century.[30] Three forms of political party are usually distinguished. Until about 1920, the parties were mainly cadre or elite parties. With the consolidation of the Western democracies between 1920 and 1960, mass-membership parties emerged. Since 1960, the parties have become dissociated from their membership base and turned into Otto Kirchheimer's catch-all parties[31] or into Angelo Panebianco's professional electoral parties.[32] The latter two are no longer committed to 'grand ideologies' or to a particular segment of the population, but seek primarily to increase votes and seats. Richard Katz and Peter Mair add to these different developmental stages a further party type, the cartel party, which has emerged since 1970.[33] This new form of party has moved closer to, and is strongly subsidised by, the state.

The question is, of course, whether Swiss parties follow these lines of party development. Especially in the case of the catch-all party and the professional electoral party, and to a lesser extent for the cartel party, the weakened link to their traditional basis would question Lipset and Rokkan's frozen party system thesis.[34] If only the names of the traditional parties survive, and they no longer represent the cleavage responsible for their emergence in terms of socio-structural basis and political orientation, the party system has changed and can no longer be considered as frozen.

Unfortunately, for most of the ideal types of party organisation, clear concepts of operationalisation are missing. Therefore, we shall concentrate on a few party characteristics, describing some features of the ideal types, such as professionalisation and financial resources of party organisations, party ties, membership figures and composition, the balance of power within the parties and the political orientation.

Professionalisation: A Slight Increase on a Low Level

In the mid-1970s, the parties of the medium-sized and larger cantons began to staff their secretariats with full-time employees.[35] A survey conducted by the author in 1996/97 shows that the cantonal parties of the four governmental parties had 74 full-time positions in total. Added to the 45 positions of the national party organisations, this amounts to a total of nearly 120 full-time posts. Henry Kerr reports for the 1970s, on the basis of personal interviews with party officials, a total of 87.5 full-time staff members at cantonal and national level together.[36] Since the middle of the 1970s, the number of full-time employees has thus increased by 40 per cent at the best. Compared to developments in other countries,[37] the increase of professionalisation in Switzerland is below average. Only Great Britain and the Netherlands have lower rates of increase, but in absolute terms these countries have a generally higher level of professionalisation. Moreover, in Switzerland, full-time employees are typically engaged in the administrative apparatus of the party, and therefore the actual level of professionalisation of the party's purely political activities is probably even lower. According to information provided by the parties themselves, about 72 per cent of the cantonal parties have become more professional in their administrative work, and 60 per cent in their programmatic and substantive activities, during the last ten years.[38] It is noteworthy that especially the two most successful parties, the SP and the SVP, claim to work more professionally with regard to substantive issues.

Nevertheless, the conclusion reached by Hans Peter Fagagnini in the mid-1970s that the party organisations in Switzerland are based on the *Milizsystem*[39] is still valid today: the number of individuals who deal professionally with politics remains very small. Professional politicians are to be found mainly among representatives of interest groups and other persons who deal with questions that lie at the basis of political decisions. These are usually lobbyists or parliamentarians.[40] The party organisations themselves employ only a small number of politically versatile collaborators.

Financial Resources: No State Funding and Increasing Difficulties

In comparison with parties of other countries, the Swiss parties have only limited financial resources, both in absolute terms, as well as in terms of growth rates over recent years. Partly responsible for this is the almost total lack of state funding. On the national level there is only a modest contribution to the parliamentary groups of about 5.5 million Swiss francs. In 1975 the ordinary budget of the four governmental parties on national level was 2.5 million francs (FDP: 0.8 million; CVP: 0.8 million; SP: 0.7 million; SVP: 0.2 million).[41] At the end of the 1980s, the total budget of the four governing parties amounted to 5.6 million francs (SP: 1.7 million; CVP: 1.6 million; FDP: 1.4 million; SVP: 0.9 million).[42] In 1999, the four governing parties reported a total budget (without election costs) of 9.4 million francs (FDP: 2.6 million; CVP: 2.3 million; SP: 3.1 million; SVP: 1.4 million). Compared to most of the other countries the budgets of the Swiss parties are very small. And even the increase in recent years is hardly impressive when we consider the average rate of inflation. In the last three decades the four parties have in real terms roughly doubled their budget. The ordinary budget of all four governmental parties together on a national level is, for instance, considerably lower than the sum an organisation like Greenpeace receives in donations.

The fact that the Social Democrats have the largest budget on national level is striking. This is due to the fact that these figures do not account for all 'costs'. Contributions to electoral or voting campaigns, to a large extent, do not show up in the 'operative budgets' of the parties on the right. If these contributions could be taken into account, it could probably be shown that in reality the bourgeois parties, because of their connections with financially strong business circles, have more funds at their disposal.

The national parties' lack of financial resources is a matter of constant concern. In the last 30 years, there have been different unsuccessful attempts to introduce a system of state financing. In 1999, for the first time, all four governmental parties jointly tried to re-start the discussion. The financial situation of the cantonal parties is only slightly better. About 37 per cent of the 90 cantonal parties in our sample claim that they dispose of more money than in previous years. For 21 per cent the financial situation has not changed, whereas 42 per cent claim to be worse off. For FDP and CVP especially, the financial situation is not very comfortable; in both parties a majority of the cantonal sections claim to have comparatively less money than in earlier days.[43] Both parties, as we have seen, are also fighting electoral problems.

The Parties on the Ground: Dealignment and Realignment

If there is a general pattern in the development of Western European party systems, it is the decline of party ties. However, there is great variation between countries, as well as between parties.[44] Various surveys have shown that an ever-decreasing percentage of the population identifies closely with a political party.[45] While in the early 1980s, after a period of decline, about 50 per cent of the voters identified with one of the governing parties, this figure had dropped to one-third by 1995.[46] In 1995, more than half of the voters declared that they did not identify with any party. Concurrently, the number of floating voters has increased significantly, particularly between 1971 and 1987.[47]

In Switzerland, the principle of party membership developed relatively late and only partially, which is evidenced by the largely unsuccessful attempts of the FDP and the CVP to introduce this principle in the 1970s and 1990s in all cantonal and local branches. One possible explanation of this can be found in the party press, which until 1970 played a relatively important role. The parties organised themselves through the party press, that is, the readers represented members and followers, and, as a consequence, there was no need to develop clear criteria for membership and to establish organisational structures for such a task.[48]

In 1963–67, according to Erich Gruner's estimates, 38 per cent of active voters were party members. In his view, the introduction of female suffrage reduced this number by half. In the 1970s, it amounted to 11 per cent of the eligible voters, which corresponds to approximately 390,000 party members. At the time, Gruner considered the Swiss parties' level of organisation to be relatively high by international comparison.[49] According to indications given by the parties themselves, they had approximately 400,000 members in the mid-1990s, just as in Gruner's time. If we take into account the fact that during these 20 years the number of voters has increased by 900,000, this implies that the percentage of party members has declined, a development which is confirmed by recent surveys. According to the studies by Longchamp between 1983 and 1994, the share of party members among the eligible voters declined from 18 to 12 per cent.[50]

The use of a more restrictive concept of membership, which eliminates those entries that (due to the lack of the principle of membership) were based on the more encompassing notion of 'followers', lowers the percentage of party members even further to seven per cent of the voters. From this perspective, the Swiss parties had only about 300,000 members in 1997. In international comparison, Switzerland still occupies a leading position in the middle field; in Germany, Holland, England and France, the parties have considerably fewer, in Austria considerably more members.[51]

As long as parties, as in the Swiss case, do not have central membership files, it is very difficult to establish trends in membership figures over time. In Switzerland, only the Social Democrats have the possibility of showing a plausible (negative) trend in their membership figures, whereas the other parties depend at the very best on estimations. About 40 per cent of the cantonal sections of the four governmental parties claim to have increased their membership figures in recent years, only about 24 per cent admit that they have fewer members.[52] If we take into account the size of the parties (weighted percentages), we get a more accurate picture of the total trend. In this perspective, a downward trend comes out clearly, since it is mainly the small and newer cantonal parties which pretend to gain members, whereas the more important bigger parties have declining figures. But even here, the result is probably too positive for the parties. For example, in the case of the Social Democrats, which experienced according to their official statistics a clear loss in recent decades, the balance turns out to be even. It is thus very likely that party officials tend to put their membership figures in too favourable a light. Anyway, the two parties suffering most from a decrease of their membership figures are FDP and CVP.

In regard to the members and voters of the different parties, most striking is the shift in the social basis of the Social Democrats and the Swiss People's Party. The Social Democrats have lost a part of their traditional membership to the Swiss People's Party. Yet they have gained a considerable number of better educated people earning higher salaries. In 1975 only seven per cent of their voters had an university degree,[53] whereas in 1999 the SP was, with 51 per cent, the party with the highest percentage of voters having a high level of education.[54] As far as income is concerned, the SP ranks with its percentage of well-off voters just behind the FDP and well ahead of CVP and SVP, while among the people from the highest income category the SP is the most popular party. The Swiss People's Party, in contrast, moved into the cities and into predominantly Catholic areas. In 1975 only eight per cent of their voters lived in urban areas,[55] in 1999 it was 38 per cent.[56] The percentage of Catholic voters increased according to the same source from 16.5 in 1975 to 34 in 1999.

The Increasing Importance of Public Office and Central Office

The balance of power between the different faces of party organisations[57] and intra-party decision-making are other important features of political parties. Professional electoral parties and cartel parties have a strong bias towards the party leaders (party in central office) and the office-holders (party in public office). In the 1980s with the rise of green parties, grass-roots democracy was very popular. In the 1990s this changed. Party leaders are not only constantly asked to present their position in the media without being able to consult their basis, but they also need enough room and competence for strategic behaviour. There has within the Swiss parties obviously been a shift towards more operative freedom for the party leaders. About two-thirds of the cantonal sections of the four governmental parties claim that leadership is more important than co-determination of the party members and almost half of them claim that there has been a shift in the priorities in this direction within the last few years (see Table 1). This change has been especially strong for the Social Democrats (SP) and the Christian Democrats (CVP).

TABLE 1
CO-DETERMINATION OF THE MEMBERS VERSUS MORE COMPETENCE TO THE PARTY ELITE

| | party members vs. party leaders | | | | | | shift in priorities | | | |
| | co-determination of the members is more important | | 'operative liberties' of the party leaders are more important | | co-determination of members has become more important | | no change | | 'operative liberties' of party leaders have become more important | |
	%	No.	%	No.	%	No.	%	No.	%	No.
FDP	41	9	59	13	33	8	29	7	38	9
CVP	21	5	79	19	25	6	29	7	46	11
SVP	47	9	53	10	40	6	20	3	40	6
SP	33	8	67	16	8	2	38	9	54	13
all gov. parties	35	31	65	58	25	22	30	26	45	39

Sources: Cantonal Parties Survey; A. Ladner and M. Brändle, *Fact-Sheets zum Wandel der Schweizer Parteien* (Bern: Institut für Politikwiesenschaft der Universität Bern 1999)

Political Orientation: There are Still Differences

In 1965, Otto Kirchheimer predicted a lessening in the importance of the parties' ideologies and a trend towards a two-party system with very few ideological differences between the two parties.[58] Obviously his predictions were wrong. Switzerland still has a multi-party system and the differences between some of the parties have even increased. Especially salient is the shift of the successful Swiss People's Party. Older studies covering the 1970s place the SVP much more in the middle and even to the Left of FDP and CVP.[59] More recent studies situate the Swiss People's Party clearly on the Right.[60] Studies analysing the parties' electoral programmes[61] reveal that the Swiss People's Party has clearly changed its political orientation to the Right as far as political issues are concerned. The Social Democrats on the other side have increased their Left orientation and consider themselves as one of the most leftist and ecological Social Democratic parties.

To sum up, despite many similarities in the development of the Swiss parties, it is impossible to discern a uniform pattern. The Swiss parties, especially if the cantonal parties are also taken into account, cover almost the entire spectrum of party types discussed in the literature. It is still possible to find cantonal-level parties that are best characterised as elite parties, especially in central Switzerland. Some parties, such as the SP, are clearly based on the principle of membership, while others – such as the former LdU or, at a lower level of organisation, the SD and the FPS – come close to the model of a electoral party. Finally, there is little evidence that the Swiss parties have moved closer to the state, a development which is typical of cartel parties. Especially salient here is the lack of public funding of the parties. Thanks to the *Milizsystem,* which even applies to the highest levels of the political system, politicians have been able to maintain a certain degree of independence. The system of concordance and the multi-party system seem to ensure that a considerable number of public sector positions are not allocated on the basis of party membership alone. However, given the high density of political offices in Switzerland, the parties have always had relatively easy access to political mandates.

PERSISTENCE OR CHANGE?

How can the Swiss party system and the Swiss parties be characterised at the end of the twentieth century in terms of persistence and change? At first glance, persistence seems to prevail. The four governmental parties control more votes than during the last 30 years and, in regard to their organisations, there have not been fundamental changes which would allow us to speak about a new party system, hardly comparable to the one in the 1960s or even in the 1920s. Despite partial support for some of the characteristics, Swiss parties cannot be described as catch-all parties in the sense of Kirchheimer,[62] nor as professional electoral parties in the sense of Panebianco,[63] or cartel parties in the sense of Katz and Mair,[64] which would mark a quite important difference from traditional parties on the basis of members and political ideologies.

However, the image of stability and persistence has to be questioned for three reasons. First, the Swiss parties, like parties in many other countries,[65] lost support from party members. Party ties have weakened. The impressively good electoral results of the four large parties together are on less firm ground than they used to be. Secondly, the cleavages responsible for the emergence of the four parties are less dominant, some have partially disappeared and, what is even more striking, there has been a switch in the social basis of the different parties. Traditional working-class voters of the Social Democrats have changed to the right-wing Swiss People's Party and, with its most recent turn towards more neo-liberal policies, the Swiss People's Party has become more attractive for voters of the Radical Party. The Social Democrats, on the other hand, have become much more popular among well-educated people with relatively high salaries. Thus, we have the same parties, but their social bases and their political claims have changed. And, thirdly, the success of the Swiss Peoples' Party has made a reorganisation of the Swiss party system more likely than ever.

NOTES

1. W. Linder, *Schweizerische Demokratie. Institutionen, Prozesse, Perspektiven* (Bern: Haupt 1999), pp.81–8.
2. P. Mair, 'Introduction', in P. Mair (ed.), *The West European Party System* (Oxford: University Press 1990), pp.1–22 at 18.
3. H.P. Fagagnini, 'Die Rolle der Parteien auf kantonaler Ebene', in *Schweizerisches Jahrbuch für politische Wissenschaft* (Bern: Haupt 1978), pp.75–94; S. Hug, 'La cohésion des partis fédéraux dans la phase référendaire', in Y. Papadopoulos (ed.), *Elites politiques et peuple en Suisse. Analyse des votations fédérales: 1970–1987* (Lausanne: réalités sociales 1994), pp.85–112 at 86; L. Neidhart, 'Funktions- und Organisationsprobleme der schweizerischen Parteien', in *Schweizerisches Jahrbuch für politische Wissenschaft* (Bern: Haupt 1986), pp.17–43 at 41; D.-L. Seiler, 'Enjeux et partis politiques en Suisse', *Pouvoirs*, 43 (1987), pp.115–38 at 119.
4. D. Caramani, 'The Nationalisation of Electoral Politics: A Conceptual Reconstruction and Review of the Literature', *West European Politics* 19/2 (1996), pp.205–24; K. Armingeon, 'Es gibt sie doch, die Schweizer Wahlen! Die Unterschiedlichkeit des Wahlverhaltens zwischen Kantonen im internationalen Vergleich', in H. Kriesi, W. Linder und U. Klöti (eds.), *Schweizer Wahlen 1995. Ergebnisse der Wahlstudie Selects* (Bern: Haupt 1998), pp.273–95.
5. GPS = Green Party, LPS = Liberal Party, EVP = Protestant People's Party, LdU = Independents' Party, SD = Swiss Democrats, formerly named National Action (NA), FPS =

Freedom Party formerly named Motorists' or Automobile Party (AP), EDU = Federal Democratic Union, Lega = League of the Tessins, PdA = Workers' Party.

6. Remarkable exceptions are the LdU, which gained 9.1, 7.6 and 6.1 in the elections in 1967, 1971 and 1975 and the Green Party with 6.1 per cent in the 1991 elections.
7. G. Sartori, *Parties and Party Systems. A Framework for Analysis*, Vol. I (Cambridge University Press 1976).
8. For example the Lega in TI, PdA in VD and GE, and LPS in most of the French-speaking cantons and in BS.
9. M. Laakso and R. Taagepera, 'Effective Number of Parties. A Measure with Application to West Europe', *Comparative Political Studies* 12/1 (April 1979), pp.3–27.
10. Since the four groups are built according to their average effective number of parties they are not necessarily homogenous as far as their trends in the 1990s are concerned. The argument here is based on the trends for the average of each group.
11. The language cleavage is not of any direct influence since there are in fact no language-specific parties. In linguistically mixed cantons like VS or FR some of the parties (CVP, FDP, SP) are organisationally divided into a German-speaking and a French-speaking party, in the electoral statistics, however, they do not appear separately.
12. R. Rose and D.W. Urwin, 'Persistence and Change in Western Party Systems, 1945–1969', in P. Mair (ed.), *The West European Party System* (Oxford: Oxford University Press 1990), pp.185–94, excerpted from 'Persistence and Change in Western Party Systems Since 1945', *Political Studies* 18/3 (1970), pp.287–319.
13. M. Maguire, 'Is There Still Persistence? Electoral Change in Western Europe, 1948–1979', in H. Daalder and P. Mair, *Western European Party Systems* (London: Sage 1983), p.78.
14. Ibid.
15. M. Pedersen, 'The Dynamics of European Party Systems: Changing Patterns of Electoral Volatility', *European Journal of Political Research*, 7 (1979), pp.1–26.
16. Due to electoral incompatibilities two (AI and AR) of the 26 Swiss cantons are not represented in the sample.
17. S.M. Lipset and S. Rokkan, 'Cleavages Structures, Party Systems and Voter Alignments: An Introduction', in S.M. Lipset and S. Rokkan (eds.), *Party Systems and Voter Alignments* (New York: Free Press 1967), pp.1–64.
18. R. Rhinow, 'Funktionen und Probleme der politischen Parteien in der Schweiz', *recht* 4 (1986), pp.105–119 at 105; C. Longchamp, *Unterstützung von Bundesrat und Verwaltung. Wandlungen im Verhältnis von Bürgerschaft und Regierung in der Mitte der 90er Jahre als eine Herausforderung an eine offene Staatstätigkeit* (Zürich: GfS-Forschungsinstitut und Bundeskanzlei und EJPD Bern 1994), p.25; I. Rickenbacher, *Politische Kommunikation* (Bern: Haupt 1995), p.13; H. Kriesi, *Le système politique suisse* (Paris: Economica 1995), p.131.
19. The lack of formal recognition by the state no longer holds, since the new Constitution of 18 April 1999, finally mentions political parties (Art. 137). In legal terms, the Swiss parties are organised as associations (*Vereine*), according to Articles 60–79 of the Civil Code (ZBG). Their statutes determine their purpose, their means, and their internal organisation.
20. A. Ladner, *Politische Gemeinden, kommunale Parteien und lokale Politik. Eine empirische Untersuchung in den Gemeinden der Schweiz* (Zürich: Seismo 1991); H. Geser *et al.*, *Die Schweizer Lokalparteien* (Zürich: Seismo 1994); A. Ladner and M. Brändle, *Fact-Sheets zum Wandel der Schweizer Parteien* (Bern: Institut für Politikwissenschaft der Universität Bern 1999).
21. H. Kriesi, 'Perspektiven neuer Politik: Parteien und neue soziale Bewegungen', *Schweizerisches Jahrbuch für politische Wissenschaft 1986* (Bern: Haupt 1986), pp.333–50 at 337.
22. E. Gruner, *Die Parteien der Schweiz*, 2. Auflage (Bern: Francke 1977), p.25.
23. E. Gruner, 'Parteien', in U. Klöti (ed.), *Handbuch Politisches System der Schweiz*, Band 2 (Bern: Haupt 1984), pp.135–62 at 150.
24. A. Ladner and M. Brändle, 'Does Direct Democracy Matter for Political Parties?', *Party Politics* 5/3 (1999), pp.283–302.
25. A. Lijphart, *Democracy in Plural Societies* (New Haven, CT: Yale University 1977), p.22; H.H. Kerr, 'The Swiss Party System: Steadfast and Changing', in H. Daalder (ed.), *Party*

Systems in Denmark, Austria, Switzerland, the Netherlands, and Belgium (London: Frances Pinter 1987), pp.107–192 at 111.

26. E. Gruner and R. Hertig, *Der Stimmbürger und die neue Politik* (Bern: Haupt 1983), p.43.
27. In Switzerland the term 'militia' is not only used in a military sense but also refers to the fact that there are hardly any professional politicians, not even on national level.
28. Neidhart, 'Funktions- und Organisationsprobleme der schweizerischen Parteien'.
29. M. Duverger, *Die politischen Parteien* (Tübingen: J.C.B. Mohr Paul Siebeck 1959); S. Neumann (ed.), *Modern Political Parties. Approaches to Comparative Politics* (Chicago: University Press 1956); O. Kirchheimer, 'Der Wandel des westeuropäischen Parteiensystems', *Politische Vierteljahresschrift* 6/1(1965), pp.20–41; L.D. Epstein, *Political Parties in Western Democracies* (New York: Praeger 1967).
30. R.S. Katz and P. Mair, 'Three Faces of Party Organization. Adaption and Change', paper prepared for the XII World Congress of Sociology in Madrid (EPRU Working Papers 1990), p.5.
31. Kirchheimer, 'Der Wandel des westeuropäischen Parteiensystems'.
32. A. Panebianco, *Political Parties: Organization and Power* (Cambridge: Cambridge University Press 1988).
33. R.S. Katz and P. Mair, 'Changing Models of Party Organization and Party Democracy: The Emergence of the Cartel Party', *Party Politics* 1/1 (1995), pp.5–28.
34. Lipset and Rokkan, 'Cleavages Structures, Party Systems and Voter Alignments'.
35. Fagagnini, 'Die Rolle der Parteien auf kantonaler Ebene', p.91.
36. Kerr, 'The Swiss Party System', p.163.
37. P. Mair, 'Party Organizations: From Civil Society to the State', in R.S. Katz and P. Mair (eds.), *How Parties Organize: Change and Adaption in Party Organizations in Western Democracies* (London: Sage 1994), pp.1–22 at 5.
38. Ladner and Brändle, *Fact-Sheets zum Wandel der Schweizer Parteien.*
39. Fagagnini, 'Die Rolle der Parteien auf kantonaler Ebene', p.91.
40. R. Wiesli, 'Schweiz: Miliz-Mythos und unvollkommene Professionalisierung', in J. Borchert (ed.), *Politik als Beruf: Die politische Klasse in westlichen Demokratien. ZENS – Europa- und Nordamerikastudien 5* (Opladen: Leske + Budrich, i.E. 1999).
41. Gruner, *Die Parteien der Schweiz*, p.221.
42. *Journal de Genève* of 5 July, 1989.
43. Ladner and Brändle, *Fact-Sheets zum Wandel der Schweizer Parteien.*
44. H. Schmitt and S. Holmberg, 'Political Parties in Decline?', in H.-D. Klingemann and D. Fuchs (eds.), *Citizens and the State* (New York: Oxford University Press 1995), pp.95–133 at 212.
45. Longchamp, *Unterstützung von Bundesrat und Verwaltung*, p.74.
46. Ibid., p.21; R. Nabholz, 'Das Wählerverhalten in der Schweiz: Stabilität oder Wandel? Eine Trendanalyse von 1971–1995', in H. Kriesi, W. Linder and U. Klöti (eds.), *Schweizer Wahlen 1995. Ergebnisse der Wahlstudie Selects* (Bern: Haupt 1998), pp.17–43.
47. Nabholz, 'Das Wählerverhalten in der Schweiz'.
48. E. Gruner, 'Eigentümlichkeiten der schweizerischen Parteienstruktur', *Politische Vierteljahres- schrift* (July 1964), pp.203–17.
49. Gruner, *Die Parteien der Schweiz*, p.218.
50. Longchamp, *Unterstützung von Bundesrat und Verwaltung*, p.22.
51. R.S. Katz and P. Mair, 'The Membership of Political Parties in European Democracies 1960–1990', *European Journal of Political Research* 22 (1992), pp.329–45 at 334; P. Mair and I. van Biezen, 'Party Membership in Twenty European Democracies, 1980–2000', *Party Politics* (Jan. 2001), pp.5–23.
52. Ladner and Brändle, *Fact-Sheets zum Wandel der Schweizer Parteien.*
53. Kerr, 'The Swiss Party System', pp.156–7.
54. Hans Hirter, *Wahlen 1999*. Swiss Electoral Studies (Forschungsgemeinschaft der politikwissenschaftlichen Institute der Universitäten Bern, Genf und Zürich 2000), p.21.
55. Kerr, 'The Swiss Party System', pp.156–7.
56. Hirter, *Wahlen 1999*, p.21.
57. R.S. Katz and P. Mair, 'The Evolution of Party Organizations in Europe: The Three Faces of Party Organization', *American Review of Politics* 14 (Winter 1993), pp.593–617.

58. Kirchheimer, 'Der Wandel des westeuropäischen Parteiensystems'.
59. G. Sani and G. Sartori, 'Polarization, Fragmentation and Competition in Western Democracies', in H. Daalder and P. Mair (eds.), *Western European Party Systems: Continuity and Change* (London: Sage 1983), p.322.
60. A. Ladner, 'Das Schweizer Parteiensystem und seine Parteien', in U. Klöti *et al.* (eds.), *Handbuch der Schweizer Politik* (Zürich: NZZ 1999), pp.213–60.
61. M. Brändle, 'Konkordanz gleich Konvergenz? Die Links-rechts-Positionierung der Schweizer Bundesratsparteien', *Schweizerische Zeitschrift für Politikwissenschaft* 5/1 (1999), pp.11–29.
62. Kirchheimer, 'Der Wandel des westeuropäischen Parteiensystems'.
63. Panebianco, *Political Parties*.
64. Katz and Mair, 'Changing Models of Party Organization and Party Democracy'.
65. Mair and van Biezen, 'Party Membership in Twenty European Democracies'.

Institutionalising the
Swiss Welfare State

KLAUS ARMINGEON

A 'welfare state' denotes a set of policies and implementing organisations that intervene in society and economy. The aims of intervention include supporting or providing full employment, health services, education, housing and social security. Of special concern are cases where there is serious loss of income due to a person's situation in the labour market, or where wage income is insufficient for subsistence. Prominent examples of intervention are public transfers paid to unemployed, aged and ill persons. These schemes and their administration make up the core of the welfare state. In its narrow sense, 'welfare state' is equated with these particular programmes.

In comparison with other countries, the Swiss welfare state has been labelled 'liberal' or 'residual'.[1] There is empirical evidence to support this classification for the years prior to the 1970s. Since then, however, much change is evident. Based on new data published by the OECD, Jan-Erik Lane detects a qualitative jump from a 'welfare society' – with a small public sector (less than 35 per cent GDP), economic efficiency and little equality – to a 'welfare state', marked by equality, low economic efficiency and a large public sector (more than 45 per cent GDP).[2] In fact, in 1970, Swiss general government receipts amounted to 36 per cent of nominal GDP. By 1997 this had increased to 55 per cent.[3] General government total outlays were around 20 per cent in 1970, but more than doubled by 1997, when they reached 49 per cent of GDP.[4] In a careful analysis of Swiss welfare state development, Herbert Obinger reaches a similar, but less dramatic, conclusion: although there has been considerable change, it has been incremental, with the liberal traits of the social security system still clearly discernible.[5]

The guiding question of the present discussion aims at this debate. Has there been a major qualitative change entailing a new type of welfare state? Or has there been gradual and incremental, although extensive, reform not

Klaus Armingeon, University of Berne

changing from one path of policy development to the other? Furthermore, how can we explain change and stability in the Swiss welfare state? In accordance with Obinger, it is argued here that, in comparative perspective, changes have been extensive, but gradual and incremental; and that these changes have not led to a qualitatively different type of welfare state. To substantiate this thesis, two types of empirical findings are presented: (1) change has brought Switzerland closer to the ideal type of a continental European welfare state; (2) convergence towards this model has been delayed, however, primarily by institutional factors. None the less, the process of convergence, once under way, could only be stalled – not stopped – by these structures.

THE CHANGING WELFARE STATE

The extent of change in welfare state characteristics will be gauged initially using indicators of public sector size (welfare state in a broad sense) and of social security transfers (welfare state in a narrow sense). In a second step, the policy changes made by creating or modifying welfare schemes will be qualitatively examined.

With respect to the Swiss public sector, a comparison of OECD indicators brings clear results.[6] Looking at general government receipts and outlays, Switzerland has shown the largest percentage increase in the last quarter century. Only Denmark, Sweden, and the three countries which democratised in the 1970s (Spain, Greece and Portugal) have growth rates of a similar magnitude. This increase is due mostly to transfers, and less to expansion of public sector employment. The growth of public sector employment is less than average and, in that regard, Switzerland is still a lean state. Only five countries in the reference group have a smaller sector. This does not apply to receipts and expenditures. In 1997 only two of the countries under study had greater revenues than the Swiss. Considering the size of public outlays, Switzerland is ranked seventh among 22 countries in 1997 (see Table 1).

A detailed analysis by Hanspeter Kriesi[7] showed that this increase, in Swiss figures, is mainly due to the former exclusion of health insurance and old age pensions from public expenditure and revenue figures. Health insurance had been voluntary until 1994, and since 1985 occupational pensions have been compulsory for the majority of employees. Including these schemes in the calculation of public revenues and expenditures leads to higher figures. But this inclusion is by no means a mere statistical change. The new law on occupational pensions made them more accessible, safer

TABLE 1

THE GROWTH OF THE SWISS WELFARE STATE IN COMPARATIVE PERSPECTIVE

	Switzerland	22 OECD countries (average)
Increase in government receipts (% GDP) 1968–97	18.7	12.1
Increase in government outlays (% GDP) 1968–97	28.1	12.8
Increase in government employment (% labour force) 1970–95	4.0	5.4
Increase in social security transfers (% GDP) 1980–95	9.3	4.8
Increase in adjusted social security transfers (% GDP), 1980–95	18.6	1.2

Notes: Increases are calculated as differences, i.e. the share in the 1990s minus the share in the 1960s/70s/80s. *Social security transfers:* All transfers from government or compulsory private insurance. *Adjusted social security transfers:* 100 * social security transfers divided by the sum of the unemployment rate and twice the rate of the population 65+.

Sources: OECD, several publications and website, Social security transfers: N.A. Siegel, 'Jenseits der Expansion? Zwischen Ausbau, Konsolidierung und Rückbau: Sozialpolitik in westlichen Demokratien nach dem "goldenen Zeitalter" wohlfahrtsstaatlicher Politik', in M.G. Schmidt (ed.), *Wohlfahrtsstaatliche Politik. Institutionen – Prozesse – Leistungsprofile* (Opladen: Leske + Budrich 2000).

and more generous for many employees. In contrast, while the reform of health insurance produced a statistical increase in public revenue, health insurance had been compulsory in some cantons before 1994. Furthermore, due to the high costs of the Swiss health system,[8] nearly all citizens had previously decided on their own membership of an insurance plan. Their insurers are private organisations, as are most occupational pension funds. High unemployment in the 1990s boosted Swiss numbers even more, due to increased reliance on unemployment benefits and social assistance. By 2000, however, Switzerland was back to full employment. As such, labour market problems no longer trigger additional expenditures and social security contributions, as they did in the 1990s.

These findings by Kriesi are supported by the analysis of Nico Siegel[9] (see Table 1). The size of the Swiss public sector has been underestimated by about ten percentage points in former statistics. This underestimation does not bias data much for the 1950s and 1960s. It becomes a serious shortcoming, however, for studies of the last two decades, when the Swiss welfare state was rapidly expanding in fields not covered by former statistical records.

Although the usability of these social security and expenditure data has been improved, serious shortcomings remain. In some other countries, corrections for similar problems probably also have to be made. In

Germany, for example, certain compulsory payments (for example, wages which have to be paid by employers in case of illness) are not included in the statistics of social security transfers; and taxes on transfers (such as on pensions or unemployment compensation) should be deducted from transfers in order to produce comparable data. As a result, the net transfers in high-spending countries are overestimated.[10] Irrespective of these flaws in the aggregate data, two conclusions can be made: (1) the Swiss welfare state has come close to the characteristics of the average OECD welfare state; (2) there was a massive growth of the Swiss welfare state in the 1980s and 1990s.

Even so, qualitative data indicate a delayed development of the Swiss welfare state. Nearly all of its major national social security schemes – which are sketched in the appendix – were introduced conspicuously late in comparison with other industrialised countries (see Table 2). This does not apply to the factory law of 1877 regulating maximum working time (11 hours), minimum working age (14 years), hygiene, and accident prevention at work.[11] This relative delay of national programmes does not mean, however, that there was no social security previously. Rather, social policy and assistance was basically the task of the 3,000 municipalities and the 26 cantons, which had different local and cantonal schemes.

This delay is partly due to the time lag between the decision to introduce such programmes and the date of implementation, if successfully enacted. Whenever a national social policy is decided upon, a constitutional referendum is required in order for the federation to be able to act. If successful, the next step is a shift of competences and resources from municipalities and cantons to the central state. Table 3 contains data on the length of time between a general constitutional decision and the implementation of the respective law.

TABLE 2

YEAR OF INTRODUCTION OF MAJOR NATIONAL SOCIAL SECURITY SCHEMES

	Switzerland	OECD average
Accident insurance	1918	1905
Health insurance (compulsory)	1911 (1994)	1924
Pension insurance	1946	1917
Unemployment insurance	1982	1929
Family allowance	1952	1944

Source: M.G. Schmidt, *Sozialpolitik in Deutschland. Historische Entwicklung und internationaler Vergleich* (Opladen: Leske + Budrich, 2nd edn 1998), Table 5, pp.180–81.

TABLE 3

FROM CONSTITUTIONAL DECISION TO ENACTMENT OF NATIONAL
SOCIAL SECURITY SCHEMES

	Year of Constitutional Decision	Year of Enactment	Time Elapsed (years)
Health insurance	1890	1914	24
Health insurance (compulsory)	1890	1996	106
Accident insurance	1890	1918	28
Pensions (1st pillar)	1925	1948	23
Pensions (1st pillar) (additional pensions)	1925	1966	41
Disability insurance	1925	1960	35
Family allowances	1945	1953	8
Maternity insurance	1945	–	> 55
Unemployment insurance (voluntary)	1947	1952	5
Pensions (2nd and 3rd pillar)	1972	1985	13
Unemployment insurance (compulsory)	1976	1984	8

Source: P. Gilliand, 'Politique sociale', in G. Schmidt (ed.), *Handbuch Politisches System der Schweiz. Band 4. Politikbereiche* (Bern: Haupt 1993), pp.111–223 at 137.

The modern form of the Swiss welfare state was primarily built in four steps: (1) in 1890, health insurance was created; (2) in 1925, inter-war social upheavals paved the way for the pension system enacted after World War II; (3) in the aftermath of World War II, plans were established for national-level programmes providing family allowances, voluntary unemployment insurance and maternity insurance; (4) in the 1970s, the system of pensions was completed, and compulsory unemployment insurance was introduced. With respect to constitutional decisions, the major foundations of the Swiss social state were laid between 1925 and 1945. Nevertheless, regarding expenditures and benefits, the relevant years are those when the respective laws were enacted. From this perspective, the Swiss welfare state developed over the past 50 years, and did so gradually. In particular, the period of 1975–85 saw many key developments in broadening welfare coverage.[12]

The benefits from Swiss social security programmes are generous. Health insurance covers the whole range of modern medical treatments (except dental). Pensions are composed of the so-called 'three pillars'. The first pillar provides universal insurance coverage. A retired couple, for example, is entitled to monthly pensions between about 950 Euro (minimum) to 1,900 Euro (maximum). In case the minimum pension is not reached, because the contribution period has been too short, an additional amount can be claimed so that the minimum income of 950 Euro for a couple is reached. Since the relation of minimum to maximum pension is

1:2, and contributions are strictly linear with income, the scheme is firmly redistributive. This is mitigated by income from the second pillar, the occupational pension. Low-paid part-time workers – frequently women – cannot contribute to this insurance. Benefits and contributions are linear with income. Income from the first and second pillar should reach at least 60 per cent of income before retirement. A third pillar consists of tax-deductible savings, favourable to medium-to-high income groups. Finally, unemployment compensation is paid for 520 days, and covers 70 per cent to 80 per cent of the former wage.

Judged by the programmes in place at the end of the twentieth century, Switzerland comes close to the typical continental European welfare state. This model is distinguished, by Peter Flora, from the peripheral welfare states of Great Britain and Scandinavia.[13] In the latter countries the state is highly centralised, the church is separate from the state, and the fragmentation of ethnic, linguistic and religious groups is low. These are conditions conducive to a universalistic and egalitarian welfare state. The continental European welfare state, however, developed in countries with lower centralisation, with an important and independent role for the Catholic Church in society, and with stronger societal fragmentation. The resulting welfare state structure, in this core of Western Europe, tends to be particularistic and inegalitarian, conserving differences due to societal stratification, gender and civil status.

Having introduced major compulsory welfare schemes for pensioners, sick people and unemployed, Switzerland is without doubt an advanced welfare state. It is contributory and not tax-based; benefits are to a large extent related to contributions; and the major schemes are oriented to a recipient model of a family led by a male bread-winner. In these regards, Switzerland belongs to the group of continental European welfare states. Nevertheless, strong liberal traits remain.[14] Administration of several schemes is often left to competing private organisations (second pillar, health insurance). The third pillar, providing income to the elderly, is organised purely according to liberal views. In health insurance, contributions are levied per capita and not per family, significant individual participation is demanded, and (with a few exceptions) dental care costs are not covered. Administrative controls are tight, for example, in unemployment insurance. And, finally, once a person becomes dependent on social assistance, the liberal face becomes particularly obvious: entitlements, benefits and administrative procedures vary strongly among municipalities and cantons; scrupulous means tests are widespread; and controls are strict. In a nutshell, judging by the scope, structure and administration of social security schemes, Switzerland is a continental European welfare state with a liberal face.

Available social security programmes aside, the legitimisation and acceptance of the state intervening in private life is another important dimension. The basic question concerns the role of government in society. In a liberal view, this role has to be limited. Social Democratic parties and centrist Conservative parties (like European Christian Democrats),[15] however, support a much stronger role – aiming to heal the imperfections and social dysfunctions of a purely market-oriented society. According to Flora, these basic orientations towards state intervention differentiate the European non-liberal states and the liberal or residual welfare states of the United States or Japan. In Japan, the state has been weak, social integration has been strong, and private enterprise has a superior role in social organisation. In the USA, ethnic fragmentation has been a prominent influence on welfare state development. Under these conditions, the state has been awarded a residual role in society. In contrast, European nation states have used the welfare state towards relative homogenisation of the population, while competition between these nation states has shaped their social institutions. Hence, the state has played a much more prominent role in society. Judging by these criteria, Switzerland has some non-European features: the central state has been and continues to be weak; linguistic and regional diversity is strong; and Switzerland hardly defines itself as a competing nation state, either in military or in economic terms. Instead, it looked for niches, facilitating the persistence of a weak central state in a fragmented society. Thus, following Flora's reasoning, the role of government in Swiss society should be seen in a similar vein to that in Japan and the USA.

We can test this hypothesis of differential welfare state legitimacy using the 'Role of government' survey, conducted under the framework of the International Social Survey Programme in 1996–98. In this survey respondents were asked whether they think government is responsible for providing jobs for everyone who wants them; to provide health care for the sick; to provide a decent standard of living for the old and unemployed; to reduce income differences between the rich and the poor; and to provide decent housing for those who cannot afford it. Those who are convinced that government is definitively responsible obviously support a strong European welfare state. The smaller this share, the more widespread are liberal orientations. Table 4 contains the results of the analysis.

Together with Australia and the USA, Switzerland belongs to the group of countries where the population holds the most liberal views with regard

TABLE 4

GOVERNMENT'S RESPONSIBILITY IN PROVIDING WELFARE
(Is it government's responsibility to ...)

Country	Provide jobs	Health care	Care for elderly	Care for un- employed	Reduce in- equality	Provide decent housing	Average
Australia	11	42	37	9	18	11	21
Canada	11	62	48	16	21	21	30
France	40	53	51	34	49	44	45
Germany (W)	28	51	48	17	25	20	32
Great Britain	29	82	73	29	36	37	48
Ireland	30	75	77	40	42	47	52
Italy	41	81	76	30	41	45	52
Japan	28	50	49	27	31	21	34
New Zealand	18	71	59	15	22	24	35
Norway	48	87	86	41	41	22	54
Sweden	35	71	69	39	43	27	47
Switzerland	15	28	28	9	24	11	19
USA	14	39	38	13	17	20	24

Notes: % saying government is definitely responsible. Unweighted data.

Source: International Social Survey 'Role of Government' 1996 (Switzerland: 1998).

to state intervention into society. Although receipts and expenditures of the Swiss welfare state, as well as its concrete programmes of social security, approach the continental European model, the underlying ideology is still very liberal. In sum, one could conclude that the welfare state is considered differently by both administrators and clients of Swiss programmes, compared with other Western European countries.

MAKING UP FOR DELAY

In international comparison, the development of Swiss social policy lags behind the pack. According to four distinct theories, this slow movement is paradoxical. From a Tocquevilleian perspective, a democratic society searches for equality, which can be realised through a welfare state.[16] Switzerland is an old democracy and, therefore, it should have become an egalitarian welfare state a long time ago. Second, affluence is correlated with the size of the welfare state. The more affluent a society, the larger the public sector. On one hand, there are the 'new, more numerous, refined public needs, ... [and] the changes in techniques of production and traffic', which demand and enable additional public tasks.[17] On the other hand, there are the functional requirements of modern society and the need to support a growing cohort of pensioners.[18] In the whole post-war period, Swiss society has been affluent. Hence, it should have had an early and large expansion of the welfare state. Third, theory about open economies argues that such economies need a large welfare state to buffer the problems and risks originating from dependence on the world market.[19] Switzerland has been an open economy for a long time,[20] without being dependent on extensive social policy buffers. According to a fourth theory, corporatism entails welfare state expenditures.[21] Although strongly corporatist, this theory does not apply to Switzerland. Obviously, these forces of expansion – democracy, affluence, economic openness and corporatism – did not work in Switzerland or were counter-balanced by other factors. If the latter, what are these factors? Why has the Swiss welfare state lagged behind for such a long time in international comparison? And why did its development accelerate so swiftly in the last two decades? These are the guiding questions addressed in this section. The methodology is a disciplined configurative analysis – that is, this case is explained on the basis of theory confirmed by empirical analyses. First, reasons for Switzerland's slow welfare state development are discussed, then the reasons why it caught up so rapidly in the years from 1975 onwards.

Delaying Welfare State Development

In a major study of the European welfare state, Jens Alber argues that the introduction of social security schemes have been a means for the stabilisation of non-democratic political systems.[22] Although the explanatory power of this argument has been put in doubt by later research,[23] it is highly plausible in cases like the reforms by Otto Graf Bismarck in Germany, where repression against Social Democracy (the stick) was combined with social security for the working class (the carrot). Switzerland is the oldest democracy in continental Europe, having enjoyed uninterrupted democratic rule for more than 150 years. As such, political stabilisation of a non-democratic order against the challenge of a politically mobilised population was not a relevant motive for welfare state reforms in Switzerland.

A second argument for the lag in welfare state development is a re-formulated argument about functional requirements. Unlike other European countries, Swiss industrialisation was not accompanied by massive urbanisation. Hence the intensification of misery and social conflicts, and the diminution of former networks of social security, were probably not as pronounced as in other countries. The need to react to these problems was not as obvious as in Manchester or Essen – simply because there were no large cities and the rural social and economic networks could contribute to social stability. In addition, after the economic crises of the late 1930s, Switzerland was not hit by serious labour market problems again until the late 1990s. In a long phase of full employment there was no urgent need for obligatory unemployment insurance, and in an economically growing society, free of major crises, pressures for welfare state expansion were difficult to substantiate. Full employment served as a functional equivalent to welfare state intervention, providing care for the unemployed. This employment record in an open economy was brought about by the public regulation of the labour market of foreigners,[24] who made up about a quarter of the labour force in 2000. If demand for labour declined, the number of foreigners was reduced, and vice versa. Technically this was achieved by not compensating for outflows of foreign labour (returning to their homelands, retiring or dying) or by increasing the inflows of foreign labour. By this way of maintaining full employment through flexible use of foreign labour, the domestic risks of being exposed to the world market could be managed, and a functional equivalent of a welfare state achieved.

Another reason for the delay of modern welfare state development could be its incompatibility with traditional political and administrative structures.[25] The Swiss central state is weak both in constitutional competences and in resources.[26] There is a long tradition of municipal social assistance, based on the concept of solidarity, whereby a member of the community is entitled to support in case of proven need. The old rule that a person in need (who has run out of entitlements for federal or cantonal benefits) has to be taken care of by his community of origin was abolished in 1975. Since that year both Swiss and foreign people in need receive support from the community where they live. Centrally organised welfare schemes are hardly compatible with such traditions of local community solidarity. One means of reconciling this incompatibility has been to combine federal norms and financing with implementation on the cantonal and municipal levels. A good example is pension insurance, which is administered by municipal institutions. These institutions already existed before 1948, and were adopted (and adapted) for the new task of old-age insurance.[27] In short, the impediments for the introduction of centrally organised social security schemes were more numerous in Switzerland than in centralised states like France, Norway or the Netherlands.

A related impediment to welfare state development is federalism. In Switzerland, each new social policy on the federal level requires a constitutional amendment, since the federal state can only govern in fields explicitly allowed for in the constitution. Municipal and cantonal administrations and populations, who either want to keep resources for themselves or prevent transfers to the federal level, have various political means to hinder any such change. Beyond the tools of direct democracy, these means include power resources stemming from co-operative federalism. The Swiss federal state has little of its own administration. Implementation is performed by cantonal and municipal institutions, and they have leeway in the application of federal norms. In addition, federal policy-making is often made in co-operation with lower levels (see Table 5).

Generally, corporatism provides favourable conditions for welfare state expansion,[28] and the Swiss version is a strong form of corporatism.[29] Typical European corporatist arrangements include some form of centralised public policy. This is not, however, the case in Switzerland. There, accords are settled in a decentralised manner, incorporating either industries or regions. In contrast to many European countries, there have never been significant attempts at a Keynesian macro-economic steering, including compensation for restraint in trade union wage demands. The Swiss mode of social partnership explains why corporatism has not become a motor of welfare state expansion.[30]

TABLE 5

RESPONSIBILITIES OF CANTONS AND THE FEDERATION IN THE FIELD OF SOCIAL SECURITY IN 2000

Programme	Extent of cover of programme	Legislation	Funding	Implementation
Old Age and Survivors' Insurance	Universal insurance	0	1	1
Disability Insurance	Universal insurance	0	1	1
Additional Pensions	Universal insurance/ means-tested	0	1	2
Unemployment Insurance	Employment-related	0	_c	1
Accident Insurance	Employment-related	0	–	0
Sickness Insurance	Universal insurance	0	1	1
Family Allowances	Employment-related	1	1b	1
Unemployment Assistance	Means-tested	2	2	2
Social Assistancea	Means-tested	2	2	2

Notes: 3-point scale: 0=federation's responsibility, 1=shared responsibility between federation and cantons, 2= cantons' responsibility; – = contributory funded.

    a social assistance for asylum seekers excluded. Moreover, a federal law regulates cost reimbursement between cantons.

    b Some cantons provide means-tested family allowances for non-employed people.

    c The federation has to cover the deficit in times of severe unemployment.

Source: H. Obinger, 'Federalism and Labour Market Policy. The Swiss Experience in the 1990s', (unpublished ms, 2000).

TABLE 6

POLITICAL COMPLEXION OF WESTERN EUROPEAN GOVERNMENTS, 1960–98
(% of total cabinet posts of respective parties, weighted by days)

Country	Right-wing Parties	Centre Parties	Left Parties
Austria	2	32	61
Denmark	42	4	51
Finland	22	37	36
France	49	11	24
Germany	19	51	29
Ireland	68	20	11
Italy	4	64	24
Luxembourg	25	47	28
Netherlands	38	42	19
Norway	20	14	66
Sweden	14	8	76
Switzerland	43	29	29
UK	68	0	32
Average	32	28	35

Notes: Right-wing parties: Liberal and Conservative parties
        Centre parties: mainly Catholic or Christian Democratic parties
        Left parties: Social Democratic and other Left parties
        For details: M.G. Schmidt, 'When Parties Matter: A Review of the Possibilities and
        Limits of Partisan Influence on Public Policy', European Journal of Political Research
        30/2 (1996), pp.155–83.

Source: K. Armingeon et al., Comparative Political Data Set (University of Berne, 2000).

Two political parties have been active promoters of social policy in Europe: Social Democrats and centrist Conservatives. Their relative strength in different countries explains some of the variation in welfare state size.[31] Both parties, however, have been weak in Switzerland, relative to the dominant Liberal Party. The Catholic centrist party became integrated into the political system at the end of the nineteenth century, while the Social Democrats have had a consistent presence in the federal government since 1959.

Table 6 demonstrates that Liberal and Conservative parties, opposing welfare state expansion, have been stronger in Switzerland in comparison with the Western European average. Furthermore, pro-welfare parties have been rather less successful than in other countries.

One of the most powerful impediments to welfare state expenditure is probably the effects of Switzerland's direct democracy structure. Numerous studies in public choice support this conclusion.[32] Their major point is that popular votes on specific legislation tend to limit politicians' ability to levy new taxes, as rational citizens will not typically accept such increases.

Ample empirical evidence shows direct democracy to be a brake on public sector expansion. If there were no direct democracy, Switzerland would have had health and accident insurance by 1900, pension insurance by 1931 and maternity insurance by 1999. In these years such laws were agreed upon in the parliament, only to be rejected by the people.[33]

Accelerating Welfare State Development

Although its welfare state expansion is limited by powerful institutional and political constraints, Switzerland has converged towards a continental European welfare model – but showing a liberal face with respect to expenditures, available schemes and public acceptance. How is such acceleration possible? Theories about welfare state development, as well as empirical findings about Swiss social and economic policy-making, provide four explanations. The first points to critical junctures: decisions at a discrete moment in time have long-lasting effects, many of which only become clear long after the point of origin. The second explanation concerns the costs and benefits of being a late-comer country. The third reason could be labelled an institutional ratchet-effect: basically, a policy which concerns and benefits a large share of the population cannot be revised in one shot, but can be changed incrementally. Ratchet-effect reform is possibly when retrenchment and expansion are combined with compensation measures. The fourth explanation relates to in-built or 'automatic' expansionary mechanisms embedded in a given social security scheme.

Policy change in extraordinary circumstances. The first explanation combines two arguments about major institutional reform in Western democracies. According to the first set of arguments, major reforms require a 'critical juncture' – seen in the synchronous occurrence of economic crises and major political changes – to make frozen political constellations 'fluid', to weaken opposition by one group, and to strengthen the position of another.[34] The second set of arguments holds that initial decisions in a given policy field have long-term effects, and that these effects often become discernible only after a long time.[35] At least two critical junctures occurred in the development of the Swiss welfare state: The first was the threat of Nazi Germany in 1939–45, combined with the preceding economic crisis of 1936. An important background factor was the general strike of 1918, which resulted in a constitutional amendment that gave the federation power to create public and national pension schemes. In that period, Social Democrats set aside their revolutionary approach and entered governments at the cantonal and temporarily (in 1943) federal level. Furthermore, economic and social policy underwent important change: interest organisations became officially incorporated into policy-making; the federal council proposed a corporatist organisation of the polity (although many proposals from this era have since been repealed);[36] and in 1946–52 the state both took a more active stance in the economy[37] and introduced pension insurance. Since then, the basic ideas behind the pension programmes have remained unchanged: The federal state provides a minimum income for all the country's elderly, while additional payments come from occupational pensions and private savings. In designing this pension plan, three institutional legacies had to be considered. (1) The federal state did not have administrative resources to implement the insurance provisions, and thus had to rely on cantonal administrations. (2) Cantonal administrations already had the organisational structure for this new insurance, stemming from federal reform during war-time. A large part of the male population had been mobilised, although in the event Switzerland did not take part in the war. Those serving were entitled to earnings-loss compensation through a programme of cantonal and private-based compensations funds. This organisation was simply adapted to run the new insurance plan. (3) The new insurance had to be compatible with the private occupational pension schemes. They had become strong in the years before, as no public insurance had been available. In 1941, a quarter of workers had entitlements to occupational pensions. In short, the option to have a single pillar system – as in Germany under Bismarck – was not feasible. This system could easily be financed as long as the politically defined minimum income for pensioners was low or the share of elderly was small and economic growth provided rising income due to the contribution-based structure of the scheme.

Much less dramatic was the second critical juncture. In the mid-1970s, Switzerland experienced a major decrease in employment. One in ten jobs was abolished. Nevertheless, this did not result in high unemployment, since the supply of labour – as it appears in the official statistics – was reduced by at least two means: one was the massive reduction of foreign labour; the other was a lack of incentives for the unemployed to register as such. Labor market offices were not very effective in finding people new jobs, and public unemployment compensation did not exist. Even so, this change in employment pattern provided a window of opportunity to implement plans for compulsory unemployment insurance which had been drafted years before.[38] This new insurance could be financed as long as declared unemployment did not soar. And in the perspective of the mid-1970s, looking back at the prior 40 years, two or three per cent unemployed seemed quite high.

Coming late. The benefits of coming late in developing a welfare state provide a lesson how one can draw from the experience of other countries. When, for example, Switzerland introduced disability insurance, it borrowed the most modern elements of other national insurance programmes. The basic principle is that integration into working life is superior to support by government handouts alone. At the same time, mental disability is treated the same as physical disability. Pensions for the disabled work the same as the basic pension for the elderly, that is, income rises with the level of wages and inflation.[39] In 1995, a policy for labour market intervention was added to the laws on unemployment compensation. Here again, Switzerland learned from other countries and introduced the principle of early activation, in that unemployed should have strong incentives to take courses, and so on, even shortly after they have become jobless.[40] The disadvantage for late-comer countries is that already at the outset of the scheme, compensations are set at a rather generous level (in international and longitudinal perspective). For 1991, the OECD calculated comparable unemployment benefit replacement rates in the first year of unemployment for an employee with a dependent spouse. In Switzerland, it was 72 per cent of prior earnings before tax. The OECD average, however, was 52 per cent.[41] A concrete factor behind its relatively high levels is a gestation effect created by Switzerland's brand of direct democracy. The longer it takes to implement a programme, the higher the expectations for it become, as exemplified by the pension insurance case. Soon after 1925, when federal pension schemes became constitutional, parliament drafted a law providing 'ridiculously low'[42] (200 Swiss francs p.a.) benefits. The draft failed in referendum. In the following 20 years, pro-welfare political parties and interest groups tried to draft improved versions, according to their views. When, in the late 1930s and 1940s, a window of opportunity opened for pension reform, these groups were able to take advantage and secure more generous legislation.

Ratchets. Four ratchet effects can be discerned in the development of welfare states. The first concerns the multiplicity of actors and decision arenas in social policy. The second involves popular initiatives taken after a social security scheme has been created. The third is the proven unwillingness of people to accept social policy retrenchment. Finally, and closely connected with the third, the fourth ratchet effect relates to compromises shaped by the exigencies of direct democracy.

Multiple decision arenas. Much mundane social policy and some types of incremental reform are not subject to popular votes. When no referendum is under way, social policy implementation and development takes place in three loosely connected arenas. The corporatist arena is made up of trade unions, employers' organisations and representatives of the federal administration. Political parties and representatives of cultural-linguistic groups bargain in the consociational arena. Finally, the federal arena sees bargaining occur between federal and cantonal authorities and among cantonal authorities themselves. These rounds are interconnected with regard to the problems to be solved and the policies to be designed and implemented. In addition, loose coupling occurs on the level of the actors. Thanks to the small size of the Swiss economic and political elites, the actors know each other, meet frequently in different settings, and some individual actors in the various rounds are the same: they are, for example, representative of a canton in the federal arena, while representing a political party in the consociational arena.[43] Welfare retrenchment requires that in all three arenas, the actors must agree on the respective measure. This agreement is necessary because interest organisations and cantonal authorities co-design and co-implement federal policies. Furthermore, even when actors pursue policies on their own, they have to be in concert with federal policy to avoid rendering the whole policy bundle ineffective. If agreement is not reached, political parties in the consociational forum have the power to call a popular vote, with all its uncertainty. Hence policy-makers are interested in avoiding this situation, particularly by building compromises.[44] The probability is high that in at least one of these arenas a majority will oppose retrenchment measures affecting their clienteles in the welfare state. In that case, for the two remaining forums, the risk of policy failure is high either in the process of formal decision making (involving parliament and the popular vote), or in the process of implementation.

Popular initiatives[45] are another ratchet. Seen formally, in Swiss history all social policy initiatives on the federal level have failed – either because they were repealed prior to a referendum or because they were rejected in a popular vote. Nevertheless, these initiatives often forced the government to present a weaker version of a reform than that demanded by its original supporters. In short, these 'counter-proposals' modified the status quo in the direction aimed at by the initiative.[46]

The third ratchet effect is caused by popular votes themselves. In the last 150 years, all laws exclusively proposing measures of welfare state retrenchment failed at the popular vote stage.[47] In part, this was because the participants in the votes are identical with the clientele of the policy. None the less, as in the cases of restrictive measures on unemployment and disability insurance, solidaristic motives are often declared in post-referendum surveys. Hence it is difficult to expand welfare schemes in a direct democracy; but very unlikely to abolish a scheme fully, which has once been approved in a popular vote.

The fourth ratchet effect is caused by this unwillingness of people to support purely restrictive measures. For the policy-maker trying to bypass this impediment, the solution lies in the combination of restrictive and innovative (or even expansive) strategies within the same reform. Guliano Bonoli presents ample empirical evidence of successful social policy reforms in 1990s, which use both retrenchment with innovation. A good example is pension reform, where women's retirement age was increased at the same time as their old-age insurance entitlements were markedly improved.[48] Under such conditions the people can be willing to support reform, even if it includes elements of retrenchment.

Built-in expansionary mechanisms. The rising expenditures of the Swiss welfare state are partly due to social policies enacted during critical junctures, which have been further, incrementally developed in following years. Major reforms consisted in enlarging the coverage of various programmes. Another part of the explanation for Swiss welfare state expansion concerns the fact that major schemes were developed under varying economic conditions and with regard to different social and demographic structures. Public pension insurance is the major example. When it was created, about ten per cent of the population was aged 65 or over. In 1998 this proportion had increased to 15 per cent. In 1960, 459,000 persons received pensions from the first pillar – in 1998 it was 1,630,000 persons. The life expectancy of a 65-year-old male was another 12 years in the early 1950s, but jumped to 17 years by 1998.[49] Another example is unemployment. In 1997 it reached five per cent, after hovering between zero and one per cent between 1950 and 1990. Hence, a large share of the dramatic expenditure increases in health care, pensions and unemployment benefits in the 1990s is simply due to changes in demographic and economic conditions that enlarged the number of those entitled to benefits.[50]

CONCLUSION

Judging by its types of social security schemes, public receipts and expenditures, and social security transfers in particular, Switzerland has converged towards the Western European welfare state model. This does not, however, apply to the structures of its schemes, which maintain some strong liberal traits; or to the relatively small number of public sector employees; or to the strong role that municipalities and cantons play in social policy. In addition, the attitudes of the Swiss people towards state intervention are much closer to those in the USA than to any other Western European country (for which data are available). It is a Western European welfare state with a liberal face.

No major 'qualitative jump' from one model of the welfare state to the other has happened in recent years, even though one might assume this given the sharp rise in social security spending in the 1990s. Rather, key decisions were taken during critical historical periods, most of which took place around 50 years ago. These policies, however, were incrementally modified in the post-war period, bringing ever increasing coverage of the population with ever more generous schemes.

Development of the Swiss welfare state was long held back by the distribution of political power (for example, the weakness of pro-welfare parties), and by institutions (like direct democracy and federalism). However, once the critical hurdle of introducing a programme was passed, these structures were not very effective in retrenching social policy or in limiting expenditures. Rather, they tended to work in the other direction, like a ratchet, helping ease the expansion of social policy, while at the same time impeding restrictive measures.

These findings are supported by analyses showing that in the period 1980–95, Switzerland expanded social security benefits more than any other in the group of economically advanced OECD countries (controlling for percentages of elderly and unemployed). In contrast, other countries, notably the Netherlands and New Zealand, were successful in reducing the size of the welfare state in the same period.[51]

Nevertheless, considering the problems of financing the rising costs of the welfare state in OECD countries, the prospects for the Swiss welfare state are not so dim as these findings initially suggest. First, although its description as a lean, residual welfare state is no longer true, the contrary is also false. In international comparison, Switzerland is just average, neither fat nor lean, especially when the high level of economic affluence is controlled for. Considering that the welfare state has important positive functions for the integration of society and the working of the economy,[52] Switzerland probably has the welfare state it needs.

Second, some European countries have financed their welfare state through debt. This is not true for Switzerland, which has sound public finances.[53]

Third, the Swiss welfare state is largely contribution-based. Income taxes are still low in international comparison.[54] One of the fastest growing and most cost-intensive schemes is the second pillar of old-age insurance. It is administered by private and public funds, with contributions (both from the individual and the employer) assigned to the employee. Besides retirement income, these assets can be used to finance houses. In many funds, once the age of retirement is reached, employees can decide whether they want to have monthly payments or the whole capital in a lump sum. Hence, this important and expanding sector of the Swiss welfare state is a mixture of an insurance scheme and a compulsory, tax-deductible savings plan (with restrictions on spending prior to retirement).

Finally, the social policy reforms of the 1990s indicate the large capacity for reform in the Swiss political system.[55] By combining the restriction of some programmes with modernisation and expansion in others, a third way has been found between neo-liberal retrenchment and the continuation of the old statist welfare policies that were so popular in the Scandinavian countries until the 1980s. It could be that this is the way to the welfare state of the twenty-first century.

APPENDIX
WELFARE STATE PROGRAMMES IN SWITZERLAND, 2000, ON THE FEDERAL LEVEL
(Social assistance is exclusively dealt with by municipalities and cantons)

1 Age: 1st pillar
Type: Old Age and Survivors' Insurance (AHV). The so-called '1st pillar', effective since 1.1.1948.
Contributions (in percentage of earnings): Employer 4.2%, Employee 4.2%. Self-employed: 7.8%.
Assessable Contribution Ceiling: No ceiling
Benefits: Retirement benefits. Single: Minimum 630 Euro; Maximum 1,260 Euro/Married couple: 150% of single retirement pension, i.e. minimum 950 Euro, maximum 1,900 Euro.
Benefits payable from 65 years (men) and 62 (2000), 63 (2001), 64 (2005) (women) to death.
Insured: All residents except foreigners in the diplomatic service.

2 Age: 2nd pillar
Type: Swiss Pension Fund Law (occupational insurance), the so-called '2nd pillar', effective since 1.1.1985.
Contributions (in percentage of 'co-ordinated earning'): between 7% and 18% depending on age and sex. Employer's share at least 50% of total contributions.
Assessable contribution ceiling: Co-ordinated earning. No contributions are paid for annual earnings below 15,000 Euro. Those who earn less do not have to pay contributions and are not entitled to benefits. For the part of annual earnings above 45,000 Euro, no contribution has to be paid, although some pension funds – e.g. in the public sector – insure and pay benefits for earnings above this threshold. The assessable 'co-ordinated wage' is the income between the minimum (15,000 Euro) and the maximum minus the minum (45,000 Euro-15,000 Euro = 30,000 Euro).
Benefits: Retirement benefits equalling 7.2% per year of accrued retirement assets as retirement pension. Guaranteed interest rate on assets: 4%. In some funds, the whole assets can be

obtained at the time of retirement as a lump sum. Before retirement age assets can be used to amortise mortgages for houses and flats. Alternatively, they can be used as securities, pledgeable to banks who are financing houses/flats of the employee.
Benefits payable: From age of retirement to death.
Insured: all employees over 25 years of age and with annual salaries exceeding 15,000 Euro.

3 Age: 3rd pillar
Type: Tax-deductible savings/contributions to life insurance, the so-called third pillar.
Contributions: Voluntary, up to the annual amount of 3,600 Euro (employees), or 18,000 Euro (persons, not entitled to membership in 2nd pillar, i.e. mostly self-employed).
Benefits: Savings can be used at the time of retirement or for financing houses/flats.
Accessible by all employees and self employed.

4 Age/disability: additional pensions
Type: Additional pensions, effective since 1966.
Financing: From tax revenues, 10–35% of cost covered by federal state, remaining costs covered by cantons.
Benefits: The constitution states that pensions for age and disability have to cover the cost of living (subsistence level). In some cases – if the contribution period to the funds of the age insurance of the first pillar have been too short – normal pensions are below this subsistence level. In this case, additional pensions are paid to achieve the subsistence level. Eligibility is restricted to Swiss citizens and foreigners, who lived for an uninterrupted period of at least 10 years in Switzerland. For refugees the requested period is 5 years.

5 Disability
Type: Disability Insurance.
Contributions (in % of earnings): 0.7% employer, 0.7% employee. Self-employed: 1.4%.
Benefits: Disability benefits, corresponding to the single retirement pension of the first pillar.
Benefits payable: From: Immediately for permanently disabled, otherwise 360 days waiting period, to: recovery, beginning of old age pension, or death.
Insured: All residents except foreigners in the diplomatic service.

6 Military service/loss of earnings
Type: Income Replacement Scheme.
Contributions (in % of earnings): Employer 0.15%, employee 0.15%. Self-employed: 0.3%.
Benefits: for loss of earnings during military service, depending on income and marital status.

7 Sickness
Type: Sickness insurance, effective since 1911; compulsory since 1994.
Financing: Insured has to pay per capita contributions, independent from income and marital status. Children have a reduced contribution, but contribution still has to be paid per capita. State subsidies.
Benefits: Usual medical treatments, excluding dental. Insured have to pay the first 150 Euro for doctor bills, and (up to an annual maximum level) they have to cover 10% of medical treatment costs.
Insured: All residents. Compulsory insurance in (mostly) private funds.

8 Accidents/occupational diseases
Type: Accident Insurance/Occupational diseases, effective since 1918.
Financing: Employers pay contributions according to danger classification of the job. Employees pay for non-occupational accidents.
Benefits: Medical treatment, disability benefits, death benefits.
Insured: All employees.

9 Unemployment
Type: Unemployment insurance, effective since 1984.
Contributions in % of earning: Employers 1.5%, employees 1.5%, temporarily increased for covering additional expenditures due to the employment crises of the 1990s.
Assessable contribution ceiling: Annual income of 62,000 Euro; temporarily, 1% of the annual income between 62,000 and 156,000 Euro has to be paid to cover additional costs of the unemployment crisis of the 1990s.
Benefits: Between 70% and 80% of previous income (ceiling: 62,000 Euro p.a.), depending on dependants.
Benefits payable: Monthly incomes below 1,900 Euro from the 1st day of unemployment, otherwise: from the 6th day of unemployment.
Duration: Maximum 520 days.
Insured: All employees.

10 Damages from military services
Type: Military insurance, effective since 1901.
Financing: Federal state.
Benefits: Covering the costs/losses of incomes due to damages during military services.

11 Families
Type: Family allowances, effective since 1953.
Financing: Employer's contribution.
Benefits: Children allowances.
Covered: Only employees in agriculture.

NOTES

1. G. Esping-Andersen, *The Three Worlds of Welfare Capitalism* (Princeton: Princeton University Press 1990).
2. J.-E. Lane, 'Welfare States or Welfare Societies?', *Statsvetenskaplig Tidskrift* 101 (1998), pp.145–65; J.-E. Lane, 'The Public/Private Sector Distinction in Switzerland', *Revue Suisse de Science Politique/Schweizerische Zeitschrift für Politikwissenschaft* 5 (1999), pp.94–105.
3. OECD: Analytical Databank, OECD website.
4. Organisation for Economic Co-operation and Development OECD, *Historical Statistics. 1960–1995* (Paris: OECD 1997), p.73; OECD: Analytical Databank, OECD website
5. H. Obinger, *Politische Institutionen und Sozialpolitik in der Schweiz. Der Einfluß von Nebenregierungen auf Struktur und Entwicklungsdynamik des schweizerischen Sozialstaates* (Frankfurt am Main: Lang 1998); H. Obinger, 'Wohlfahrtsstaat Schweiz: Vom Nachzügler zum Vorbild?' in H. Obinger and U. Wagschal (eds.), *Der gezügelte Wohlfahrtsstaat. Sozialpolitik in reichen Industrieländern* (Frankfurt am Main/New York: Campus 2000).
6. In the following Switzerland is compared to 21 other OECD countries: Australia, Austria, Belgium, Canada, Denmark, Finland, France, Germany, Greece, Ireland, Italy, Japan, Luxembourg, Netherlands, New Zealand, Norway, Portugal, Spain, Sweden, United Kingdom and the United States of America. Due to missing values, this reference group may include less countries in some of the statistical analyses.
7. H. Kriesi, 'Note on the Size of the Public Sector in Switzerland', *Revue Suisse de Science Politique* 5 (1999), pp.105–8.
8. M.G. Schmidt, 'Warum die Gesundheitsausgaben wachsen. Befunde des Vergleichs demokratisch verfasster Länder', *Politische Vierteljahresschrift* 40 (1999), pp.229–45.
9. N.A. Siegel, 'Jenseits der Expansion? Zwischen Ausbau, Konsolidierung und Rückbau: Sozialpolitik in westlichen Demokratien nach dem "goldenen Zeitalter" wohlfahrtsstaatlicher Politik', in M.G. Schmidt (ed.), *Wohlfahrtsstaatliche Politik. Institutionen – Prozesse – Leistungsprofile* (Opladen: Leske + Budrich 2000).
10. M.G. Schmidt, *Sozialpolitik in Deutschland. Historische Entwicklung und internationaler Vergleich* (Opladen: Leske + Budrich 2nd edn. 1998), pp.198–9, n.725.

11. P. Gilliand, 'Politique sociale', in G. Schmidt (ed.), *Handbuch Politisches System der Schweiz. Band 4. Politikbereiche* (Bern: Haupt 1993), pp.111–223 at 119.
12. Obinger, *Politische Institutionen und Sozialpolitik in der Schweiz.*
13. P. Flora, 'Europa als Sozialstaat?', in B. Schäfers (ed.), *Lebensverhältnisse und soziale Konflikte im neuen Europa* (Frankfurt am Main/New York: Campus 1993), pp.754–62.
14. See in particular Obinger, *Politische Institutionen und Sozialpolitik in der Schweiz.*
15. K. van Kersbergen, *Social Capitalism. A Study of Christian Democracy and the Welfare State* (London/New York: Routledge 1995).
16. J.-E. Lane and S.O. Ersson, *Politics and Society in Western Europe* (London/Thousand Oaks/New Delhi: Sage 4th edn 1999), chapter 11.
17. Adolph Wagner, quoted J. Kohl, *Staatsausgaben in Westeuropa. Analysen zur langfristigen Entwicklung der öffentlichen Finanzen* (Frankfurt am Main/New York: Campus 1985), p.29.
18. H. Wilensky, *The Welfare State and Equality. Structural and Ideological Roots of Public Expenditures* (Berkeley/Los Angeles/London: University of California Press 1975).
19. D.R. Cameron, 'The Expansion of the Public Economy. A Comparative Analysis', *American Political Science Review* 72 (1978), pp.1243–61.
20. P. Bairoch, 'La Suisse dans le contexte international aux XIXe et XXe siècles', in P. Bairoch and M. Körner (eds.), *La Suisse dans l'économie mondiale* (Genève: Librairie Droz 1990), pp.103–40.
21. K. Armingeon, *Neo-korporatistische Einkommenspolitik. Eine vergleichende Untersuchung von Einkommenspolitiken in westeuropäischen Ländern* (Frankfurt am Main: Haag & Herchen 1983); Lane and Ersson, *Politics and Society in Western Europe*, p.337.
22. J. Alber, *Vom Armenhaus zum Wohlfahrtsstaat. Analysen zur Entwicklung der Sozialversicherung in Westeuropa* (Frankfurt am Main/New York: Campus 1987).
23. D. Berg-Schlosser and S. Quenter, 'Makro-quantitative vs. makro-qualitative Methoden in der Politikwissenschaft - Vorzüge und Mängel komparativer Verfahrensweisen am Beispiel der Sozialstaatstheorie', *Politische Vierteljahresschrift* 37 (1996), pp.100–118.
24. G. von Rhein-Kress, *Die politische Steuerung des Arbeitsangebotes. Die BRD, Österreich und die Schweiz im internationalen Vergleich* (Opladen: Westdeutscher Verlag 1996); K. Armingeon, 'Wirtschafts- und Finanzpolitik', in U. Klöti *et al.* (eds.), *Handbuch der Schweizer Politik* (Zürich: NZZ-Verlag 1999), pp.725–66; M.G. Schmidt, *Der schweizerische Weg zur Vollbeschäftigung. Eine Bilanz der Beschäftigung, der Arbeitslosigkeit und der Arbeitsmarktpolitik* (Frankfurt am Main/New York: Campus 1985); M.G. Schmidt, 'Vollbeschäftigung und Arbeitslosigkeit in der Schweiz. Vom Sonderweg zum Normalfall', *Politische Vierteljahresschrift* 36 (1995), pp.35–48; H. Obinger, 'Federalism and Labour Market Policy. The Swiss Experience in the 1990s' (unpublished ms, 2000).
25. Schmidt, *Sozialpolitik in Deutschland.*
26. For a general overview of the Swiss political system, see H. Kriesi, *Le Système Politique Suisse* (Paris: Economica 1995); W. Linder, *Swiss Democracy. Possible Solutions to Conflict in Multicultural Societies* (Houndsmill: Macmillan 1994); W. Linder, *Schweizerische Demokratie – Institutionen, Prozesse, Perspektiven* (Bern: Haupt 1999).
27. Linder, *Schweizerische Demokratie*, pp.160–61.
28. Lane and Ersson, *Politics and Society in Western Europe*, p.337.
29. A. Siaroff, 'Corporatism in 24 Industrial Democracies: Meaning and Measurement', *European Journal of Political Research* 36 (1999), pp.175–205.
30. K. Armingeon, 'Swiss Corporatism in Comparative Perspective', *West European Politics* 20 (1997), pp.164–79.
31. M.G. Schmidt, 'When Parties Matter: A Review of the Possibilities and Limits of Partisan Influence on Public Policy', *European Journal of Political Research* 30 (1996), pp.155–83; Lane and Ersson, *Politics and Society in Western Europe*, pp.338–40.
32. B.S. Frey, 'Direct Democracy: Politico-Economic Lessons from Swiss Experience', *American Economic Review* 84 (1994), pp.338–42; G. Kirchgässner, L.P. Feld and M.R. Savioz, *Die direkte Demokratie. Modern, erfolgreich, entwicklungs- und exportfähig* (Basel/Genf/München: Helbing & Lichtenhahn 1999); H. Obinger and U. Wagschal, 'Zwischen Reform und Blockade: Plebiszit und Sozialstaatstätigkeit', in M.G. Schmidt (ed.), *Wohlfahrtsstaatliche Politik. Institutionen – Prozesse – Leistungsprofile* (Opladen: Leske + Budrich 2000).

33. Obinger, *Politische Institutionen und Sozialpolitik in der Schweiz*; Obinger and Wagschal, 'Zwischen Reform und Blockade'.
34. P. Gourevitch, *Politics in Hard Times. Comparative Responses to International Economic Crises* (Ithaca/London: Cornell University Press 1986); J.T.S. Keeler, 'Opening the Window for Reform', *Comparative Political Studies* 25 (1993), pp.433–86; A.P. Cortell and S. Peterson, 'Altered States: Explaining Domestic Institutional Change', *British Journal of Political Science* 29 (1999), pp.177–203.
35. P. Pierson, 'Increasing Returns, Path Dependence, and the Study of Politics', *American Political Science Review* 94 (2000), pp.251–67.
36. Schweizerischer Bundesrat, 'Botschaft des Bundesrates an die Bundesversammlung über eine Partialrevision der Wirtschaftsartikel der Bundesverfassung (3616)', *Bundesblatt* 89 (1937), pp.833–900.
37. E. Gruner, '100 Jahre Wirtschaftspolitik. Etappen des Interventionismus in der Schweiz', *Schweizerische Zeitschrift für Volkswirtschaft und Statistik* 100 (1964), pp.3–70.
38. D. Freiburghaus, *Präventivmassnahmen gegen die Arbeitslosigkeit in der Schweiz. Methoden der Wirkungsanalyse und erste Ergebnisse* (Bern: Haupt 1987).
39. H.P. Tschudi, *Die Sozialverfassung der Schweiz (Der Sozialstaat)* (Bern: Schweizerischer Gewerkschaftsbund 1986).
40. Organisation for Economic Co-Operation and Development OECD, *Arbeitsmarktpolitik in der Schweiz (Deutsche Uebersetzung der offiziellen französischen Ausgabe)* (Paris/Bern: OECD/Schweiz. Bundesamt für Industrie und Gewerbe 1996).
41. Organisation for Economic Co-Operation and Development OECD, *The OECD Jobs Study. Evidence and Explanations. Part II* (Paris: OECD 1994).
42. G. Bonoli, 'Pension Policy in Switzerland. Institutions and the Politics of Expansion and Retrenchment', in U. Klöti and K. Yorimot (eds.), *Institutional Change and Public Policy in Japan and Switzerland* (Zürich: Universität Zürich: Institut für Politikwissenschaft/ Abteilung für Internationale Beziehungen 1999).
43. H. Kriesi, *Entscheidungsstrukturen und Entscheidungsprozesse in der Schweizer Politik* (Frankfurt am Main/New York: Campus 1980); H. Kriesi, 'The Structure of the Swiss Political System', in G. Lehmbruch and P.C. Schmitter (eds.), *Patterns of Corporatist Policy-Making* (London/Beverly Hills: Sage 1982), pp.133–61.
44. See K. Armingeon, 'Renegotiating the Swiss Welfare State', in G. Lehmbruch and F. von Waarden (eds.), *Renegotiating the Welfare State* (London: Routledge and Kegan Paul 2000).
45. A referendum concerns a law approved by parliament, or a proposed constitutional change. It is a reaction to decision-making in the parliamentary arena. An initiative is a demand for an constitutional amendment, proposed by 100,000 citizens. For further differences, see Linder, *Swiss Democracy*, and Papadopoulos in this volume.
46. H. Obinger, 'Soziale Sicherheit in der Schweiz', in E. Talos (ed.), Soziale Sicherung im Wandel. Österreich und seine Nachbarstaaten. Ein Vergleich (Wien/Köln/Weimar: Böhlau 1998), pp.31–102.
47. Obinger and Wagschal, 'Zwischen Reform und Blockade', pp.90–123.
48. G. Bonoli, 'Switzerland: Institutions, Reforms and the Politics of Consensual Retrenchment', in J. Clasen (ed.), *Social Insurance in Europe* (Bristol: Policy Press 1997), pp.107–29; G. Bonoli, 'La réforme de l'Etat social suisse: Contraintes institutionnelles et opportunités de changement', *Revue suisse de science politique* 5 (1999), pp.57–77; Bonoli, 'Pension Policy in Switzerland'.
49. All data from H. Ritzmann-Blickenstorfer, *Historische Statistik der Schweiz/Statistique historique de la Suisse/Historical Statistics of Switzerland. Unter der Leitung von Hansjörg Siegenthaler* (Zürich: Chronos 1996); Bundesamt für Statistik BFS, *Statistisches Jahrbuch der Schweiz 2000* (Zürich: Neue Zürcher Zeitung 1999).
50. Kriesi, 'Note on the Size of the Public Sector in Switzerland', pp.105–8.
51. N.A. Siegel, 'Jenseits der Expansion? Zwischen Ausbau, Konsolidierung und Rückbau: Sozialpolitik in westlichen Demokratien nach dem "goldenen Zeitalter" wohlfahrtsstaatlicher Politik', in Schmidt (ed.), *Wohlfahrtsstaatliche Politik*, pp.54–89.
52. Schmidt, *Sozialpolitik in Deutschland*.

53. K. Armingeon, 'Wirtschafts- und Finanzpolitik', in Klöti *et al.* (eds.), *Handbuch der Schweizer Politik*, pp.725–66.
54. M. Eggler and E. Rotzetter, 'Die Steuerbelastung der Schweiz im internationalen Vergleich', *Volkswirtschaft* (1992), pp.51–6; U. Wagschal, 'Deutschlands Steuerstaat und die vier Welten der Besteuerung' in Schmidt (ed.), *Wohlfahrtsstaatliche Politik*.
55. See in particular Bonoli, 'La réforme de l'Etat social suisse', pp.57–77.

The Growth of the Public Sector
in Switzerland

JAN-ERIK LANE and REINERT MAELAND

Switzerland's public sector, relatively speaking, is today larger than that of all the other OECD Member countries. From the income side, Switzerland has passed Sweden as an extreme welfare state; total government revenues are close to 60 per cent of GDP. This is astonishing, as the general image of Switzerland has been one of a country with a relatively small public sector.[1] The Swiss public choice school has long argued that the special Swiss political institutions were conducive to a strong market society, which would help to moderate public expenditures.[2] Both this image and this theory is wrong, as the Swiss institutions have not held down public sector expansion. More recently, the expansion of the Swiss social state has been acknowledged by Swiss scholars but hardly to its full extent.[3] In international social science research, Switzerland continues to be treated as an exception, a so-called outlier.

How can we model the sharp growth of the Swiss public sector since 1960? We suggest the employment of an alternative framework to that of traditional welfare state theory, namely quantitative budgetary analysis. Welfare state theory has resulted in a large literature offering so-called determinants of the growth of government.[4] However, no conclusive findings have been arrived at concerning which factors have the most weight when public expenditures are pushed upwards over a long period of time. This is basically a *macro* approach, focusing upon the impact of major aggregates such as population growth, age distribution of the population, the overall size of political parties, the position of organised interests, and so on.

Within a budgetary framework, the fundamental approach is *micro* based, although it admits the aggregation of expenditure items into huge aggregates. In a couple of articles from the 1970s, Aaron Wildavsky and his associates showed how illuminating a budgetary approach, using econometrics, could be for modelling and interpreting the growth in public

Jan-Erik Lane, University of Geneva; Reinert Maeland, Lund University.

expenditure.[5] The advantage of the Wildavsky approach is that it allows for two things at the same time: (a) econometric exposition of the data; and (b) decision theory interpretation of the resulting statistical parameters. This study takes a preliminary step towards the analysis of public sector expansion in Switzerland using the Wildavsky framework.

Public sector expansion is both a macro and a micro phenomenon. It shows up in enormous aggregates, but it results from the growth of millions of expenditure items, all calculated in relation to the development of GDP. The budgetary framework is basically a micro framework focusing upon how each small budgetary item changes from one year to another, corresponding to incremental decision theory.[6] By marrying the macro or aggregate perspective with the micro one, we hope to describe how overall public expenditures have developed over the last 40 years, and to identify some decision mechanisms that help account for the growth, concentrating upon the yearly changes – the so-called increment in the language of bounded rationality theory.[7]

THEORY: WAGNER, BAUMOL AND WILDAVSKY

It would seem natural to apply traditional welfare state theory to the Swiss case, as this theory has been developed into a set of hypotheses tested in several studies in relation to other OECD countries. Two circumstances, however, encouraged us to use another framework, especially given public sector growth theory's failure to deliver a coherent set of hypotheses tested and confirmed in empirical research, despite several attempts. In public sector growth theory one predicts aggregate public expenditures from other factors such as GDP, the age composition of its population, the party composition of government, the place of interest organisations, as well as the bargaining strength of the bureaucracy – summarised as either demand-side or supply-side forces.

First, public sector growth theory never managed to integrate two entirely different theories – on the one hand, the demand-side hypotheses entailing that public sector growth was real and wanted; on the other hand, a set of supply-side hypotheses that entailed that public sector growth was a fiction merely driven by inefficiency losses, mainly in the form of higher unit costs. Figure 1 shows that the demand-side theory (Wagner's Law) and the supply-side theory (Baomol's disease) can predict the same level of public expenditures, making it difficult to choose between them.

The demand-side theories focus upon the shift from D1 to D2, which would explain why the public sector has expanded from Q1 to Q2, with the

FIGURE 1

DEMAND- AND SUPPLY-SIDE EXPLANATIONS OF GOVERNMENT GROWTH

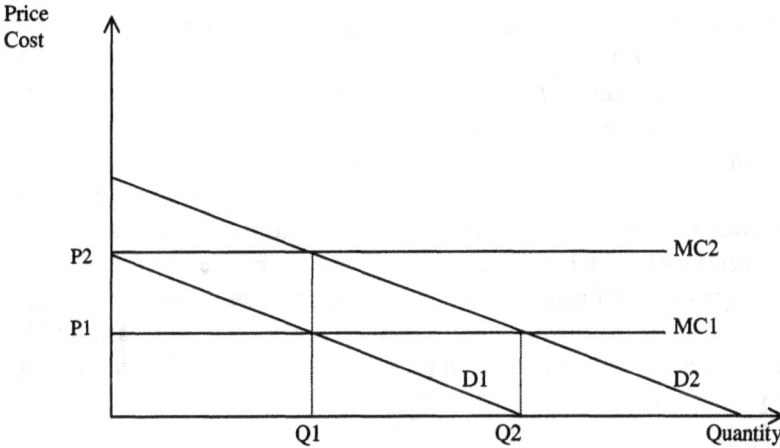

attendant explosion in costs, from Q1 X P1 to Q2 X P1. At the same time, the supply-side theory explains the same cost explosion by focusing upon the shift in price from P1 to P2, reflecting the change from one supply S1 (MC1) (marginal cost at P1) to another supply S2 (MC2) (marginal cost at P2). The public sector is as large today as it was forty years ago, but price has more than doubled, leaving the same huge bill to be paid for taxes or user fees, Q1 X P2 = Q2 X P1.

Public sector growth is probably a function of both the demand- and supply-side forces, but to predict and verify what constellation of demand and supply forces results in which level of public expenditures has not been possible, despite immense efforts in various detailed country studies.

Second, public sector growth theory, especially the welfare state version, lacks a mechanism through which external forces, or the context of budget-making get transplanted into expenditures. At the end of the day, any increase in public expenditure must be based upon a micro decision to do exactly that, namely increase outlays on one or more programmes from one year to another. We suggest that this micro decision-making process can be modelled in conjunction with the effort to predict macro outcomes.. Thus, the budgetary mechanism is the link between forces calling for more expenditures and the real decision to do just that.

A decision approach is a micro one. It focuses upon a decision concerning one expenditure item. Public sector growth, however, is a macro process, covering decisions relating to an immense mass of single expenditure items. Thus, the need for aggregation forces us to focus upon major macro outputs, such as the overall growth rate in public expenditures from one year to another, totally or in several sectors. Such outputs may be derived from modelling the growth process in accordance with Wildavsky's equations.[8] The Wildavsky equations belong to an incrementalist decision framework, as budget decisions are looked upon as marginal ones, adding or subtracting from a base that remains stable from one year to another.

The Wildavsky equations model the appropriations behaviour as a yearly decision process where, in other words, this year's appropriation is a function of last year's appropriation and an error term. It is a stochastic process in which the decision parameters may be identified through the employment of estimators in econometric techniques. The critical question is not the exact nature of the yearly change, not whether there is an addition or a subtraction, but if a decision process is stable or not. Either the budget is growing regularly or diminishing regularly, or the budget changes are volatile.

The Wildavsky equations focus upon appropriations as well as requests. Since we only have access to data about the appropriations for a few major outputs we will focus upon them in order to model how they have grown in the Swiss public sector and whether there have occurred significant shift-points. A *shift-point* involves an unexpected major change that moves the appropriation to a considerably higher (or lower) level. In order to detect these shift-points one may use a special regression technique, the so-called Kalman filter technique.

Public sector growth results from millions of decisions, some of which increase the budget, whereas others leave it intact or decrease it. The final outcome of all the behaviour that goes into each expenditure decision is summarised in the yearly change, or the increment. Whether one adheres to a demand approach or to a supply-side approach, it is the increment that summarises all the forces that increase or decrease public spending. If one understands the logic of the increment, then one has a key for explaining public sector growth. We see public sector growth as basically expenditure-driven, where the income side is decided afterwards. The expenditure increment also tends to determine the decision-making on incomes, at least in most cases. Except for the exceptional period where politicians do not know what to do with all their revenues, it is the expenditure side of the budget that is initially considered. Revenues are then determined by either the setting of tax rates or charges or the use of bonds.

When processes of public sector growth take place over a long period of time, then one would seek answers to at least three questions:

(1) Is there a stable incremental rule that increases the public sector linearly?

(2) Is there a stable incremental rule that relates the size of the public sector to another basic aggregate such as the GDP?

(3) Is the use of stable incremental rules the same over all outputs or items of public expenditures?

The remainder of the discussion endeavours to answer these questions through an enquiry into the growth rates of the Swiss public sector. We wish to show that the growth rates have been neither stable nor linear and, also, that they have varied over all kinds of public expenditures. The analysis of the increments allows us to pinpoint the occurrence of major decisions when public expenditures are moved to a higher level of ambition – the so-called shift-points. Future analysis of public sector growth in Switzerland should concentrate upon the making of these critical decisions.

THE DATA

We have used only one source of information concerning public sector expansion during the post-war period in Switzerland, namely the various series stated in the country's official statistical yearbook.[9] The collection of these data series required some standardisation as well as interpolation in order to arrive at time series that consist of comparable yearly data. All series were transformed into inflation-free statistics. The following series will be examined: (1) GDP; (2) public consumption or provision of services; (3) social security transfers; (4) Education; (5) health; (6) social assistance; (7) welfare state expenditures; (8) total revenues (taxes + social security charges).

It is not known whether these series are available in another form than the official Swiss statistical publication. Unfortunately, this yearbook has changed its manner of presentation a few times, partly in response to policy changes. We have devoted considerable effort to making the series uniform over the period during which the yearbook has been published, that is, since the early 1950s. All these series are real costs, and the deflator is the conventional consumer price index, published by the Statistical Office in Bern. The objective here is to analyse growth rates in order to nail down the silent revolution that has taken place in Switzerland transforming the country from a market economy with a small public sector to a mixed economy with a large public sector.

We start by examining the base of all calculations of the public sector, namely the Gross Domestic Product. All talk about public sector growth is basically about proportions, meaning the relative size of the two sectors of society – the public and the private sectors. If the growth rate in the economy is meagre, then the public sector will expand automatically. However, the typical finding in comparative research on public sector expansion in Western Europe has been a high positive income elasticity between GDP and public expenditures. When GDP increases by one money unit, then total public expenditures increase by more than one money unit. Since public expenditures started at a low level after the Second World War, the growth rates of the public sector will tend to be higher than those of the GDP. This suggests that public sector expansion is a major trend.

GDP GROWTH

Switzerland, it is well known, is one of the richest countries in the world. The affluence of the Swiss was largely created after the Second World War, when a number of circumstances combined to favour economic growth. In the 1950s there were almost Japanese growth rates, but they have come down considerably with time. Figure 2 shows the negative trend (r = -.50). It is based upon the real GDP series created by the Swiss National Bank covering the entire period 1950 to 1999 using a specially calculated deflator.

FIGURE 2
ECONOMIC GROWTH 1950–99

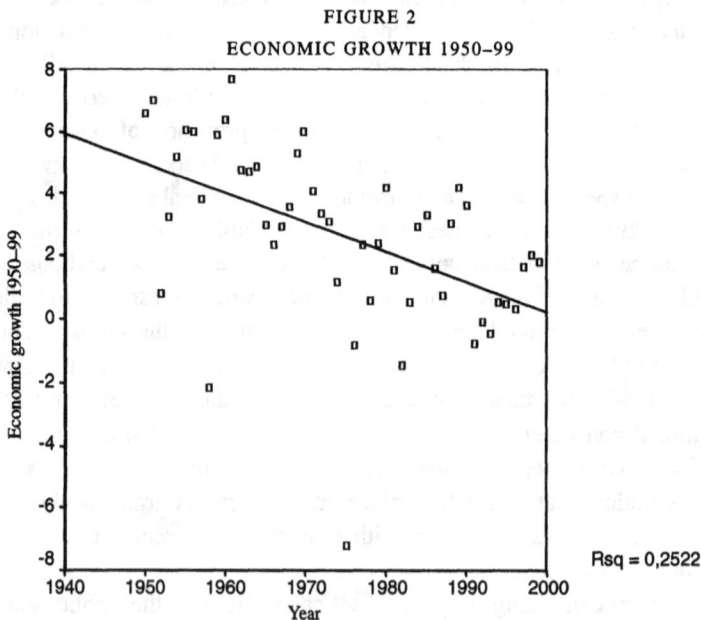

Sources: Economic growth: GDP in 1990 prices. Thomas Koch (personal communication 2000).

FIGURE 3

ECONOMIC GROWTH RATES, 1956–97

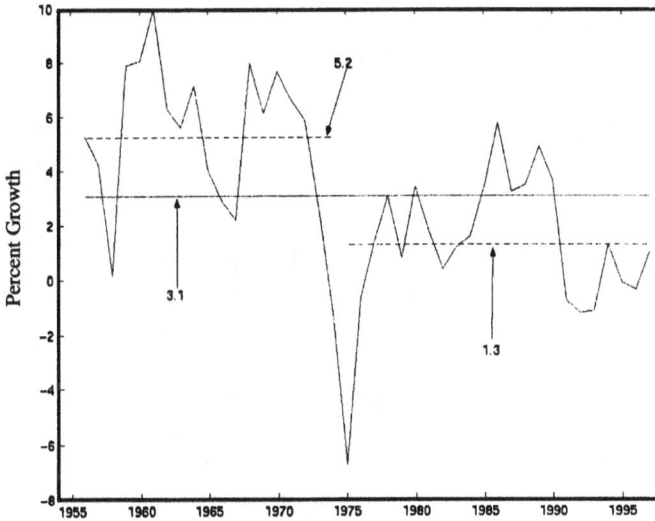

In Figure 3 the various growth rates for the time periods selected in this analysis are given, using the consumer price index as deflator in order to achieve comparability with the public sector expansion rates to be given below. As Figure 3 shows, economic growth rates were almost consistently high during the 1950s and 1960s, but have since become much more modest. The average GDP growth rate is 3.1 per cent for the entire period of roughly 40 years.

It appears from Figure 3 that the 1980s and 1990s have been rather meagre in terms of economic expansion. Thus, the difference in mean growth in output between the first period and the second period studied is substantial. Before the oil crisis, average economic growth reached an impressive 5.2 per cent. Since 1975, however, average economic growth has been only 1.3 per cent. Considerable effort has been devoted to explaining why economic growth has been close to zero during the 1990s. One hypothesis relates to the maturing of the economy, meaning that affluence drives down economic growth by saturation. Another suggests the peculiar openness of the Swiss economy. Switzerland is harbouring several multinationals that expand mainly outside the country, while at the same time the country protects itself against foreign competition in the labour market and in agriculture through a policy of splendid isolation. We suggest, against these views, that public sector growth may explain the meagre growth rates in GDP, at least to an extent.

Given such a low growth rate in the economy – about one per cent in the 1990s – it is hardly surprising that the public sector might grow at the expense of the private sector. Since the public sector started expanding from a low level after the Great War and the economy was at a high level, growing slowly, the public sector had to expand, not only absolutely but also relatively speaking. However, this fact cannot explain the virtual explosion in public expenditure items. Other factors also impinge upon the growth of Swiss government.

'Public sector expansion' or the 'growth of government' or the 'rise of the tax state' – all these expressions denote the same phenomenon. We will use the classical Musgrave framework to analyse public sector growth. Although it was first formulated in 1959, it retains its validity and fertility for enquiry into processes of government expansion.[10] According to Musgrave, the 'state' means only the allocative and redistributive functions of government. Thus, public regulation is not taken into consideration and public enterprises are left outside the public sector in so far as they are financed through user fees.

The fundamental distinction when classifying public expenditure items in the Musgrave system is that between allocation and income maintenance. Allocative items of expenditure consist of the costs for the provision of services that are handed over to the citizens without charge. Transfer payments make up social security; it involves the mailing of cheques in order to maintain income when people face adversity. The costs of public regulation are not entered into this calculus of the size of the public sector. Nor are public enterprises considered to belong to the consolidated public sector. Some of these would be joint stock companies, or, in other words, private sector institutions. At the same time, the cost of paying for losses of the public enterprises, as well as the costs associated with state debts, do enter the public sector.

All levels of government are included in the Musgrave framework: national, regional and local, independently from whether the system is federal or unitary. This approach to the public sector is based exclusively upon money, or the costs of the public household. It is open to the criticism that money does not measure everything about the role of government in society. Admitting that only using money as the measuring rod amounts to a limited approach to the public sector, and acknowledging that other frameworks may offer valuable insights into what government can do for people, we nevertheless insist upon the strict employment of the Musgrave approach.

Although it involves a partial view of the public sector, it remains illuminating when applied strictly. We begin by enquiring into the expansion of the allocative part of the public sector, which is called 'final government consumption' in the National Accounts System of the OECD.

EXPANSION OF ALLOCATION

The allocative part of the public sector imposes a restraint upon consumer choice, as citizens have to accept the provision of these services and pay for them by taxes. In one view, the allocative part of the public sector is the core of government, since there is simply no choice. Markets are not employed to allocate these services, as they are decided upon by means of budget allocation. A few Swiss cantons and communes have started to operate so-called internal markets, but even in this case there is no real consumer choice.

The allocative programmes include payment for public goods, infrastructure that is gratis, and the welfare state programmes that involve the provision of services. Figure 4 shows that the rate of expansion has been larger than that of the growth in GDP, or 4.6 per cent/year.

Allocative programmes grew especially rapidly during the first half of the post-war period.[11] The average growth rate was 7.4 per cent for the first

FIGURE 4

GROWTH RATES IN ALLOCATION, 1956–96

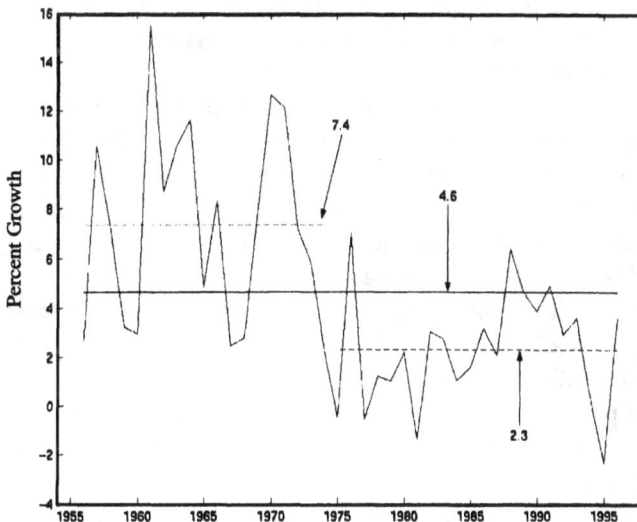

period, but only 2.3 per cent for the last period. However, for both periods resources had to be transferred from the private sector in order to pay for this part of the public sector. The overall pattern of budget-making is such that it hardly indicates the occurrence of incremental decision-making. Instead, one observes a number of shift-points, meaning that the yearly increases jump considerably. Evidently, major new expenditures have been undertaken during some years.

The Swiss welfare state provides a comprehensive programme structure including all levels of education, all kinds of health care and many aspects of social care. Although there is private supply, the bulk of these services is provided through public organisations, financed through taxes or obligatory charges. The Swiss welfare state also comprises considerable income assistance, almost all of which is placed outside the allocative part of the public sector in the Swiss accounting practice as well as in the Statistical Yearbook. Social assistance or poverty relief is, however, paid for by means of the regular budgets of the lower-level governments. In addition, the federal government budget provides for income support to farmers.

EXPANSION OF SOCIAL SECURITY

For a long time the OECD did not display any substantial costs for the Swiss welfare state in relation to its income-maintenance programmes. This partly reflected the fact that the federal government's ambitions to redistribute money were small. Things have, however, changed rather dramatically. Today the public sector comprises a number of large income maintenance programmes which carry considerable costs.[12] Figure 5 shows the growth rates in social security costs.

Social security spending has increased immensely, the average growth rate being 7.4 per cent. Income maintenance is one major element in the Swiss public sector and it explains a considerable part of the public sector expansion. The major ingredients in social security – general pension, supplementary pension and sickness insurance – have been greatly expanded both in terms of coverage and level of compensation.

Figure 4 indicates the occurrence of stable incremental decision-making in relation to social security. Only in the first part of the period are there shift-points, indicating new policies with considerably higher ambitions. When the policy is changed, costs tend to jump. Very important decisions have been taken in the Swiss social security system, transferring semi-private systems for pensions and sickness insurance into the public sector. During the latter part of the period, expenditures have grown at five per cent

FIGURE 5

GROWTH RATES IN SOCIAL INSURANCE EXPENDITURES, 1956-96

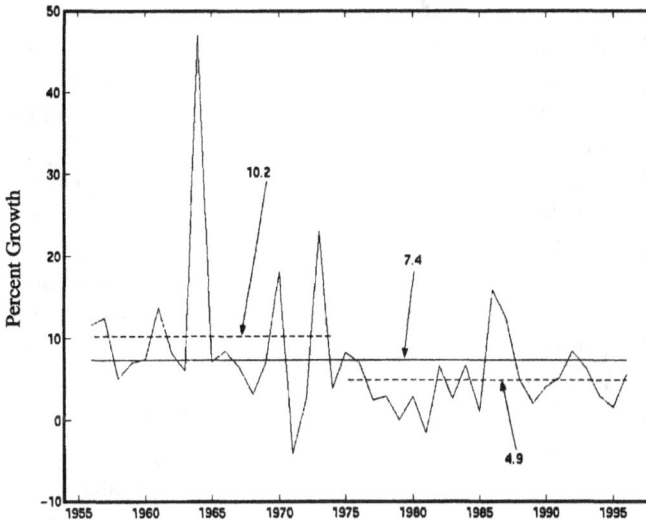

– faster than the growth in GDP. This has occurred with only one major shift-point in 1986.

During the post-war period, social security changed in quantity as well as in quality. It provides a whole programme structure for the maintenance of an income at a high level of consumption, not just a basic floor. The redistributive ambition is very high, although much of the redistribution is to the same individual over his/her life cycle.

The high growth rate in social security in both periods must change the division between the public and the private sectors when continued for such a long period. Social security is one of the two pillars of every well elaborated welfare state. The other is allocative welfare programmes. We now show that the major allocative welfare state programmes have been expanded considerably more than other kinds of allocative public sector programmes during the period in question.

EXPANSION OF WELFARE STATE PROGRAMMES

The allocative welfare state is concentrated upon three expenditures: education, health care and social care. In a mature welfare state, these programmes tend to be gratis or nearly free and they each comprise a number of expenditure items. These items respond to the variety of needs within a population for different kinds of education, health care and social care. The allocative welfare state is complex, covering an immense number of small programmes. It can be invaded by supply-side pressures, resulting in a large number of small expenditure items which when added up cost a great deal. Research into the growth of the Swiss welfare state has not arrived at a stage where it is possible to decide whether demand- or supply-side forces have been most important.

Looking initially at education, one observes in Figure 6 that average growth has been higher than GDP growth, or 4.7 per cent per year. In Switzerland, it is not only primary and secondary education that are free. Tertiary education is almost gratis as well. The expansion of education has followed GDP growth much more closely than has the development of social security. Educational expenditures expanded greatly in the first part of the period (9.6 per cent), but its rate of expansion during the second part has been much lower (1.7). During the second part there has been clear incremental decision-making, increasing the budget for education marginally. The increments have become smaller and smaller, indicating almost zero growth in the late 1990s. In the first period there are shift-points, which may reflect a change in accounting practice.

Health care has become a major programme in the Swiss welfare state, although there is both public and private production. Figure 7 shows how the costs of health-care provision have increased. It covers the costs for all publicly provided or publicly financed health care services, regardless of who provides these services and how they are financed. Switzerland, as is commonly known, uses a peculiar system of financing health care, involving private insurance companies. Membership in these companies is obligatory, and the system lacks strong elements of competition.

The average growth rate for this programme, six per cent, is considerably higher than the GDP growth rate. Its expansion is the most incremental of the budgetary items studied here. It tends to grow by a few per cent in real terms every year. At the outset of the period, we have shift-points reflecting major decisions concerning the system's construction. After these systemic decisions, budget-making became incremental. By the 1990s, the growth rate was tending towards zero in real terms.

It is interesting to compare the incremental pattern of health care budgeting, probably responding rather well to the quantitative growth in demand, with the highly unstable development of social care. Figure 8 shows that budget-making for social care comprises several shift-points, where resources have either been increased or decreased in a non-incremental fashion. Despite all the volatility, the average growth rate is 6.3 per cent.

FIGURE 6
GROWTH RATES IN EDUCATION EXPENDITURES, 1961–97

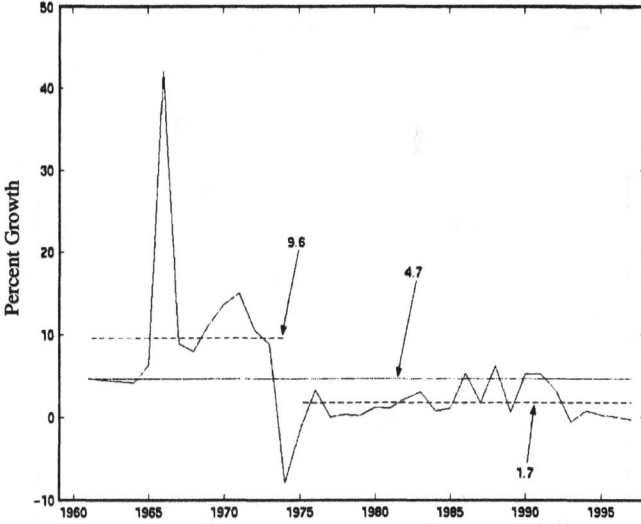

FIGURE 7
GROWTH RATES IN HEALTH CARE EXPENDITURES, 1961–97

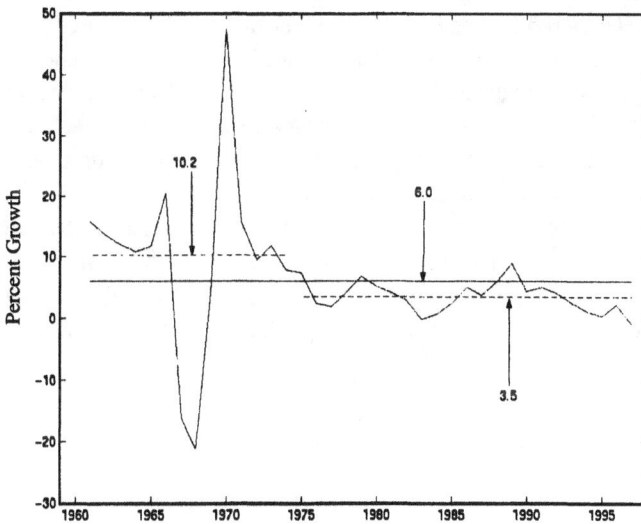

FIGURE 8

GROWTH RATES IN SOCIAL CARE EXPENDITURES, 1961–97

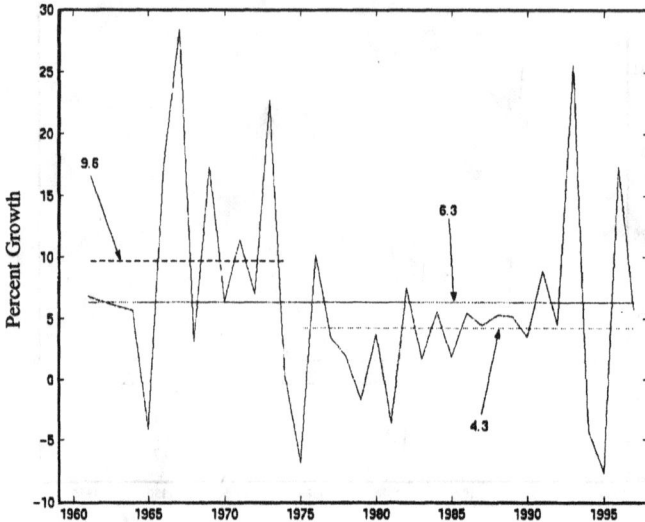

When new responsibilities are assumed in social care, costs may jump considerably. Such single decisions move expenditure levels considerably higher in a one-shot change, which smaller subsequent yearly increases do not undo. Heavy reductions in public budget-making happen seldom. Thus, the immense shifts that have often taken place in social care expenditure call for more profound analysis. It could be the case, for example, that some of these shift-points result from mere changes in accounting practices. This possibility must be investigated more closely, especially for those years when the tables in the Statistical Yearbook have been changed significantly.

When social security increases by seven per cent and allocative welfare expenditures jump by five or six per cent, whilst at the same time GDP growth amounts to only three per cent, the outcome is clearly welfare state expansion at a very rapid rate. Let us look at all the welfare state expenditures together.

THE SWISS WELFARE STATE: TOWARDS A MIXED ECONOMY

A complete welfare state fully supplies three kinds of services: (1) tax-financed education, health care and social care; (2) income maintenance at a high level of protection, usually around 70 per cent of normal income; (3)

labour market retraining, involving courses to reactivate unemployed to occupational life. The Swiss welfare state now fulfils these criteria. Public expenditure for each one of these programmes has been expanded considerably since the Second World War. Figure 9 displays the growth rates of the Swiss welfare state, comprising the total costs of the major allocative and income maintenance programmes.

The average annual growth rate amounts to 6.4 per cent. That is, it has expanded twice as fast as the growth in total resources. The expansion involves a peculiar mix of discretionary decision-making during the first period and highly incremental decision-making during the second period. The shift-points during the first period reflect the many important decisions involved in bringing Switzerland up to a West European level of social spending. The positively incremental pattern during the second period has maintained this level of social spending.

What does this all add up to? When the welfare state grows faster than GDP for any length of time, then resources have to be moved from the private sector to the public sector. The demarcation between the public and the private sectors is, thus, shifted in favour of the first, driving out the second. The rate of expansion in real welfare state spending could be compared with the pace of development in other kinds of allocative public expenditures – see Figure 10, where the growth rates are much smaller.

FIGURE 9

GROWTH RATES IN WELFARE STATE EXPENDITURES, 1961–97

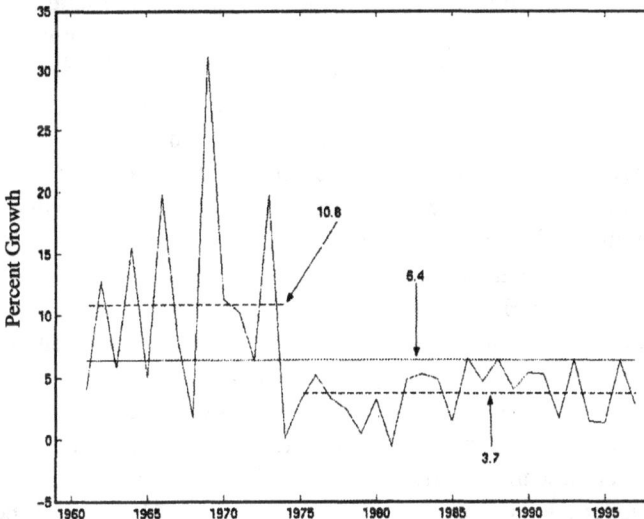

FIGURE 10

GROWTH RATES IN EXPENDITURES FOR PUBLIC GOODS AND
INFRASTRUCTURE, 1961–97

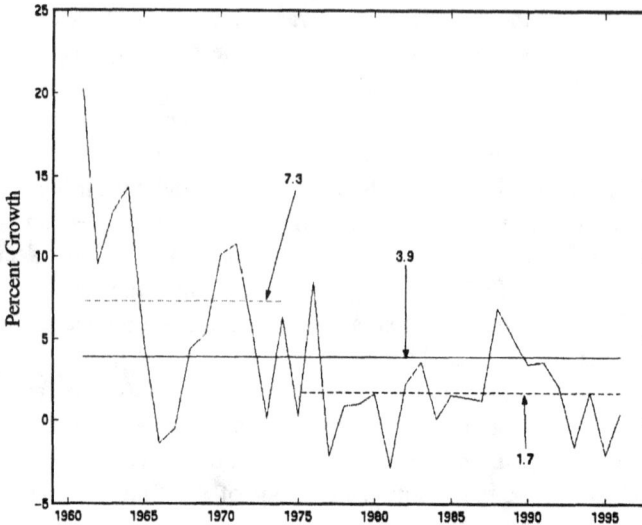

Following the seminal trends in Figures 9 and 10, Switzerland must be characterised as a mixed economy, or one in which the public and the private sectors are of equal size. The country can no longer be described as a market economy with a dominant private sector, or as a hesitant welfare state. It is now fully in line with the West European welfare state. Nor is it any longer correct to classify Switzerland as a conservative welfare state in contradistinction to the Nordic countries adhering to the radical Social Democracy model. The public sector is larger in Switzerland than in the Scandinavian countries and Finland. It is more generous.

The growth in public expenditure cannot continue along the average path outlined in Figure 9. There was a marked tendency for growth rates to decline in the 1990s, but welfare expenditure is only controllable by government to a certain degree – or perhaps one should say 'governments' in relation to Switzerland, as a considerable part of the welfare state is decided at a level below the federal government. The Swiss welfare state will mature, and we may soon see negative growth rates.

Several Swiss regional and local governments have started experiments with New Public Management in order to increase efficiency. It is too early to tell whether these management reforms will result in savings sufficient to have consequences upon aggregate public sector costs. It may well be that public sector productivity is a theme that has been missed out in the Swiss context. There has been little research into internal or external efficiency in the allocative part of the Swiss welfare state. With regard to the redistributive part, one has the impression that it is not quite *comme il faut* to question whether these generous programmes really are incentive-compatible.

EXPLOSION OF THE TAX STATE

All that remains now is to draw a few final conclusions about the Swiss tax state. Schumpeter predicted that the twentieth century would become the century in which government became as huge as the entire set of markets in the so-called capitalist democracies.[13] Swiss people and foreigners long believed that the country was not following the secular West European trend of development. This, however, was merely a figment of imagination. Switzerland may be special in many ways, but, in terms of the size of government, it is exactly where mainstream political science theory would predict.

Figure 11 shows the evolution of one side of the Swiss tax state, namely the taxes. The average growth rate is higher than GDP growth, or four per cent per year. However, the process of expansion has been volatile, as these revenues depend upon the economy, fluctuating in relation to the business cycle, as well as government decisions, which are discretionary in this regard.

FIGURE 11

GROWTH RATES IN THE TAX STATE, 1961–96

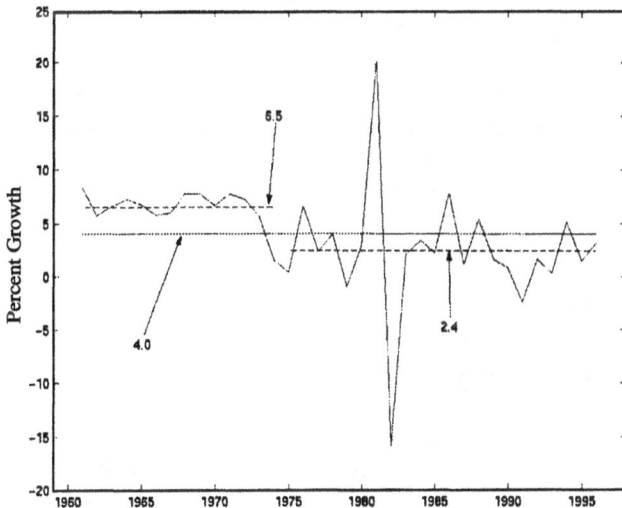

FIGURE 12

GROWTH RATES IN TOTAL SOCIAL SECURITY CHARGES, 1961–96

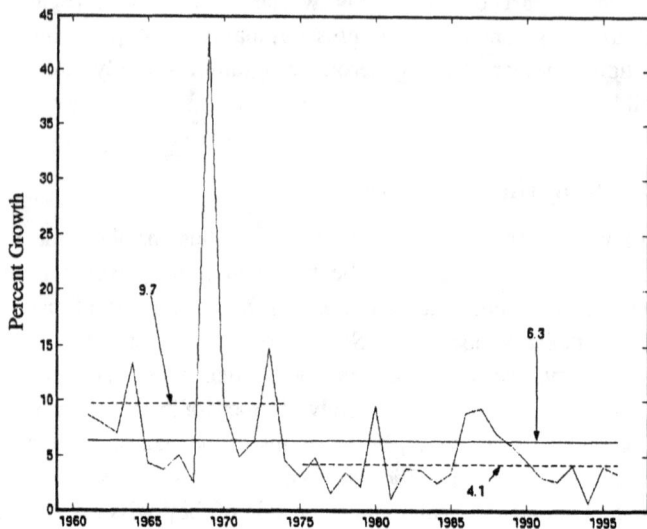

However, an even faster rate of expansion is to be found in the other part of the Swiss tax state, namely in social security charges. Here, the average growth has been more than six per cent/year. And it has been a very stable incremental process with the exception of one year (1968), which probably is more reflective of institutional changes than a true shift-point. Figure 12 shows the growth in social security revenues, which, incidently, includes a huge savings of more than ten per cent. It is true that a person can lower what s/he has to contribute in ordinary taxes by paying into the social security scheme (pensions) or by deducting various cost items, but this does not reduce the aggregate combined tax-load from ordinary taxes and social security charges.

If the economy grows by three per cent on average for 40 years but the tax state expands by more 4–6 per cent on average, the public sector obviously is bound to drive out the private sector rather quickly. This is what has happened in Switzerland – with a vengeance. Neither demand-side theory following Wagner's framework nor supply-side theory in accordance with Baumol's approach could have predicted such a revolution within such a short period of time. It is indeed the most significant social change of the twentieth century in Switzerland. Why this major social change has not been fully recognised by Swiss social scientists remains a mystery.[14] According to one scholar, public sector expansion is just a matter of changing labels on programmes.[15] It is claimed that the Swiss social security system is so close to a private actuarial system that its costs should not be classified under the public sector. This involves a misunderstanding of social security in Switzerland, which is basically a set of obligatory schemes. It also shows a lack of understanding of the dynamism in public budget-making. As the Swiss public sector has expanded every year in such a manner that it has grown faster than GDP in real terms.

CONCLUSION

The Swiss public sector today is the largest one, when compared with all the other advanced countries. It has even bypassed Sweden, a country whose misguided effort to create the most egalitarian society ever pushed their welfare expenditures beyond all reason. The Swiss public sector stands today at 57 per cent of GDP – an incredibly high figure compared with countries like Australia, New Zealand, the US, Japan and Ireland. Total allocative costs amount to about 115 billion Swiss francs, total social security costs are about 95 billion, whereas GDP stands at 370 billion francs, according to most recent estimates in the Satististical Yearbook for 1997.

From the income, the Swiss tax state is clearly the largest one in the OECD set. Taxes provide governments with some 108 billion francs and social security charges deliver another 114 billion. Together this makes 222 billion francs, or 60 per cent of GDP. This is hardly economically sound. No country with such high levels of public expenditure has been able to maintain steady and comfortable rates of economic growth, a fact that is undeniable whatever one may think about the advantages and disadvantages of big government.[16]

Let us now take a final look at the growth of total public sector income in Switzerland during the post-war period. Figure 13 shows the evolution of all kinds of government taxes and charges, except user fees for public enterprises. The yearly growth rate has been 4.9 per cent on average, which is much higher than GDP growth. During the second period analysed here growth in total revenues shows no sign of abating, constituting 3.2 per cent.

Consider, finally, Figure 14. It shows a time-series analysis of the rate of growth in the Swiss economy regressed upon the size of the public sector (expenditure side) for each year since 1956. The parameter linking the two series is clearly negative, or r = -.63. There is only one interpretation possible : The larger the public sector, the smaller the rate of expansion in the economy.

FIGURE 13
GROWTH RATES IN TOTAL REVENUES, 1961–96

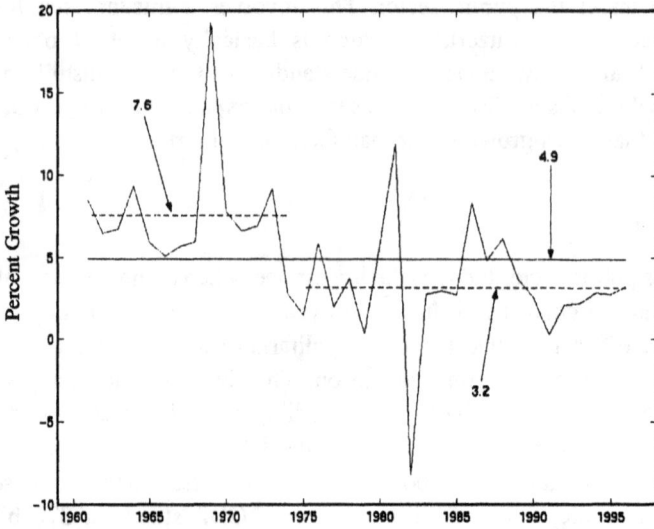

FIGURE 14
ECONOMIC GROWTH v. QUOTA OF TOTAL EXPENDITURES AND GDP, 1961–96

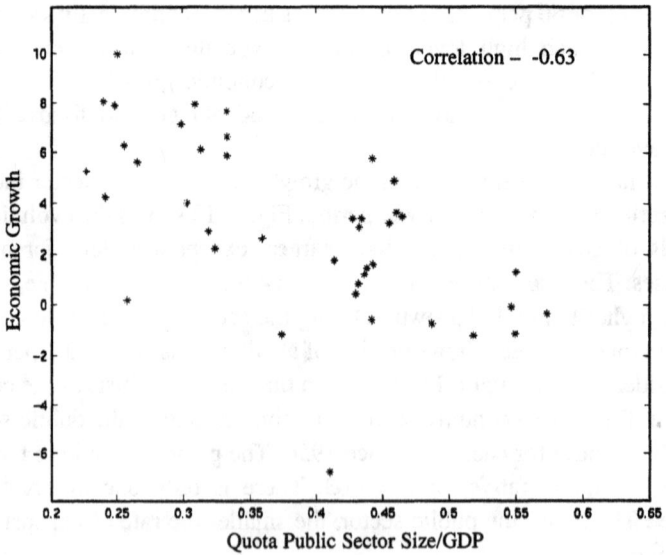

Economic growth depends upon many things, and public expenditures constitute only one set of factors. Some public expenditures may increase growth, whereas others may reduce growth. Economic growth in an open economy like Switzerland's depends critically upon the business cycle and external interactions. As the world economy keeps expanding and growth picks up in Europe, Switzerland will enjoy higher rates of economic growth in the early years of this new century. This will push down the relative size of the Swiss tax state. As long as nothing fundamental is done about the public sector, however, high economic growth in Switzerland will not be sustainable for long.

Many things have been done to energise public enterprises, which, strictly speaking, do not enter the public sector in the OECD National Accounts system. But there remains much to be done in market-testing these companies, several of which have been accustomed to an easy ride as virtual monopolies. The federal government has done more in relation to deregulation and privatisation than many of the regional or local governments.

NOTES

We are grateful to Simon Hug for giving us economic support when building up the data basis for this research on public sector growth in Switzerland. The economic help came from a project with the Swiss Science Foundation: Grant no: 5004-0487882/1.

1. One finds the following analysis in a major textbook on Switzerland:

   Im internationalen Vergleich nimmt sich der schweizerische Sozialstaat allerdings bescheiden aus. Seine Leistungen beanspruchen geringere Anteile des Sozialprodukts als in den meisten europäischen Ländern, und dies trotz der Tatsache, dass die Schweiz zu den reichsten Ländern gehört, aber keineswegs geringere soziale Ungleichheiten ausweist. Nach Armingeon (1996a:76) gehört die Schweiz damit weder zu den konservativen Wohlfahrtsstaaten wie Oesterreich und Deutschland noch zu den sozialdemokratischen Wohlfahrtsstaaten wie diejenigen Skandinaviens, sondern zu den liberalen, die in reichen Staaten wie Japan oder den USA mit einer eher schwachen politischen Linken vorzufinden sind.

   This quotation is taken from W. Linder, *Schweizerische Demokratie, Institutionen – Prozesse – Perspektiven* (Verlag Paul Haupt, 1999), p.52. Armingeon has changed his opinion – see his contribution to this volume.
2. B.S. Frey and I. Bohnet, 'Democracy by Competition: Referenda and Federalism in Switzerland', *Publius: The Journal of Federalism* 23 (1993), pp.71–81; W.W. Pommerehne and F. Schneider, 'Fiscal Illusion, Political Institutions and Local Public Spending', *Kyklos* 31 (1978), pp.381–408; W.W. Pommerehne, 'The Empirical Relevance of Comparative Institutional Analysis', *European Economic Review* 34 (1990), pp.458–69.
3. In international research one reads from a recent article that Switzerland provides a social protection that is half that of Sweden – see F. Castles, 'Social Protection in the Post-War Era: the OECD Experience', *Social Security (Institute of National Insurance in Israel* 56 (1999), pp.138–60.
4. J.A. Lybeck, *The Growth of Government in Developed Economies* (Aldershot: Gower 1986);

J.A. Lybeck and M. Henrekson (eds.), *Explaining the Growth of Government* (Amsterdam: North-Holland 1988).

5. A. Wildavsky, *The Revolt against the Masses and Other Essays on Politics and Public Policy* (New York: Basic Books 1972).

6. A. Wildavsky, *The Politics of the Budgetary Process* (Boston, MA: Little, Brown & Co. 1984 [1964]); A. Wildavsky, *Budgeting: A Comparative Theory of the Budgetary Process* (Boston, MA: Little Brown & Co. 1986 [1975]); A. Wildavsky, *The New Politics of the Budgetary Process* (Boston, MA: Little, Brown & Co. 1988).

7. H.A. Simon, *Models of Man* (New York: Wiley 1957)

8. J.-E. Lane, A. Westlund and H. Stenlund, 'Analysis of Structural Variability in Budget-Making', *Scandinavian Political Studies* 4/2 (1981); J.-E. Lane *et al.*, 'Budget-Making for Social Purposes', *Scandinavian Political Studies* 6 (1983); J.-E. Lane and A. Westlund, 'Choice and Constraint in Budget-Making', *Theory and Decision* 23/3 (1987), pp.217–30; A. Westlund and J.-E. Lane, 'The Relevance of the Concept of Structural Variability to the Social Sciences', *Quality and Quantity* 17 (1983), pp.198–201.

9. *Statistisches Jahrbuch der Schweiz, 1950–1998* (Zürich: Verlag NZZ 1997).

10. R.A. Musgrave, *The Theory of Public Finance* (New York: McGraw-Hill 1959); R.A. Musgrave and P. Musgrave, *Public Finance in Theory and Practice* (New York: McGraw-Hill 5th edn. 1989). See also H.S. Rosen, *Public Finance* (Homewood: Irwin 1988).

11. OFS, *Kosten des Gesundheitswesens 1995. Definitive Ergebnisse 1994 und 1995. Entwicklung seit 1960* (Bern: Office fédéral de la statistique 1997); S. Spycher, T. Bauer and B. Baumann, *Kinderkosten und deren Ausgleich in der Schweiz – Empirische Analyse und Reform-Modelle* (Chur: Rüegger 1995).

12. P. Gilliand and S. Rossini, *La protection sociale en Suisse* (Lausanne: Réalités sociales 1997); M. Rossi and E. Sartoris, *Solidarität neu Denken* (Locarno: A. Dadò 1999); J.H. Sommer, *Das Ringen um soziale Sicherheit in der Schweiz* (Diessenhofen: Rüegger 1978); P. Gilliand, *Politique sociale en Suisse*. Lausanne: Réalités sociales 1988); S. Cattacin and V. Tattini, 'Les Politiques Sociales', in *Handbuch der Schweizer Politik* (Zürich: NZZ Verlag 1999), pp.808–39. See also IDA FiSo, *Rapport sur les perspectives de financement des assurances sociales* (Bern: OFAS 1996); IDA FiSo, *Analyse des prestations des assurances sociales* (Berne: OFAS 1998).

13. J.A. Schumpeter, *Die Krise des Steuerstaats* (Graz/Leipzig: Leuschner & Lubensky 1918), p.74.

14. W.W. Pommerehne, 'Institutional Approaches to Public Expenditure – Empirical Evidence from Swiss Municipalities', *Journal of Public Economics* 9 (1978), pp.255–80; L.P. Feld and F. Schneider, 'State and Local Taxation', *International Encyclopedia of the Social and Behavioral Sciences* (Oxford: Elsevier 2001, forthcoming); L.P. Feld and J.G. Matsusaka, 'Budget Referendums and Government Spending: Evidence from Swiss Cantons' (St Gallen University, mimeo 2000). The approach here is cross-sectional, but what we lack is the longitudinal approach.

15. H. Kriesi, 'The Size of the Public Sector in Switzerland', *Swiss Political Science Review* 5/2 (1999), pp.105–13.

16. J.M. Buchanan, A. Musgrave and A. Richard, *Public Finance and Public Choice – Two Contrasting Visions of the State* (MIT Press 1999).

The Political Economy of Switzerland: A Monetarist Success?

The political economy of Switzerland has attracted international attention because of the high level of affluence that has characterised the country during the post-war period. The puzzle is, of course, did economic policy-making by the government and political institutions play a major role in accomplishing the Swiss success story? Many have replied 'yes'. Here we argue that they are most probably wrong. If any actor made a decisive contribution, then it was the central bank which has not been tempted by Keynesian discretionary intervention measures but has practised monetarism in one form or another, especially a rule-based version underlining credibility in the long run.

The key role of the Swiss National Bank in steering the economy towards low levels of inflation has prevailed against demands for policies to boost output and employment in the short run. However, Switzerland has a strong system of organised interests on both sides of the economy, labour and enterprise. Some argue that Switzerland has a corporatist political economy, which explains part of the success story. This is a questionable argument which needs more research. The interesting thing about Swiss corporatism is that it is neither of the strong Scandinavian type nor of the weak US kind. It is somewhere in between, which may help explain why the central bank rather than the government has prevailed when it comes to economic policy-making.

Below we briefly discuss the institutions of the Swiss political economy and then focus upon the outcomes in order to substantiate our argument that this is a case of successful monetarism. We start, however, with the counter-argument, namely that corporatism is the key to understanding the Swiss political economy, as favoured by Peter Katzenstein[1] and Manfred Schmidt.[2]

Jan-Erik Lane, University of Geneva.

ORGANISED ECONOMIC INTERESTS

It is a well-known fact that Switzerland has a carpet of organised economic interests, spanning agriculture, industry and the service sector. However, what is not so clear is whether Switzerland practises lobbyism typical of the Anglo-Saxon model or corporatism characteristic of the Scandinavian model. This remains an unresolved problem for research both in Switzerland and in comparative enquiry.

It is not the place here to go into a lengthy description of how organised economic interests operate in Switzerland – for such an investigation see Klaus Armingeon and Simon Geissbühler.[3] Even when the facts are known the puzzle remains: does Switzerland lean towards lobbyism or towards corporatism? Table 1 gives a few well-known rankings of the degree of

TABLE 1

SCALES OF MACRO-CORPORATISM

Country	Corp1	Corp2	Corp3	Corp4	Corp5	Corp6
Austria	5.0	5.0	5.0	5.0	5.0	5.0
Belgium	3.2	3.0	1.5	3.0	3.5	2.8
Denmark	3.5	3.5	4.0	4.0	3.5	3.5
Finland	3.4	3.5	2.5	4.0	3.5	3.3
France	1.8	2.5	1.0	1.0	1.0	1.7
Germany	3.5	3.5	5.0	3.0	2.0	3.5
Greece	–	–	–	–	–	1.0
Iceland	–	–	–	–	–	3.0
Ireland	2.1	–	–	2.0	2.0	2.0
Italy	1.7	2.5	1.5	1.0	1.0	1.5
Luxembourg	–	–	–	–	–	3.0
Netherlands	4.2	3.5	5.0	4.0	2.0	4.0
Norway	4.9	4.0	5.0	5.0	5.0	4.9
Portugal	–	–	–	–	–	1.5
Spain	–	–	–	–	–	1.3
Sweden	4.7	4.0	5.0	4.0	5.0	4.7
Switzerland	3.5	2.0	5.0	3.0	2.0	3.4
United Kingdom	1.7	2.5	1.0	1.0	2.0	1.7
Canada	1.0	1.0	1.0	2.0	1.0	1.2
United States	1.0	1.0	1.0	2.0	1.0	1.2
Japan	2.9	2.0	2.5	–	1.0	2.9
Australia	1.4	3.0	1.0	–	2.0	1.7
New Zealand	1.3	3.0	1.5	–	–	2.0

Note: Corporatism scales reproduced on a 1 to 5 scale; CORP1: Lijphart and Crepaz; CORP2: Calmfors-Drifill; CORP3: Bruno-Sachs; CORP4: Schmitter; CORP5: Cameron; CORP6: Siaroff; CORP2 to CORP6

Sources: A. Siaroff, 'Corporatism in 24 Industrial Democracies: Meaning and Measurement', *European Journal of Political Research* 36 (1999), pp.175–205; A. Lijpart and M.M.L. Crepaz, 'Corporatism and Consensus Democracy in Eighteen Countries: Conceptual and Empirical Linkages', *British Journal of Political Science* 21 (1991), pp.235–46.

TABLE 2

TRADE UNION DENSITY AND *DRITTELPARITÄT*

Country	TRIP1	TRIP2	TRIP3	TRIP4	TUD1	TUD2	TUD3
Austria	48	9	1	1	58	60.8	58.2
Belgium	85	10	1	1	68	–	77.5
Denmark	69	9	1	1	83	88.9	86.0
Finland	86	10	1	2	81	86.6	90.0
France	115	10	1	2	15	17.7	12..0
Germany	75	10	1	2	38	41.5	40.1
Greece	66	10	1	2	–	–	25.0
Iceland	–	–	1	–	–	–	–
Ireland	60	9	1	1	48	61.2	58.4
Italy	102	10	1	2	51	42.0	62.7
Luxembourg	–	–	1	–	–	–	–
Netherlands	94	10	1	2	28	34.4	30.2
Norway	99	10	1	2	64	67.9	67.7
Portugal	68	9	1	1	–	–	30.0
Spain	124	10	1	2	–	–	–
Sweden	84	10	1	2	91	94.4	96.1
Switzerland	51	5	0	0	32	34.4	30.0
United Kingdom	80	7	1	1	44	49.8	46.1
Canada	28	5	0	0	33	36.2	34.6
United States	11	2	1	0	17	17.4	–
Japan	41	5	0	0	29	28.8	26.8
Australia	54	9	1	1	51	56.7	53.4
New Zealand	56	6	1	1	41	54.9	50.5

Note: TRIP1: Total number of ILO conventions ratified; TRIP2: Number of basic ILO conventions ratified; TRIP3: Ratification of Tripartite consultation; Convention no 144; TRIP4: Summary index of TRIP1-TRIP3.

Sources:World Bank, *World Development Report* (1995), pp.150–51. Trade union density 1: B. Western, 'A Comparative Study of Working-Class Disorganization: Union Decline in 18 Advanced Capitalist Countries', *American Sociological Review* 60 (1995), pp.179–201; trade union density 2: K. Armingeon, 'Arbeitsbeziehungen und Gewerkschaftsentwicklung in den achtziger Jahren. Ein Vergleich den OECD-Ländern', *Politische Viertalsjahresschrift* 30 (1989), pp.603–28; trade union density 3: OECD, *Employment Outlook* (1994), p.184.

corporatism in a country. It seems hard to arrive at an agreement concerning the extent of macro-corporatism in various countries. Much of the disagreement among observers concerns Switzerland as a matter of fact. How can one and the same country be placed both close to lobbyism and close to the Scandinavian model? We suggest that both these rankings are wrong, as data indicate that Switzerland is somewhere in between the two polar types.

If one argues that the institutions governing the labour market and organised interests appear in two forms which are somewhat different from each other, then perhaps things become less ambiguous. Firstly, one dimension refers to trade union density. Secondly, another dimension deals with the occurrence of *Drittelparität*, as measured by a country's acceptance of international conventions concerning tripartite consultation. Table 2 presents data about these two aspects of the political economy of organised interests.

We see from the comparative data in Table 2 that Switzerland cannot be classified as having a corporatist political economy, because it lacks tripartite institutions. However, its trade unions have more members than the US counterparts and a few sectors of the economy are very strongly protected, especially agriculture. In Switzerland organised interests constitute a power factor, but it is not formalised as within a corporatist regime. Organised labour is definitely stronger than in countries adhering to the Anglo-Saxon model.

CORPORATISM AND *KONKORDANZ* ARE DIFFERENT

Some scholars today argue that corporatism in the political economy is but a prolongation of the consensus regime in the wider political system. Thus, we read that the strong position of organised interests in Switzerland provides them with a veto role similar to that of other groups in society.[4] We suggest that one should distinguish clearly between the institutions of corporatism and those of 'amicable agreement'.

Arend Lijphart has always been very careful to point out that his consensus model, of which Switzerland is regarded as the best concrete example, consists of two dimensions, which are independent of one another. The first is called the 'consensus dimension' and the other the 'federal dimension'. For the measurement of the occurrence of the institutions of the first kind, the consensus dimension, Lijphart offers three indices, one from 1984, another scale from 1991 and a third from 1999. Table 3 gives the country scores for these indices, the higher the scores the stronger the institutions of consensus, where also two alternative scales of *Konkordanz* democracy are given (Gerhard Lehmbruch and Manfred Schmidt).

Konkordanzdemokatie occurs in those countries which tend to have grand coalitions. A grand coalition involves all major players being brought on board, thus negating the adversarial government–opposition interaction that is a characteristic feature of the Westminster model. Which countries practice oversized coalitions?

One may distinguish between a minority government, a simple majority government and oversized coalitions, where the line separating the last two is somewhat arbitrary. Let us use the criterion of more than 60 per cent support in parliament. Table 4 records the occurrence of various kinds of government between 1945 and 1999.

The country where the average support in parliament for the government was the highest between 1945 and 1994 was no doubt Switzerland. The Swiss political system is an example of *Konkordanz*. But is *Konkordanz* linked to corporatism? The institutions of corporatism and *Konkordanzdemokratie* may co-exist in space and across time. Wherever there is corporatism, *Konkordanzdemokratie* is also present. Table 5 shows the correlations between the six scales measuring corporatism as well as the scales tapping the existence of *Konkordanzdemokratie* or consensus democracy.

Some countries rank very high on the scales of corporatism, but they are classified as competitive democracies, like the Scandinavian ones. Some

TABLE 3

INDICES OF *KONKORDANZDEMOKRATIE*

Country	Lehmbruch	Schmidt	Lijphart84	Lijphart91	Lijphart99
Austria	2	−.84	−1.50	−.37	.33
Belgium	2	.74	.55	.64	1.08
Denmark	1	.89	.78	.77	1.25
Finland	1	1.65	1.49	1.47	1.53
France	0	.11	.18	.16	−1.00
Germany	1	−.11	−.68	−.07	.67
Greece	0	−.90	–	–	−.73
Iceland	0	.30	.06	–	.52
Ireland	0	−.73	−.61	−.73	.01
Italy	1	1.18	.10	1.04	1.07
Luxembourg	2	−.30	−.08	–	.43
Netherlands	2	1.58	1.69	1.40	1.23
Norway	0	.30	−.42	.24	.63
Portugal	0	.50	–	–	.36
Spain	0	−.11	–	–	−.59
Sweden	0	.14	−.48	.08	.82
Switzerland	2	1.88	1.65	1.67	1.77
United Kingdom	0	−1.30	−1.16	−1.25	−1.21
Canada	0	−1.55	−.81	−1.48	−1.12
United States	0	−.97	−1.11	−.96	−.54
Japan	0	.01	−.12	−.04	.70
Australia	0	−.95	−.67	−.92	−.78
New Zealand	0	−1.36	−1.42	−1.32	−1.00

Sources: The Lehmbruch and Schmidt scales are taken from M. Schmidt, *Demokratietheorien* (Opladen: Leske und Budrich 1995), who constructs it himself following various texts by Lehmbruch. Schmidt's own index is an adaptation of Lijphart's scales. Lijphart's scales goes back to A. Lijphart, *Democracies: Patterns of Majoritarian and Consensus Government in Twenty-One Countries* (New Haven, CT: Yale U.P. 1984); A. Lijphart and M.M.L. Crepaz, 'Corparatism and Consensus Democracy in Eighteen Countries: Conceptual and Empirical Linkages', *British Journal of Political Science* 21 (1991), pp.235–46; and A. Lijphart, *Patterns of Democracy: Government Forms and Performance in Thirty-Six Countries* (New Haven, CT: Yale U.P. 1999).

TABLE 4

TYPES OF GOVERNMENTS AFTER WORLD WAR II, 1950–99

Country	Number	Months in power	Parliamentary support (%)	Number of parties	Average duration (%)
Austria	19	31.2	70.9	1.7	65.1
Belgium	29	20.9	62.2	3.4	43.1
Denmark	30	19.5	41.2	2.0	40.6
Finland	41	14.7	56.3	3.0	30.6
France	39	14.9	58.1	4.1	25.1
Germany	18	31.8	57.9	2.2	66.1
Greece	38	13.5	59.3	1.0	28.2
Iceland	21	29.4	54.9	2.2	61.1
Ireland	21	27.5	51.1	1.5	55.2
Italy	49	12.5	50.5	3.1	20.8
Luxembourg	14	43.4	68.1	2.0	71.0
Netherlands	19	30.6	60.6	3.3	61.1
Norway	25	24.3	44.0	1.8	50.5
Portugal	17	18.4	58.4	1.5	38.1
Spain	9	33.8	49.6	1.0	70.5
Sweden	23	25.6	46.5	1.5	64.8
Switzerland	14	44.3	79.5	3.9	92.3
United Kingdom	19	30.8	54.6	1.0	51.3
Canada	18	31.0	54.2	1.0	51.7
United States	14	41.1	48.5	1.0	85.7
Japan	36	16.9	52.3	1.3	37.1
Australia	26	22.9	58.1	1.7	63.5
New Zealand	25	23.9	55.9	1.2	65.9

Sources: J.-E. Lane, D. McKay and K. Newton, *Political Data Handbook: The OECD Countries* (Oxford: Oxford U.P. 1996); and updatings from Keesing's *Record of World Events*, as well as various issues of *Political Data Yearbook* issued by the *European Journal of Political Research*.

TABLE 5

CORPORATISM AND *KONKORDANZ*

Corporatism index	*Konkordanz* index			
	Lehmbruch	Schmidt	Lijphart91	Lijphart99
Corp1 (L-C)	.54 (.011)	.64 (.002)	.61 (.004)	.61 (.003)
Corp2 (C-D)	.31 (.117)	.28 (.135)	.28 (.143)	.28 (.143)
Corp3 (B-S)	.54 (.013)	.59 (.007)	.57 (.008)	.62 (.004)
Corp4 (Schm)	.39 (.073)	.39 (.073)	.35 (.101)	.49 (.031)
Corp5 (Came)	.32 (.104)	.32 (.109)	.29 (.130)	.36 (.079)
Corp6 (Siar)	.51 (.007)	.52 (.014)	.47 (.012)	.62 (.001)

Note: Spearman's rank-order correlation. The correlations have been computed on the basis of Tables 1–5. In parentheses, the significance values are given.

countries are truly *Konkordanzdemokratie*, but they do not rank very high on the scale of corporatism like Switzerland.

Interestingly, uncertainty concerning how Switzerland is to be classified with regard to corporatism affects the macro correlations for the OECD set. When Switzerland is considered corporatist as in Corporatism 1 and Corporatism 3, then there is modest interaction. But when Switzerland is ranked lower on the scales of corporatism, then there is little or no interaction. Corporatism is not necessarily linked with *Konkordanz*. Let us try the monetarist argument and see where it will take us.

THE SWISS LABOUR MARKET

Let us first look at the main outline of the Swiss labour market. Table 6 presents data about the growth in population, the working population and employment. Along with the steady growth of the population the labour force has expanded to meet the needs of the economy for trained manpower. The rate of growth in the active labour force is somewhat stronger than the growth in the population, because women in Switzerland have markedly increased their participation in the economy. Thus, the so-called labour quota for women has increased from 33 per cent in 1960 to 44 per cent in 1996. It remains though considerably lower than that for Swiss men.

The Swiss labour market has used much foreign labour, which has played a major role in bringing about a healthy economic growth record, especially in the 1950s and 1960s. As shown in Table 7, the number of foreigners was small up until the 1950s when it started to rise dramatically. As economic growth is a function of investments, technological changes and labour force expansion, the impact upon total output of such an increase in foreign labour was a sharp and strong one. In the 1980s there was a reduction in the number of foreigners, which may actually merely reflect a change in the status of several foreigners, as Switzerland changed its naturalisation procedures. However, in the 1990s the influx of foreigners was again strong, resulting in a situation where almost 20 per cent of the population are non-Swiss – 19.3 per cent in 1996.

THE SWISS NATIONAL BANK

In rankings of central bank independence Switzerland scores consistently very high.[5] The regime that governs the relationship between the monetary authority and the government is worth analysis when Swiss political institutions are examined. Economic policy-making is always highly

TABLE 6

THE SWISS LABOUR MARKET

	1960	1965	1970	1975	1980	1985	1990	1994	1995	1996
Population (.000)	5,328	5,945	6,181	6,321	6,335	6,485	6,751	7,019	7,062	7,081
Working pop. (.000)	2,717	3,025	3,143	3,108	3,166	3,354	3,821	3,785	3,802	3,803
Labour quota	49.3	49.2	48.3	46.9	47.8	49.7	53.2	52.8	52.7	53.0
Unemployed	1,227	299	104	10,170	6,255	30,345	18,133	171,038	153,316	168,630
Unemployment quota	0.06	0.01	0.004	0.3	0.2	1.0	0.5	4.7	4.2	4.7
Men										
employed (.000)	1,790	2,017	2,075	2,026	2,021	2,114	2,327	2,250	2,259	2,236
Labour quota	66.0		64.4	62.6	62.2	63.9	65.4	63.2	63.2	62.9
Unemployed (.000)			84	7,804	3,696	16,421	9,827	97,966	85,473	96,829
Unemployment quota				0.4	0.2	0.8	0.4	4.4	3.9	4.4
Women										
working (.000)	927	1,008	1,067	1,082	1,145	1,239	1,494	1,535	1,543	1,567
Working quota	33.0		32.9	32.0	34.1	36.3	41.6	42.9	42.8	43.5
Unemployed (.000)			20	2,366	2,559	13,924	8,306	73,072	67,843	71,801
Unemployment quota				0.2	0.2	1.2	0.6	5.2	4.8	5.1

Source: Statistisches Jahrbuch der Schweiz 1998.

TABLE 7

COMPOSITION OF THE POPULATION, 1900–1995 (THOUSANDS)

	1900	1920	1930	1941	1950	1960	1970	1980	1990	1995
Switzerland, total	3,315 6,366	3,880 6,874	4,066 7,062	4,266	4,715	5,429	6,270			
Men	1,627	1,871	1,958	2,060	2,272	2,663	3,089	3,115	3,390	3,449
Women	1,688	2,009	2,108	2,205	2,443	2,766	3,180	3,251	3,484	3,614
Swiss	2,932	3,478	3,711	4,042	4,430	4,844	5,190	5,421	5,628	5,699
Foreigners	383	402	356	224	285	585	1,080	945	1,245	1,364

Source: Statistisches Jahrbuch der Schweiz 1998

relevant for politics, and the position of the central bank in the wider political system is one key element determining the amount of centralisation–decentralisation in the political system.

The formal and real independence of the Swiss central bank reinforces the generally high level of decentralisation in the Swiss political system, although it cannot be interpreted as an historical legacy or as an institutional response to the social fragmentation of the country. The central bank of the Swiss Confederation is the Swiss National Bank, dating back to 1907. Article 39 of the Federal Constitution states that the bank should 'regulate the country's money circulation', 'facilitate payment transactions' and 'pursue a credit and monetary policy serving the interests of the country as a whole'.

One may be tempted to interpret the Swiss central bank as a monetarist device, following an inspiration from the international success of this macroeconomic doctrine. This would then be a case of policy diffusion, Switzerland adopting the German model of a central bank. Yet the key article of the Constitution of 1978 concerning the regulation of economic activity clearly states the aims of the Confederation's economic policy as 'balanced development of economic activity', which includes not only monetarist objectives but: 'The prevention and combating of unemployment and inflation'.

Counter-cyclical notions are far from absent from the policy considerations of the Swiss National Bank. It seems as if the role of this central bank in the political system is more an indigenous phenomenon than merely international policy diffusion.

Background

The Swiss National Bank was founded by means of the Swiss National Bank Law that came into force on 16 January 1906. Actually, the proposal to establish a state bank had previously been rejected by the people, but it began its operations on 20 June 1907. Legally speaking, the central bank is a joint-stock company governed by certain provisions of federal law. Formally, it is administered under the supervision of the Confederation in accordance with the provisions of the National Bank. Its shares are listed on the Zurich stock exchange. These shares may be held by Swiss citizens, Swiss public corporations, Swiss general partnerships and limited partnerships as well as by legal entities established in Switzerland. Interestingly, the federal government does not hold any shares, as two-thirds of the capital of 50 million Swiss francs is held by the cantons or cantonal banks. The remaining shares belong to private persons.

The bank has its legal and administrative head office in Berne, whereas the seat of the governing board is in Zurich. The Bank operates six branches and has 17 agencies operated by cantonal banks. The controlling bodies of the central bank include first the General Meeting of Shareholders and second a number of bodies such as the Bank Council, the Bank Committee, the Local Committees and the Auditing Committee. However, due to the Bank's public function, the powers of the General Meeting are not as extensive as with ordinary joint-stock companies. The Bank Council supervises the 'progress and conduct of business', as at its quarterly meetings with the Governing Board there is an opportunity of discussing policy in detail. The Bank Council comprises 40 members representing the economy as well as the different regions of Switzerland. It may be noted that 15 of these 40 members are elected by the General Meeting but 25, including the president and vice-president, are designated by the federal government

Thus the National Bank is basically owned by the cantonal governments, but the federal government recruits its chief decision-makers. The Confederation's power over the National Bank's policy is weakly based upon the Article 2, section 2 of the National Bank law, where it is stated that the Federal Government and the National Bank should inform each other ahead of taking economic and monetary decisions and that there is mutual obligation to co-ordinate measures. Such co-ordination takes place within the framework of periodic meetings between the federal government's Delegation for General Economic Policy and the National Bank's Governing Board. Furthermore, there are the frequent informal contacts between the head of the Finance Department and members of the Bank's Governing Board. Yet, the central bank acts with a large amount of discretion.

To conclude, we may say that the central bank is constituted in the form of a joint-stock bank, administered with the co-operation and under the supervision of the Confederation. Formally, the federal government possesses a number of important powers to approve decisions and elect candidates, which may give it a long-term influence on the Bank's management through its capacity to choose people. Yet the only sanctioning powers of the federal government include the approval of the annual report and annual accounts before their publication and before their adoption by the annual general meeting. It may also sanction the most important regulations issued by the Bank Council.

Goals and Instruments

The instruments for steering the money market involve the central bank influencing the sight deposits by buying and selling assets or by granting or not renewing credits on the due date. The instruments allowed for conducting monetary policy operations are specified in the National Bank

Law, where a revision of the National Bank Law as per 1 November 1997 expanded the range of instruments. The following instruments are currently of practical significance: (a) repo transactions; (b) foreign exchange swaps; (c) advances against securities (Lombard loans). Repos and foreign exchange swaps are with the National Bank. In lending against securities, the central bank decides the terms applying to short-term loans which the commercial banks can take out in order to cover liquidity shortages.

The central bank has adhered to the basic quantity theory of money, stating that accelerated expansion of the money supply is conducive to a rise in inflation, whereas a slowdown in the growth of the money supply reduces inflation. However, the Bank does not use the monetarist approach in a naive fashion, as it argues that 'the price level does not react immediately to changes in the money supply; the time lag is considerable – in Switzerland it is two to three years'.

The National Bank acts in relation to both the price level and unemployment. Its objective function is not merely that of applying monetarism, although it underlines the importance of a low level of inflation. Thus, the central bank considers price level stability important 'particularly because (relative) prices in our market-economy system govern the production and consumption of individual goods'. The central bank argues that 'changes in the price level are liable to give misleading signals', which result in costly mistakes in planning and investment. For the central bank, the prevention of inflation is especially important, and it considers that 'protracted changes in the price level are, as a rule, due to malfunctioning of the monetary system', upon which it may have an impact through the use of its instruments of monetary policy.

Switzerland's monetary sovereignty is divided into the coinage prerogative and the banknote-issuing privilege. While the coinage prerogative is vested in the Confederation, the National Bank has the sole right to issue banknotes. The National Bank, however, does not only supply the economy with banknotes that meet high requirements with respect to quality and security, but it also puts the coins into circulation via its network of branches. The central bank can control the money supply: it expands (narrows) the monetary level by purchasing (selling) domestic or foreign assets and by granting (or reducing the volume of) credits.

The National Bank employs its principal assets directly for implementing monetary policy. Thus, the central bank acquires assets in order to supply the economy with base money, which assets of course represent the real countervalue to the monetary base. For controlling the monetary base, the central bank employs mainly repos, foreign exchange swaps and domestic assets. Foreign exchange swaps are made up of dollar reserves which are hedged in the forward market. Unhedged foreign exchange is held in key currencies; these reserves can be sold in the market in order to support the external value of the Swiss franc. But the gold holdings cannot be used for interventions. The Swiss franc is still linked to gold by law, which means that the central bank can only buy and sell gold at the official price, which is below the market price. Yet both gold holdings and foreign exchange balances are important as a national emergency provision, contributing to ensure that Switzerland remains solvent *vis-à-vis* foreign countries even in emergencies.

It should be emphasised that the National Bank is the only institution which can autonomously create new money, but it is subject to the supervision by the political authorities. The Swiss approach to a central bank entails that this supervision should not make the central bank subordinate to the political authorities. What is feared is that the central bank could be misused for directly or indirectly financing various public expenditures. The National Bank Law states what assets the National Bank may acquire and it lays down the instruments to be employed for their management. The National Bank endeavours to manage its assets as profitably as possible within the limits set by legal provisions and by its monetary policy mandate. The revision of the National Bank Law, which became effective on 1 November 1997, did increase its discretion to manage its gold and foreign exchange reserves. Thus, the National Bank can now invest its foreign exchange reserves in more markets and currencies. Moreover, the revised law enables the central bank to use a part of the gold reserves for gold lending.

Money-market steering involves the Governing Board laying down guidelines for money market operations on a quarterly basis. The money market is controlled via sight deposits and money market rates, where sight deposits are non-interest-bearing funds held by the banks at the National Bank. The demand for sight deposits is determined by the liquidity requirements under banking law as well as by the liquidity requirements under banking law. The banks have to hold a minimum of 2.5 per cent of their short-term liabilities in sight deposits, banknotes or postal cheque balances. The banks require sight deposits for processing cashless payments in the Swiss Interbank Clearing System (SIC). The central bank controls the level of sight deposits, meaning that it controls, in addition, the level of short-term interest rates in the money market.

NATIONAL BANK PRACTICE

The National Bank has faced up to extreme exchange rate fluctuations as well as to a changing demand for liquidity. Monetary decisions have involved both expansion and diminution of the money supply. A spectacular example was the massive expansion in the supply of money in autumn 1978 as a response to the strong appreciation of the Swiss franc within a short time. Other examples were the economic developments in 1996 and the strength of the Swiss franc, which again forced the central bank to expand the supply of money beyond the limits originally set. A contrary example was the reduction in the supply of money during 1988 and 1989, when the demand for sight deposits among the banks fell sharply because of changes in liquidity requirements and the introduction of a new interbank payment system (SIC). In reality, the central bank did not always reach its monetary targets because it has been willing to accept deviations from targets in the case of external disruptions.

In 1971 the United States ended the Bretton Woods system by moving away from the convertibility of the dollar into gold. The surge in inflation that followed resulted in a collapse of the system of fixed exchange rates. The switch from fixed exchange rates around the world afforded the central bank more discretion in steering the money supply in accordance with the needs of the economy, using the monetarist assumption of a close correlation between the money supply and the price level, in the short-run or long-run perspective. The central bank has adhered to the concept of money supply control and aimed at a money supply growth that will guarantee a stable price level, but its practices in doing so have changed over the years.

Since the events in 1971 involving the lifting of the exchange rate constraint, the National Bank has orientated its policy to money supply targets. This focus on targets has governed its own activity in the money and financial markets as well as provided a guideline to the public. At the outset the money supply target was fixed at the end of every year for the next year, orientated to the money supply and later to the monetary base. However, in 1990 the central bank moved away from this practice of fixing a money supply target for the following calendar year. The rule has been that in the medium-term average the monetary base should expand by about one per cent per year.

The National Bank publishes its 'Conclusions for Monetary Policy' in its *Quarterly Bulletin* and on the Internet, where it describes the current monetary environment and outlines its plans for monetary policy in the coming quarter. It also provides a projection of the expected development

of the monetary base in the next three months. All this is done to make clear
to the markets what the policy of the central bank will be in the near future.
The central bank has developed a practice to the effect that any short-term
monetary policy presupposes flexibility. This entails discretion on the part
of the central bank as rigidly adhering to money supply targets would lead
to excessive exchange rate volatility, since Switzerland is a small country
with a strong international involvement. Yet it practices considerable
restraint in order to smooth fluctuations, as not every change in the
exchange rate requires an adjustment of monetary policy.

What the National Bank first and foremost wishes to avoid is a policy
oriented to the very short term which would lead to less rather than more
stability. As the central bank does not know about all the factors that trigger
the exchange rate change in specific cases and cannot quantify their effects
early enough, it refrains from reacting to minor disruptions. On the contrary,
it allows for deviations from the envisaged money supply expansion for
extraordinary situations.

OUTCOMES

Economic policy has a set of objectives, among which is full employment
given that one specifies a target for the level of unemployment that is in
agreement with non-accelerating inflation. Of the two kinds of economic
policy – fiscal and monetary policy – it is the latter which belongs to the
National Bank when it is a matter of the Swiss economy. Fiscal policy is
conducted primarily by the federal government. In relation to Swiss
economic development after the Second World War, there have been three
major outcomes that are relevant for assessing the conduct of economic
policy. They are: (1) rapid economic growth between 1950 and 1974; (2) an
extremely low level of unemployment during almost the whole post-war
period with the exception of the 1990s; (3) a low level of inflation during
the 1990s. Let us briefly examine these outcomes and attempt to find
indications that economic policy-making has mattered.

The Swiss economy is at a level of affluence that makes it one of the richest
countries of the world. This is a result of a long period of economic growth
after the Second World War, which left Switzerland unscathed amidst a Europe
in ruins. The Swiss unemployment figures are truly interesting (see Table 8).
The level of unemployment during the 1960s must constitute the lowest figures
ever in modern history. For more than ten years Switzerland recorded levels of
unemployment close to zero. It should be strongly emphasised that economists
in Switzerland have reservations about these figures, as they underestimate real

unemployment. It was not until a uniform public insurance system was created in the 1970s that reliable figures about people looking for a job could be retrieved. People who need state unemployment support must simply register in order to receive the money. Figure 1 gives the absolute number of unemployed, and it has been suggested that the low figures in the 1960s and 1970s should be multiplied by a factor as high as 70.

Now, such a low level of unemployment must, according to Okun's Law, result in a high level of total output. Figure 2 contains a simple approximation of Okun's Law for Switzerland, predicting economic growth (GDP) from the level of unemployment, measured by the logarithm of absolute numbers of unemployed. The negative correlation – r = -.51 – constitutes strong evidence that the high level of employment has been conducive to the affluence of the country. Now, is there any indication in the data that economic policy has contributed to the low level of unemployment? Another way of asking the same question is to try to estimate a Phillips' curve for Switzerland. If economic policy has favoured low levels of unemployment, then one would find clear signs of inflation in the Swiss economy, at least for some periods of time (see Figure 3).

Although there is a tendency towards a negative relationship (r = -.48) between inflation and unemployment in the Swiss data, the Phillips' curve relationship is weaker than one might have expected, at least if a corporatist economic regime had been in place. The trade-off between full employment and monetary stability is there, but it is not a forceful one. Yet what is noticeable is that the central bank has not been willing to accept much inflation in order to reduce the output gap and bring down unemployment. The political economy regime in Switzerland is distinctly monetarist with the entailment that a low level of inflation has been the prime concern, especially during the 1990s. Let us look at another estimate of the Swiss Phillips' curve using data for the entire time period although they are shaky when it comes to unemployment. The surface correlation in Figure 4 amounts to r = -.37, again indicating a trade-off between inflation and unemployment. However, the policy preference of the central bank has mainly been for a low level of inflation. Now, the central bank can to some extent affect the inflation by its monetary policy. Has it had an impact upon output?

Monetarist policy-making can be conducted in various ways. Simple monetarism involves the money authority controlling one mass of money – for instance M1 – and adds and subtracts to this mass according to the situation. More elaborate versions of monetarism include the use of other money definitions – for instance M3, but also the targeting of interest rates as the crucial parameter and not simply the mass of money. The Swiss

TABLE 8

INFLATION, UNEMPLOYMENT AND ECONOMIC GROWTH, 1950-98

Year	Inflation	Unemployment	Economic growth GDP	Real GDP	Nominal GDP
1950	−1.5	0.6	6.6	91,943.00	20,703.00
1951	4.8	0.3	7.0	98,877.00	22,690.00
1952	2.6	0.4	0.8	99,653.00	23,975.00
1953	−0.7	0.3	3.2	102,983.00	25,164.00
1954	0.7	0.3	5.2	108,647.00	26,666.00
1955	0.9	0.2	6.1	115,657.00	28,765.00
1956	1.5	0.2	6.0	123,024.00	30,927.00
1957	2.0	0.1	3.8	127,936.00	32,899.00
1958	1.8	0.2	−2.2	125,199.00	33,824.00
1959	−0.6	0.1	5.9	133,030.00	35,923.00
1960	1.4	0.0	6.4	142,093.00	39,512.00
1961	1.8	0.0	7.7	153,961.00	44,450.00
1962	4.3	0.1	4.8	161,693.00	49,293.00
1963	3.4	0.0	4.7	169,707.00	54,204.00
1964	3.1	0.0	4.9	178,359.00	60,083.00
1965	3.4	0.0	3.0	183,825.00	64,349.00
1966	4.8	0.0	2.4	188,258.00	69,102.00
1967	4.0	0.0	2.9	193,907.00	74,383.00
1968	2.4	0.0	3.6	201,077.00	79,427.00
1969	2.5	0.0	5.3	212,352.00	86,061.00
1970	3.6	0.0	6.0	225,855.00	95,863.00
1971	6.6	0.0	4.1	235,511.00	108,900.00
1972	6.7	0.0	3.3	243,654.00	123,401.00
1973	8.7	0.0	3.1	251,355.00	137,516.00
1974	9.8	0.0	1.2	254,313.00	149,189.00
1975	6.7	0.4	−7.2	237,244.00	148,190.00
1976	1.7	0.7	−0.8	235,252.00	150,099.00
1977	1.3	0.4	2.3	240,802.00	154,148.00
1978	1.0	0.3	0.6	242,232.00	160,371.00
1979	3.6	0.3	2.4	248,124.00	167,634.00
1980	4.0	0.2	4.2	259,004.00	180,095.00
1981	6.5	0.2	1.6	263,092.00	193,488.00
1982	5.7	0.4	−1.5	259,311.00	203,628.00
1983	3.0	0.9	0.5	260,624.00	210,110.00
1984	2.9	1.1	2.9	268,512.00	224,064.00
1985	3.4	0.9	3.3	277,692.00	237,206.00
1986	0.8	0.7	1.6	282,211.00	248,492.00
1987	1.4	0.7	0.7	284,287.00	257,175.00
1988	1.9	0.6	3.0	293,131.00	272,726.00
1989	3.2	0.5	4.2	305,854.00	293,316.00
1990	5.4	0.5	3.6	317,304.00	317,304.00
1991	5.9	1.1	−0.8	314,764.00	333,661.00
1992	4.0	2.5	−0.1	314,366.00	342,364.00
1993	3.3	4.5	−0.5	312,852.00	349,799.00
1994	0.9	4.7	0.5	314,518.00	357,463.00
1995	1.8	4.2	0.5	316,104.00	363,329.00
1996	0.8	4.7	0.3	317,111.00	365,833.00
1997	0.5	5.2	1.6	322,429.00	371,371.70
1998	0.0	3.9	2.0	329,066.00	380,940.10

Sources: Inflation: Thomas Koch (personal communication 2000); Unemployment: 1950–82: Schmidt. 1985: 19 and 1983–98: OECD (various years) Economic Outlook. Paris: OECD; Economic growth: GDP in 1990 prices; Real GDP and Nominal GDP: Thomas Koch (personal communication 2000).

FIGURE 1

UNEMPLOYED – YEARLY AVERAGES IN ABSOLUTE NUMBERS SINCE 1955

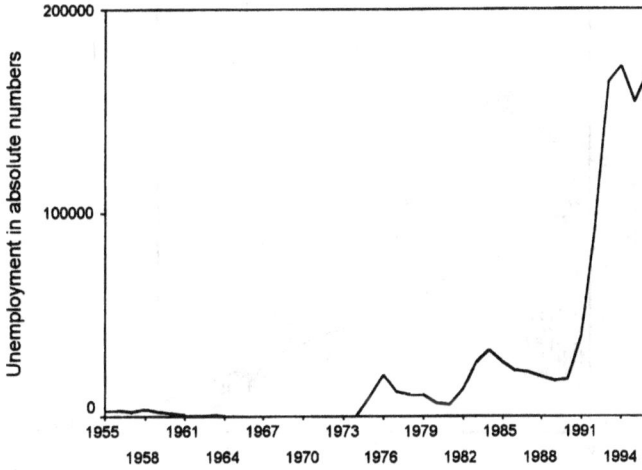

Source: Statistisches Jahrbuch der Schweiz, 1960–98

FIGURE 2

OKUN'S LAW IN SWITZERLAND: ECONOMIC GROWTH AND UNEMPLOYMENT

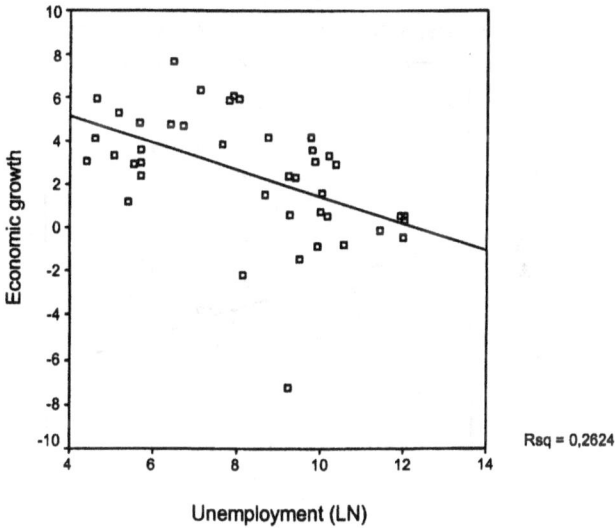

Sources: Economic growth: Thomas Koch (personal communication 2000); Unemployment: Statistisches Jahrbuch der Schweiz (various years).

FIGURE 3

INFLATION AND UNEMPLOYMENT IN PER CENT 1975–98

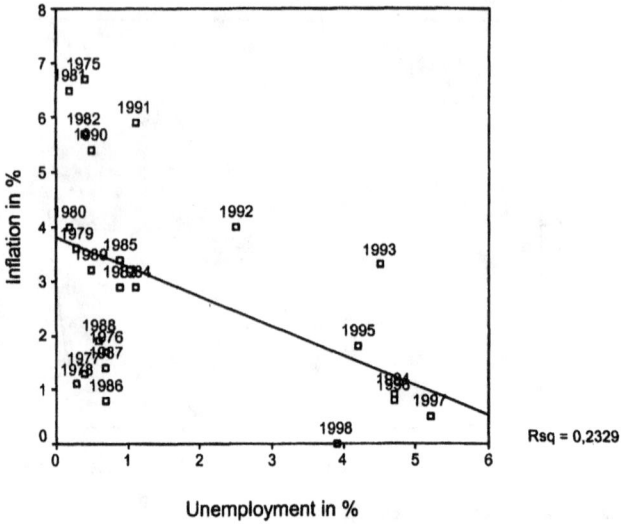

Sources: Inflation: Thomas Koch (personal communication 2000); Unemployment: 1975–82: Schmidt, 1985: 19 and 1983–98: OECD (various years) Economic Outlook. Paris: OECD.

FIGURE 4

INFLATION AND UNEMPLOYMENT 1955–

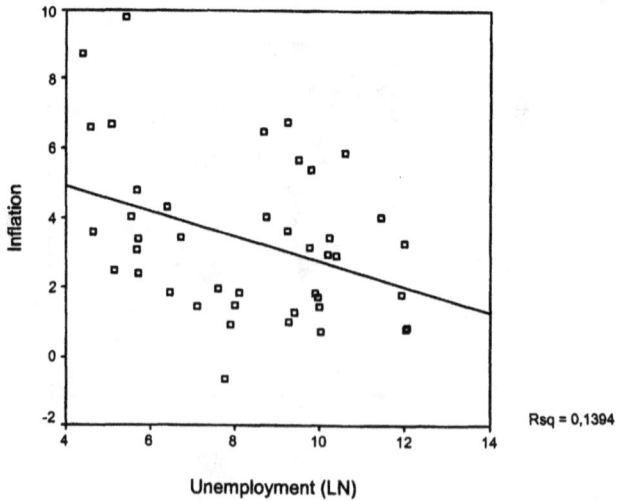

Sources: Inflation: Thomas Koch (personal communication 2000); Unemployment: Statistisches Jahrbuch der Schweiz (various years).

National Bank moved from simple monetarism in the 1970s to refined monetarism in the 1990s, using more and more a rule-based approach. In a monetarist regime the money authority increases the supply of money in proportion to the growth in output.

Correlating total output with the money basis M1, one arrives at a very high positive correlation in the Swiss figures for 1950–97. For the GDP and M1 the correlation is r =.90, confirming moneterism. One may discuss the nature of this relationship, as a larger output evidently needs more money to transact all the goods and services. However, what is apparent is that the central bank has managed to stay away from stagflation, or the occurrence of both inflation and unemployment. Thus, the central bank has not given in to the temptation to try to boost output and employment by excessive money expansion.

Figure 5 offers some evidence of successful monetarism in Switzerland, showing how money expansion one year is related to output growth the following year. The relationship is not a very strong one, but it is positive, r = .30. The conclusion is that more attention should be directed upon the independent Swiss National Bank and its efforts to create a long-term positive climate for economic development by means of a monetarist regime. However, output depends of course upon other factors as well, which we cannot include here.

FIGURE 5

ECONOMIC GROWTH AND LAGGED MONEY SUPPLY GROWTH (M1) 1950–

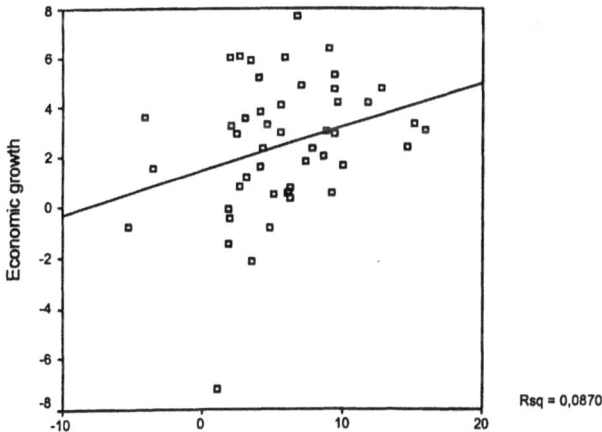

Sources: Data on economic growth and monetary growth: Thomas Koch (personal communication 2000).

210 THE SWISS LABYRINTH

CONCLUSION

The purpose of this study is to invite a debate about the Swiss political economy. It is a most interesting case from a theoretical point of view. How could Switzerland achieve such a balanced mix of low inflation, low unemployment and moderate economic growth over such a long period? The standard answer has been to draw attention to the role of organised interests, suggesting that Switzerland has a corporatist regime of some sort.

There is another interpretation that should be tried, namely to focus upon the role of the Swiss National Bank. Its power to effect monetary policy makes it a key player in the political economy of the country. The available evidence suggests a successful monetarist regime, but more research is needed.

NOTES

The following persons were highly helpful in making possible this short account, written for the purpose of stimulating debate: Svante Ersson (Umea) undertaking all the work upon the final version, Enzo Rossi (Bern) providing me with insights about the Central Bank and Sylvia Dumons (Geneva) as always being instrument here and there. All responsibility for this new interpretation rests with me alone. Thomas Koch (Zurich) provided me with up-to-date series on the Swiss economy.

1. P.J. Katzenstein, Small States in World Markets: Industrial Policy in Europe (Ithaca, NY: Cornell University Press 1985); P.J. Katzenstein, Corporatism and Change: Austria, Switzerland, and the Politics of Industry (Ithaca, NY: Cornell University Press 1984).
2. M.G. Schmidt, Der Schweizerische Weg zur Vollbeschäftigung. Eine Bilanz der Beschäftigung. der Arbeitslosigkeit und der Arbeitsmarktpolitik (Frankfurt am Main: Campus 1985).
3. K. Armingeon and S. Geissbühler (eds.), Gewerkschaften in der Schweiz: Herausforderungen und Optionen (Zurich: Seismo 2000).
4. H. Abromeit, Interessenvermittlung zwischen Konkurrenz and Konkordanz (Opladen: Leske + Budrich 1993).
5. See rankings in A. Cukierman, Central Bank Strategy, Credibility, and Independence: Theory and Evidence (Cambridge, MA: MIT Press 1992); and W. Bernhard, 'A Political Explanation of Variations in Central Banks Independence', American Political Science Review 92 (1998), pp.311–27.
6. G. Rich, 'Monetary Targets as a Policy Rule: Lessons from the Swiss Experience', Journal of Monetary Economics 39 (1997), pp.113–41.

Switzerland and the European Integration Process: Engagement without Marriage

CÉDRIC DUPONT and PASCAL SCIARINI

The rapid expansion of the process of integration within the European Community since the mid-1980s has put the issue of economic and political relationships between Switzerland and the EC at the top of the Swiss political agenda.[1] In particular, there has been much public discussion on the form and nature of the links to be developed with the EC. In this context, the government – Federal Council – has redefined its policy line and has tried to implement new strategies and tactics. These efforts have met considerable resistance, however, not only domestically but also on the external front, and have not brought the country as large and secure an access to the Single Market as is the case for all other Western European countries.

How can one explain this course of events? A widespread interpretation focuses on the characteristics of the Swiss political system that grants strong assenting power to Eurosceptic citizens and the cantons. From this perspective, the government has little steering power and is constantly facing the threat of popular rejection of any new approach to the process of European integration, especially any approach that comes close to accession. A major case in point was the rejection of the treaty on the creation of a European Economic Area (EEA) in 1992, which has increased Switzerland's isolation in Western Europe.[2] According to this view, major domestic institutional reforms are necessary before Switzerland can participate fully in the process of European integration.[3] Without such reforms, especially in the area of direct democracy, the Swiss will not go beyond economic engagement with the EC.

The following account aims to provide a more nuanced analysis of the sources of variation in foreign policy-making, one that carefully examines the influence of perceptions on the design of policy lines. Switzerland's stance towards the process of European integration, from the late 1950s to the late 1990s, can be seen as the result of trade-offs between perceived

Cédric Dupont, Graduate Institute of International Studies, Geneva; Pascal Sciarini, Graduate Institute of Public Administration, Lausanne risks and opportunities, with no clearly predetermined outcome from domestic political structures. Misperceptions about the range of feasible options at the external level have often reinforced domestic political difficulties and even overshadowed them sometimes. From this perspective, then, weak steering ability by the government does not come necessarily, or uniquely, from the domestic political system.

Analytically, we proceed from the assumption that a state's integration policy has internal as well as external aspects and that it thus can be fruitfully understood as a search for a balance between the internal and the external level. We conceptualise and measure this balance as a search for coherence. Governments are concerned with coherence because it generally helps them achieve their underlying objectives. Exogenous shocks, such as the one created by the Single European Act (SEA) tend to disrupt coherence in that it creates discrepancies between the current policy line and the new context. To avoid inefficiency, governments must adjust and find a coherent path of action. These efforts are analysed with the help of analytical tools from the rational choice literature. Thus, our assumption is that decision-makers are strategic actors that try to choose the best possible and feasible course of action under both domestic and external constraints and given their broad objectives.

We begin with a brief description of the analytical framework that guides the empirical study. The following section outlines the historical background of Switzerland and the process of European integration from the late 1950s (failure of the wide free-trade zone inside the Organisation for European Economic Cooperation (OEEC) and subsequent creation of the EC and European Free Trade Association (EFTA)) to the mid-1980s. We then consider in greater detail the most recent episodes of Swiss European integration policy, that is, the attempt to participate in the EEA and then the efforts to design special bilateral ties to the EC. We conclude with a general assessment of the relative influence of domestic institutional factors and a discussion of the need for institutional redesign in a rapidly changing Europe.

POLICY-MAKING IN AN INTERDEPENDENT WORLD: AN ANALYTICAL
FRAMEWORK

Figure 1 depicts the major dimensions of foreign policy making. On the basis of pre-established goals, the government undertakes an evaluation of an optimal course of action. This includes both an assessment of the intrinsic features of different courses of action and of the fit or misfit of the various options with the domestic and external environments.

FIGURE 1

EUROPEAN INTEGRATION POLICY-MAKING

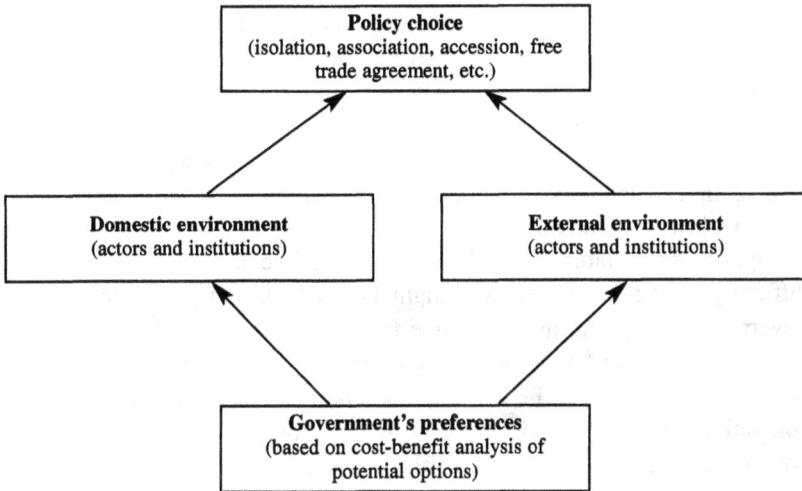

Governments tend to commission reports that undertake cost-benefit analyses of various policy options according to a politico-economic logic. Applied to the case of the definition of Swiss policy towards the EC, any agreement between Switzerland and the EC has redistributive consequences inside the country, with winners and losers. Gains and losses are not restricted to short-term material interests but also to issues of policy autonomy. The government is thus concerned with the implications of different options on the country's core political system, such as the type of democracy, and the basic organisational mode of the state. Apart from reflecting the pure preferences of the government, the choice of a policy option also incorporates interactive constraints coming from the domestic and external environments. The government must confront other actors, domestic and international, and must condition its choice according to the preferences and power of these other actors. The impact of this interdependence with other actors depends in turn on the institutional setting, both domestic and international. A particular feature of the assessment of strategic interdependence is its subjective nature. Contexts are not naturally given but are perceived by actors and these perceptions are often sources of great difficulty.

To sum up our argument so far, Figure 1 suggests an approach to policy-making that views governments as maximisers under constraints. Given the demanding requirements of such a process, governments often tend to rely on simplifying schemes to design optimal courses of action.[4] We contend that the search for coherence is such a scheme. A coherent policy choice is one that is perceived to fit the underlying objectives as well as the domestic and external environments. Intuitively, this corresponds to a reactive behaviour on the part of governments. They adjust to the context hoping to get to a desirable balance.

Yet such a balance is often hard to achieve and may inhibit policy change. Indeed, the search for coherence may compel a government to settle to such a low common denominator between the two sets of constraints that the option of the status quo is the most appropriate one. In some cases, the difficulty in gaining coherence might be so high and so inhibiting that governments may opt, in a proactive fashion, for incoherence in the short term. They deliberately choose to give priority to one set of constraints, external or domestic, while working on making the other set of constraints compatible with the policy option in the longer term. Alternatively, government might bypass the difficulty and reconsider the objectives, which induces a reassessment of preferences and might open up the possibility of a fit with the constraints.

Furthermore, the search for coherence by governments yields poor results when governments misperceive domestic and external contexts. The uncertainty related to the strategic interdependence may push the government to see a balance where objectively there is none. From this perspective, the use of coherence is surely not a guarantee of efficiency.

Whereas the concept of coherence may be relatively easy to grasp, the problem of measurement is a tricky one. Both the external and domestic environments consist of complex sets of constraints, and it might appear difficult to evaluate whether a specific policy line is coherent with them. In order to bring this complexity into tractable form, we use tools from the rational choice/strategic behaviour literature. These tools are particularly suitable to analyse decision-making processes when actors face alternative courses of action and thus enable us to measure the coherence of a chosen policy in a straightforward way.[5]

The key idea is to use the game-theoretical concept of equilibrium to diagnose whether the chosen means are consistent with their respective contexts. An equilibrium is generally defined as a situation where no one actor alone can improve the situation. The concept of equilibrium nicely captures the intuitive notion of a 'fit' between means and context, and offers a rigorous measurement tool that can be used across different cases. Whereas equilibrium analysis is generally performed inside the structure of well-specified games, that is, of schematic depictions of strategic interactions between the government and its main (external or internal) interlocutor, we refrain from doing so in this article. We rely on the insights from our prior formal work,[6] presenting an informal argument on coherence, discussing the various episodes of Swiss policy-making on matters of European integration, the underlying objectives of the government, the set of options considered and the perceived contexts. This enables us to assess the relative influence of different factors in the effort to design a coherent policy line.

HISTORICAL BACKGROUND: SWITZERLAND AND THE PROCESS OF EUROPEAN INTEGRATION FROM THE LATE 1950s TO THE MID-1980s

From the OEEC to EFTA–EC (1955–60): Mutual Restraint

Beginning with the conference in Messina in June 1955 and institutionalising with the Treaty of Rome and the creation of the EC and Euratom in 1957, Western European states were split between those in favour of integration and those in favour of looser relationships. The former were mostly interested in the building of a customs, and even economic, union, whereas the latter wanted to establish a free-trade zone. From the Swiss perspective, the main issue was how best to secure, within this context, an access to European markets for the Swiss export industry. Such an objective was of great importance given the high economic dependence of the country on external trade. The government considered three main policy options.[7] The first was a tight relationship with the pro-integration camp, which meant either accession to the EC or an association agreement with it.[8] A second option consisted in seeking a large multilateral free-trade accord within the Organisation of European Economic Cooperation (OEEC) that would include both the pro-integration and the free-trade camps. Third, the government could refrain from any new initiative and stick to the status quo.

From the government's viewpoint, the multilateral initiative within the OEEC was the preferred option. If successful, such an initiative would bring large economic gains with little political cost. In contrast, a close relationship with the EC (through accession or association) was more costly because it would have forced Switzerland to surrender policy autonomy over foreign trade issues, which was seen as a threat to the policy of neutrality, and to modify domestic legislation on social and fiscal matters. Opting for the status quo had no immediate costs but no secured economic gains. Whereas the multilateral option within the OEEC was the most preferred, it was also the most uncertain at the external level. Indeed, it depended on the ability and willingness of the French and the British to narrow the gap between their individual visions of a free-trade zone.[9]

The assessment of the uncertainty at the external level was central in the choice of the government. Even though the multilateral initiative inside the OEEC was risky, it provided the best balance between the preferences of the government and the domestic and external environments. At the domestic level, it was acceptable to the Vorort, the executive board of the Swiss Federation of Commerce and Industry, which was the most powerful domestic actor on external economic issues. In contrast, the Vorort was strongly opposed to the development of tighter links with the EC, and concerned with the risk of isolation attached to the status quo.

In short, the government's choice was coherent. It clearly fitted into the domestic context and was also consistent with the external environment as long as there was some positive prospect for a minimal (not limiting policy autonomy) agreement between the British and the French. The latter's unilateral decision to quit the negotiation process in November 1958 definitely ruined the hopes of the Swiss government. The first attempt by Switzerland to cope with the existence of the EC was thus a failure. Domestic politics did influence the choice of the government but ultimately it was the external environment that caused policy failure.

France's decision to withdraw from the negotiation process on the creation of an OEEC wide free-trade zone forced the Federal Council to revisit its policy line. The primary objective remained providing the Swiss industry with good access to European markets, but available options had changed due to the clear-cut division inside the OEEC between EC members and all the other countries. The Swiss government could opt for a closer bilateral relationship with the EC, which could have materialised through a range of means including accession (the most ambitious), association, customs union, free-trade zone and a GATT type of trade agreement (the least ambitious). Alternatively, the Federal Council could develop a counter-project to the EC with the other members of the OEEC. Lastly, the government could sit back and wait for better times.

Among these options, a free-trade agreement with the EC was intrinsically the most beneficial. It could bring large economic gains without the political costs linked to more ambitious solutions such as adhesion or association with a customs union. The Federal Council explicitly ruled out accession in its 1960 report on the process of European integration, arguing not only that this would require a surrender of policy autonomy over trade issues but that it would also hurt core political values, such as neutrality, federalism and direct democracy as well as require a fundamental change of farm policy.[10] The build-up of an alternative economic scheme with the other OEEC members was, given the structure of Swiss external trade, economically less promising than a closer relationship with the Six. Yet, this was the option chosen by the Federal Council.

The external context was central to that choice. Uncertainty about the behaviour of other states was very high, in particular on the EC side. Low and middle course options faced the risk of EC rejection. Accession was not a much safer bet either. In contrast, the development of a counter-project to the EC had a good chance of being implemented. Uncertainty about this option pertained to its mid-term implications for Western Europe and the relationship with the EC. Given that, at the domestic level, the creation of a small free-trade zone did not meet any opposition from the Vorort (it did not raise enthusiasm either), the Federal Council chose to pursue it as the only coherent option available. As a consequence, Switzerland was a founding member of the European Free Trade Association (EFTA) that aimed at creating a free-trade area among six countries – Austria, Denmark, Norway, Portugal, Sweden, Switzerland and the United Kingdom. While successful in the short run, the EFTA option failed to reach its main goal, namely an efficient collective platform to negotiate good access to EC markets.[11]

To sum up, the Swiss government had to face considerable external difficulties in the late 1950s while trying to achieve its prime objectives with respect to the process of European integration. The uncertainty of that process, still in its infancy, undermined several options that could bring significant economic gains without extensive political implications. The Swiss chose the one that was thought to be the least weakened by that uncertainty. Yet, they knew that it could not be a long-lasting solution. One can therefore wonder whether the government could not have chosen a more ambitious policy line, that is, to become part of the EC or at least very closely associated with it. In its 1960 report, the government ruled out such a policy line on the basis of its incompatibility with core political and institutional values. There is no doubt that the government gave considerable importance to domestic constraints but it is unclear what would have happened if it had actively tried to gain access to the EC. The next episode brings some responses to this counterfactual thought.

The Association Attempt (1961–63): Aborted Marriage?

The limits of EFTA, as a common platform to manage relationships with the EC and minimise economic discrimination in Western Europe, became manifest when the UK and Denmark officially applied for EC membership in early 1961. The threat to EFTA's future pushed the Federal Council to reconsider the policy line it had just started to implement. As an alternative to the actual option of betting on EFTA, the government re-examined the case of closer bilateral relationship with the EC through accession or association.[12]

At the external level, the uncertainty about the EC's likely responses had diminished, in particular with respect to association schemes. In May 1961, the EC proposed to EFTA members that had not applied for membership to organise their bilateral relations on the basis of the status of association (article 238 of the Treaty of Rome). The specific form of such an avenue was not fully determined, however. In particular, the issue of external tariffs was still open, even though the EC had a preference for a customs union over a free-trade zone. On accession, the EC had not made public any firm stance.

The Swiss government reacted to new elements in the external environment with a significant rethinking of its policy line.[13] It chose to pursue the avenue of an association treaty with the EC, showing a readiness to accept a customs union if the EC insisted on it. That constituted a major, and very surprising, policy shift. Barely one year earlier, the government had dismissed the option of a customs union on the ground that it would imply a surrender of policy autonomy over trade issues. Clearly, for the first time the government gave priority, and much importance, to the evolution of the external context because it was highly concerned with the increased risk of economic discrimination that could come from an enlarged EC.

Designed inside the federal administration, the new policy line never materialised at the external level. France's veto on the British membership application put relationship with all EFTA members on hold. But inside Switzerland, preparatory work on the new policy line revealed the extent of domestic constraints on the government's behaviour. In particular, the Vorort opposed the new option out of fear of sharing a common external tariff with EC countries. The peak industrial and trade association was also wary of possible implications for domestic competition policy. It acknowledged that a closer bilateral relationship with the EC had become necessary, but was not ready to pay the political and economic price for it. Similarly, the Swiss Farmers' Union opposed any liberalisation agreement that would threaten the highly protectionist Swiss agricultural policy.

The government chose a path that did not fit into the domestic environment. It did so because it gave priority to external developments, with the hope of subsequently winning support at home. De Gaulle's veto on the British membership application put an abrupt end to the audacious move by the Swiss government. And, as a consequence, it prevents us from making a concrete assessment of the influence of domestic constraints on Switzerland's policy towards the process of European integration. On the one hand, the association project suggests that the Swiss government was domestically not as severely constrained as it publicly claimed, especially with respect to the three institutional cornerstones (neutrality, direct democracy and federalism). Thus, it was ready to endorse the limitation of the policy of neutrality resulting from membership of the customs union. On the other hand, one can conjecture that the government made a very risky bet with its association project. For the first time since 1945, the Federal Council chose to confront the Vorort in an area that was largely considered to be its private domain.[14] Strong dissent could therefore be expected, and given the traditional weight of interest groups in Swiss politics it is hard to conceive how the government could have bypassed opposition and implemented a tight relationship with the EC. As revealed by the initial reaction of the Vorort, interest groups knew that the best way to protect their vested interests was to resort to the claim that the policy line would endanger core domestic political values. Doing so, they could portray themselves as defenders of Swiss identity.

The 1972 Free-Trade Agreement and its Aftermath: Institutionalised Partnership

In May 1967, the UK – together with Denmark, Ireland and then Norway – submitted a new membership application to the EC. This new wave of demands ultimately received a positive response from the EC, mostly due to de Gaulle's resignation from the French presidency. The EC chose to reconsider globally the issue of its relationship with EFTA countries during the Hague conference in December 1969. At the Hague, the EC member states expressed their willingness to find an overall solution to the economic division of Western Europe. To that end, they opened the door to full membership for those countries that were willing and able to join the club. In addition, they also envisaged the establishment of particular ties with those EFTA countries that, for domestic reasons, were not ready for accession.

These new developments at the external level pressed the Federal Council to re-examine its policy line on European integration. Like its EFTA partners, Switzerland was greatly concerned with the prospect of UK accession to the EC. As the largest EFTA country, the UK was a key player in the free-trade zone. Accordingly, the Federal Council swiftly dismissed the 'wait and see' (status quo) scenario, which would in fact imply a worsening of Switzerland's situation in Europe. Options that would lead to full or almost full integration into the EC, such as EC membership or participation in the customs union, were also rejected for reasons of loss of policy autonomy. As an alternative, the Federal Council had a preference for a so-called *sui generis* agreement, which would take the form of a free-trade agreement with the EC.[15] Given past EC wariness of a free-trade zone, the Swiss government could not be sure of the external feasibility of this option. Uncertainty regarding the EC attitude was not limited to the option of a *sui generis* agreement, but also applied to other options, for instance, to a membership application with a reserve on neutrality. But the potential net gains (high economic gains at low political costs) of a *sui generis* agreement were much higher than those of any other options. Backed by the Vorort,[16] still the main actor in the domestic game, the Federal Council opted for a project that would possibly lead to the creation of a wide free-trade zone in Western Europe.

After a short bargaining process, the EC–EFTA talks led to the conclusion of bilateral (between each EFTA country and the EC) free-trade agreements on industrial goods. The agreement provided Swiss export-oriented sectors with better access to the European market, while leaving both the fundamental institutions and the domestic economy untouched.[17] Therefore, it is not surprising that all the peak associations, as well as the unions and all major political parties supported the agreement. The high level of consensus existing among the elite translated into an overwhelming majority in the popular vote for ratification.[18]

The free-trade agreement boosted trade flows between EFTA and EC countries. From the Swiss government's perspective, this was a clear and strong proof of the merits of its pragmatic approach to the process of European integration. The period of stagnation experienced by the integration process during the 1970s and early 1980s only served to reinforce this conviction and made any policy revision meaningless.

DESIGNING THE EUROPEAN ECONOMIC AREA (1986–92): THE
FAILURE OF ARRANGED MARRIAGE

In the mid-1980s, the outlining of the Single Market programme by the members of the EC sparked off a new era in the economic and political integration of Western Europe. The adoption of the Single European Act (SEA) not only revitalised the EC but also sent shock waves to close EFTA neighbours. The latter's responses came in two steps.[19] First, between 1986 and the end of 1988, EFTA countries defined independently from each other, and thus differently, their responses to the Single Market programme. But in a second stage they were forced to reassess collectively their individual policy lines, following a proposal in January 1989 by the President of the EC Commission, Jacques Delors, to build a closer and more structured partnership between EFTA and EC countries. We analyse in the next two subsections how Switzerland reacted to these new circumstances.

1986–88

Whereas the prospect of a single European market brought about dramatic change in some EFTA countries, in particular in neighbouring Austria,[20] the Swiss government made minor change to its policy line on European integration. Having hardly reacting to the SEA before late 1987, it started to elaborate its official stance with the publication of a special report to the federal parliament in August 1988.[21] In this report, the government discussed three strategic options – EC membership, the median way or *'troisième voie'*, and isolation (*'Alleingang'*). Despite the changes occurring in the EC, the Federal Council saw no compelling reason to reconsider the median way of selective economic engagement as implemented through the 1972 free-trade agreement. Such an option was still perceived to be the best tool to achieve the government's prime objectives – to gain access to the Single European market while avoiding any political commitment that might endanger Switzerland's fundamental institutions.

The median way nicely fitted into the domestic environment. Due to both the far-reaching implications of the Single Market and the 1977 constitutional change that had extended the application of the instruments of direct democracy to foreign policy issues, the dominant actor was no longer the Vorort but the federal parliament.[22] Concerned with possible economic discrimination against Swiss firms in Europe, the Swiss parliament did not see isolation as a credible solution. But it felt equally concerned with the likely consequences of EC membership on Switzerland's institutions and political autonomy. Consequently, Swiss MPs almost unanimously endorsed the median way strategy.

While coherent domestically, the choice for a median way was highly problematic externally. It was indeed very demanding for the EC. First, unlike Austria, Switzerland was not ready to adapt its legislation unilaterally, but mainly wanted to obtain the recognition of the compatibility of Swiss legislation with the *acquis communautaire*. Second, Switzerland was looking for a selective integration over matters of special interest for the Swiss export sector.[23] Third, this *à la carte* participation was also demanding in the sense that it would require a multiplication of separate bilateral negotiations.

In sum, the Swiss favoured a solution that was domestically optimal in the short term, but was hardly feasible at the external level. The question of feasibility is, however, difficult to assess even in an *ex-post* analysis due to the contextual change that occurred in early 1989. Jacques Delors's proposal to create an encompassing EC–EFTA framework made the Swiss median way virtually irrelevant, at least in its traditional form of *à la carte* participation. Delors envisioned a new approach of a 'more structured partnership with common decision-making and administrative solutions in order to increase the efficiency of our action'.[24] The aim was to create a large market – the European Economic Area (EEA) – regrouping members from both organisations.[25]

1989

The Swiss government reacted very positively to Delors' proposal. It considered that the EEA project would be the crowning achievement of its pragmatic policy line. The government was convinced that the EEA would not only bring very high economic gains but would also be a very attractive political solution. Indeed, the Federal Council was confident that the EEA would grant co-decision powers to EFTA members over the evolution of the economic area. Investing in the EEA project, as a continuation of the median way, was thus the preferred option of the government in comparison to a membership application or an isolationist stance.

The EEA option had no difficulty fitting into the domestic context, but it was more problematic at the external level. The Swiss government misperceived coherence at the external level and misinterpreted Delors' message and the EC's intent. First, the Federal Council did not properly evaluate the implications of Delors' proposal with respect to both the scope and the form of the negotiations with the EC. The Swiss government thought the EEA would be a mere continuation of its past strategy of *à la carte* participation. Accordingly, when the EEA talks started, the Swiss wanted the four freedoms of movement (goods, capital, services and persons) to apply wherever and whenever this would prove to be beneficial.[26] The EC, however, was opposed to any permanent derogation that would threaten the 'homogeneity of the European space'. In other words, the EEA talks shifted the focus from the traditional sectoral talks on selected matters to global talks on the whole *acquis communautaire*. In addition, they also shifted the focus from bilateral (Switzerland–EC) to multilateral (EFTA–EC) negotiations with an obligation for the EFTA countries 'to speak with one voice'. This obligation prevented Switzerland from voicing its demands for specific solutions.[27]

Second, the Swiss government misread the EC's stance on the issue of co-decision. Since 1987 the EC had repeatedly stated that the relationships with the EFTA countries should not endanger the autonomy of EC's decision-making process.[28] In spite of this, the Swiss government believed – at least, it claimed so – until the last rounds of negotiations that it would obtain a balanced EEA, that is, an EEA with a co-decision right.[29]

This government's misperception and related behaviour had unfortunate consequences, both internationally and domestically. Internationally, the EEA negotiation process turned out to be a bitter experience for the Swiss government, which had to find out that there was no way it could obtain *à la carte* participation.[30] Domestically, the high demand strategy by the Swiss government, especially on the issue of co-decision, gave rise to unrealistic, and unachievable, expectations among voters. No wonder, then, that the EEA agreement, especially with respect to the co-decision procedures, was seen as a major diplomatic defeat in Switzerland.

It was only after several months of tough bargaining and costly stalemate that the Swiss became aware of the inconsistency of their position and switched to membership as the priority solution. They announced this new policy line on the day the EEA talks were concluded in September 1991. At that time, EC membership was still inconsistent with the domestic environment, but the government apparently chose to bypass the domestic constraints.[31] This decision did not prove to be successful, however. A sense of defeat due to this sudden change of course pervaded the general public, and nurtured a movement against participation in European affairs.

To sum up, in the second half of the 1980s the Swiss government proved unable to design a coherent policy line with respect to European integration. This inability was due to both an erroneous reading of the external situation and the priority given to the respect of domestic constraints. Regarding perceptions, the Swiss government misread the external context by overestimating the opportunities offered by the EEA talks. It therefore committed itself to pursuing for several months a strategy that was a dead-end. Regarding constraints, given the prospects of a possible popular vote, the Swiss government admittedly faced more stringent domestic constraints than its EFTA partners. However, as is suggested by the Austrian case, the early introduction of the membership option into the internal debate might have led to a learning process in favour of EC membership among the Swiss public. Instead, the persistent pursuit of the median way by the Swiss government, which was certainly in line with short-term domestic preferences, precluded a serious internal discussion of the membership option, at least as a long-term strategy. As a consequence, when the government actually did turn to this option, the public was completely unprepared for such a policy. The end result of this poor policy management was the public rejection of the EEA treaty in December 1992.

At the time of the signing of the EEA agreement in May 1992, a majority of Swiss citizens were still ready to endorse it according to opinion polls.[32] In addition, the EEA treaty was overwhelmingly accepted in parliament[33] (the key domestic actor), had the support of cantonal governments, and of three (the Socialist Party, the Radical Party, and the Christian Democrat Party) out of the four parties that had seats in the Federal Council. Opposition came only from the Swiss People's Party, as well as from the extreme right (the Swiss Democrats and the Car Drivers' Party) and from factions of the Greens. Within the economy, the trade unions and the peak association representing export-oriented interests (the Vorort) supported the treaty, whereas the domestic economy was either split (the Swiss Association of Small Businesses) or opposed (the Swiss Farmers' Union).

The referendum campaign on the EEA treaty reached a level of intensity hardly met before. In the 'no' camp, the referendum campaign was led by the powerful Action for an Independent and Neutral Switzerland. According to a quantitative analysis of newspapers advertisements, the elite's political communications were far more evenly distributed between *pro* and *contra* arguments than was suggested by parliamentary votes or parties' voting recommendations.[34] The 'no' camp tried successfully to dramatise the debate with emotional arguments about sovereignty and neutrality, the decline of direct democracy and federalism, and immigration. The opposition seized the opportunity to use the confusion between EEA and EC membership to launch – especially in the German-speaking region – a fundamental debate on the future of the country and its main institutions. On 6 December 1992, the EEA agreement was rejected by 50.3 per cent of the voters and 16 cantons out of 23, on a very high – for Swiss standards – 78.3 per cent turnout.[35]

BACK TO BILATERALISM (1993–2000): ENGAGEMENT WITHOUT MARRIAGE

The popular rejection of the EEA agreement left Switzerland in a very difficult situation. All other EFTA countries had secured privileged access to EC markets and a majority of them was clearly heading towards accession. There was thus a very high risk of discrimination. The government had to react, and it re-examined its policy line. It considered four options, that is, EC membership, a new EEA negotiation, bilateral agreements or the status quo. From the government's perspective, EC membership was still the preferred option because it was considered to be the only one that could secure full access to the Single Market while at the same time giving some control over its evolution. But, given the results of the vote on the ratification of the EEA, the membership option was clearly incoherent with the domestic environment, as was the option of new EEA talks.[36] Accordingly, the Federal Council decided to freeze the membership application and to opt for the bilateral strategy of sectoral agreements with the EC. The search for a bilateral *ad hoc* approach was only a third best option because it would not bring a long-term economic solution and left Switzerland with no political say. But it was the only option that could fit into a very difficult domestic context.

At the external level, the bilateral route faced major problems. Fearing that Switzerland would use the bilateral talks to have its cake and eat it, the EC made clear from the outset that it would refuse a piecemeal approach. It was therefore doubtful whether the government could achieve significant results through the bilateral option. As a case in point, when the Federal Council in 1993 submitted a list of 15 issues to be negotiated, the General Affairs Council picked only five of them (public procurements, technical barriers to trade, research, road transportation and air transportation), and added two other issues of particular interest to some member states (agriculture and the free movement of persons). In addition, the EC insisted on the 'parallelism of the talks', that is that any agreement on a given topic was dependent on the acceptance of an agreement in another issue area. Given the EEA experience, the EC wanted to protect itself against a possible new popular rejection.

Negotiations eventually started in December 1994. The external suboptimality of the bilateral strategy helps explain the extreme length of the negotiation process (four years). Two issues proved especially sensitive:[37] road transportation and the free movement of people. On the free movement of persons, the EC repeatedly stated that the final agreement should include provisions for the complete freedom of movement of persons. Arguing that this goal would lead to a rejection in a popular vote, the Swiss authorities opposed any 'automatic' introduction of the free movement of persons that would imply the removal of the system of permits and quotas. Initially, the Swiss negotiators suggested only qualitative improvements of the immigration policy. After several rounds of unproductive discussion, positions progressively converged on a sophisticated system that enabled each negotiating partner to claim the final agreement as a bargaining success. The Swiss gained a long transitory period, various kinds of safeguard clauses, as well as the option to terminate the agreement after seven years; the EC gained the free movement of people, on trial from 2006, and without restrictions after 2013.

On transportation, talks also quickly reached a stalemate. Whereas the EC considered access to the Swiss territory for its 40-ton lorries a precondition for successful negotiations, the Swiss government equally strongly rejected such an outcome. After several months without any progress, the Federal Council made a proposal that relaunched the negotiation process. It suggested a trade-off between lifting the 28-ton limit and introducing new road taxes. With such a proposal, the Federal Council could at the same time allow the progressive ban of road transport through the Alps (requested by a successful popular initiative) and its transfer to rail. The bone of contention became the level of the new tax, and it took several additional rounds of talks to settle the issue on a middle ground.

Domestic coherence won strong confirmation during the ratification debate in the Swiss parliament. Only the small far-right parties (the Swiss Democrats and the Lega dei Ticinesi) opposed the bilateral agreement. They were nevertheless able to force a popular vote on the agreement, giving the last word to voters. But they then proved unable to wage a major campaign, and the bilateral agreement received great public support.[38]

The government's choice has thus brought some significant change regarding Switzerland and the process of European integration. One should, however, not overestimate the value of the bilateral agreement. Unlike the EEA treaty, bilateral agreements are static in the sense that they will not automatically be updated with the next integration steps in the EC.[39] They are at best a medium-term solution and the government needs to think ahead. There are several issues that require further co-operation. Switzerland is notably interested in asylum and immigration policy (Schengen, Dublin). The EC is pressing for collaboration over fiscal issues. It is unclear whether these issues will be addressed on an *ad hoc* basis or will require a more institutionalised relationship.

CONCLUSION: IS MARRIAGE POSSIBLE WITHOUT INSTITUTIONAL REDESIGN?

Among Western European countries, Switzerland is currently the one with the least access to the EC Single Market. This is the ultimate implication of essentially reactive policy-making in Switzerland over matters of European integration, with a clear priority given to preserving domestic consensus. Crafting responses to developments at the European level has been both difficult and slow.

The reasons for difficulty have varied over time with an important change at the end of the 1960s. Earlier, there was hardly any hope of finding a true fit between the government's prime objectives, the domestic and the external environment. Domestically, the Federal Council was highly concerned with both the institutional and redistributive consequences of a close relationship with the EC. But it faced even more stringent constraints at the external level, which were due to a mix of initial uncertainty regarding the integration process and the rigidity of some EC member states, especially France.

Later on, however, the difficulties faced by the Federal Council were less 'structural' and had more to do with perceptions, in particular of the external environment. It took the painful exercise of the EEA negotiations to open the eyes of the Swiss government and make it revise its policy line in favour of accession. The revision was stark and domestic actors were unprepared for it. The immediate sanction was the rejection of the EEA treaty by the citizens and cantons, which significantly weakened the government's ability to fulfil its prime objectives. Overall, the Swiss government has thus shown a very poor strategic understanding of the external context in the later period, first choosing a bad policy line and then revising it inappropriately. The government signally failed to achieve its declared objective of improving the playing field of the Swiss economy.

A central finding of our analysis is the overall priority given by the government to domestic constraints even at the price of external misfit. From this perspective, the central questions are whether the government could have done differently, and, as a corollary, what a different emphasis could have meant for Switzerland. We have discussed two clear efforts by the government to give priority to the external context, both of which failed to achieve results. The first one, the association attempt in 1961–63, raised a strong domestic reaction and was then wrecked by the EC. The second one, the decision to aim for accession announced at the conclusion of the EEA negotiations, stumbled at the domestic level. Clearly, this evidence does not make a compelling case for giving priority to the external level. There is no denying that domestic political constraints have largely limited the ability of the government to become engaged to the EC, not to mention its ability to conclude a marriage. As central elements of the Swiss identity,[40] the core principles of neutrality, direct democracy and federalism and related

228 THE SWISS LABYRINTH

informal practices proved especially constraining. Yet the association project of 1961–63 suggests that the Federal Council was perhaps not as severely constrained as is usually assumed. Similarly, the fact that it opted for EC membership at the end of the EEA talks tends to demonstrate that a different response to the Single Market project might have been possible from the outset. In addition, the government has, through its discourse and its actions, contributed to increasing the stringency of these constraints. Since the late 1950s, and even more so since the 1972 free-trade agreement, the Federal Council has nurtured the idea that Switzerland could always get privileged treatment from the EC. This behaviour has empowered domestic constituencies opposed to the development of closer relationship with the process of European integration.

What are the implications of this analysis for the future of Swiss–EC relationship? Public debate has so far revealed three main viewpoints. The first sees the virtue of waiting. Given the blocking power given by the constitution to Eurosceptics, there is currently little hope for a more ambitious policy, namely a membership application.[41] The government should therefore wait and see how the EC will evolve. If the latter becomes a decentralised entity, membership could fit into the domestic context and hence would be a coherent choice. In addition, domestic public opinion could change and become more amenable to a closer relationships with the EC. A second view is proactive. Rather than waiting for the external context to change, the government should reform the domestic setting, including some major institutions (such as direct democracy and federalism), in order to bridge the gap with the EC. The third view considers that the government should give priority to the external level and negotiate accession immediately, without prior institutional reform. While negotiating, it could prepare public opinion for ratification.

Our analysis brings some useful elements to the evaluation of these various viewpoints, in particular the first and third ones. The first view is a mere continuation of the reactive nature of policy-making towards the process of European integration. The shortcomings of such an approach have been shown. In particular, Switzerland has never been able to sustain the pace of change at the external level, starting with the quick erosion of EFTA and ending with the EEA episode. The fact that Switzerland has never been so isolated on matters of European integration can only increase the challenges of reactive behaviour. Therefore, waiting for external change is not likely to make policy-making easier, quite to the contrary. A wait and see position is particularly risky in a country with an extensive direct democratic system. Abrupt policy shifts require public opinion to adapt quickly to external change. This can only be the case if the government plays an active steering role.

Turning to the third viewpoint, we can draw an analogy with the association attempt in 1961–63. Both cases correspond to a situation in which the government takes the initiative despite strong domestic dissent and with an uncertain external context. Granted that it is now less likely that the EC would turn down Swiss demands than in 1961–63, the government could be encouraged to be audacious. To yield positive results, this option requires that the EC should consider it as acceptable to the Swiss people and that the government should think it will be able to convince the same people. Both challenges are tough, but with the difference from the association project that the government would not be alone in promoting an ambitious strategy. It could count on the support of a significant part of public opinion (in particular the younger voters who have put the issue on the political agenda through a popular initiative) and on a large minority of members of the parliament.

It is harder to evaluate the second viewpoint on the basis of our findings because the government has never really tried such an option before. But one can first raise doubts about the feasibility of preparatory domestic reforms. Any domestic reform is likely to be evaluated in connection with EC membership, which would help to mobilise opponents and would spread conflicts across a whole spectrum of political and economic issues. Furthermore, the experiences of other small states that joined the EC show that very different political systems can be compatible with EC membership, and thus that there is ample room for diversity.[42]

On the basis of our evaluation of the different positions, we tend to agree with the principle of the third scenario, but not with the suggested timing. We argue that 'marriage' with the EC may be possible without institutional redesign. But it requires a proactive Federal Council with a good steering capacity. The government should announce a precise time-horizon for a reactivation of its membership application (say four years) and in the meantime actively prepare public opinion for this deadline.

NOTES

We wish to thank Caroline Eggli and Derek Lutterbeck for their research assistance and we are grateful to the Swiss National Science Foundation (grant no. 4042-044244/1) for financial support.

1. For the sake of convenience, we use the European Community (EC) as a generic title for the integration process from the Treaty of Rome to the current situation.
2. A. Riklin. 'Isolierte Schweiz. Eine europa- und innenpolitische Lagebeurteilung', *Schweizerische Zeitschrift für Politische Wissenschaft* 1/2–3 (1995), pp.11–34.

3. See, e.g., S. Borner *et al.*, *Schweiz AG. Vom Sonderfall zum Sanierungsfall?* (Zürich: Neue Zürcher Zeitung 1990); R.E. Germann, *Staatsreform. Der Übergang zur Konkurrenzdemokratie* (Berne: Haupt 1994).

4. Instead of optimising, they may thus only be 'satisficing': H. Simon, 'A Behavioural Model of Rational Choice', *Quarterly Journal of Economics* 69 (1955), pp.99–108; J.G. March and H. Simon, *Organizations* (New York: John Wiley 1958).

5. Game-theoretic models of decision-making have opened new perspectives for the study of foreign policy. See the discussion of G.T. Allison's *Essence of Decision: Explaining the Cuban Missile Crisis* (Boston: Little Brown 1971) by J. Bendor and T.H. Hammond, 'Rethinking Allison's Model', *American Political Science Review* 86 (1992), pp.301–22, and, among others, the work of B.B. de Mesquita and D. Lalman, *War and Reason* (New Haven: Yale University Press 1992), or R. Powell, *Nuclear Deterrence Theory* (New York: Cambridge University Press 1990).

6. C. Dupont and P. Sciarini, 'Impossible efficacité? La politique suisse d'intégration européenne en perspective historique et comparative' (unpublished ms, Institut HEI et Département de science politique, Geneva, 1999); C. Dupont, P. Sciarini and D. Lutterbeck, 'Catching the EC Train: Austria and Switzerland in Comparative Perspective', *European Journal of International Relations* 5/2 (1999), pp.189–224; C. Dupont, C. Eggli and P. Sciarini, 'Entre cohérence et efficacité. Les négociations bilatérales Suisse-Union européenne' (paper presented to congrès suisse de science politique, Balsthal, 12–13 Nov. 1998).

7. See, e.g., A. Enz, 'Die Schweiz und die Grosse Europäische Freihandelszone', *Studien und Quellen. Zeitschrift des Schweizerischen Bundesarchivs* 16/17 (1991), pp.157–61; B. Hurni, 'The Failure to Establish the Large Free Trade Area', in P. du Bois and B. Hurni (eds.), *EFTA from Yesterday to Tomorrow* (Geneva: European University Institute 1987), pp.27–35.

8. The specific contours of the association status with the EC remained opaque until the mid-1960s due to a multiplicity of interpretations by the EC itself on the content of such an option.

9. France was mostly seeking to protect the newly formed EC and thus wanted to restrict tariff-setting autonomy and economic policy autonomy inside the future zone, whereas the UK, concerned with the Commonwealth, dismissed such restrictions. From the Swiss government's perspective, the opposition between France and the UK did not preclude a minimal agreement, mostly because the Swiss perceived that Germany would push France to accept such an accord.

10. Federal Council, *Message to the Federal Assembly regarding Switzerland's Participation in the European Free Trade Association* (Berne: Feuille fédérale 1960), pp.888–90.

11. See, e.g., W. Kaiser 'Challenge to the Community: The Creation, Crisis and Consolidation of the European Free Trade Association, 1958–72', *Journal of European Integration History* 3/1 (1997), pp.7–33.

12. The government did not wait for the EC to answer the UK and Danish demands in order to avoid accepting a *fait accompli*.

13. M. Zbinden, 'Das EWR-Projekt: eine Wiederholung des Assoziationsversuches von 1961–1963', *Annuaire suisse de science politique* 32 (1992), pp.221–48; M. Zbinden, *Der Assoziationsversuch der Schweiz mit der EWG 1961–1963* (Geneva: HEI 1999).

14. For an assessment of the role of the Vorort on trade and monetary issues post Second World War, see C. Baumann, C. Dupont and M. Peter, 'Forme et logique des engagements internationaux de la Suisse: quelques enseignements du cas des relations avec les institutions de Bretton Woods', *Revue suisse de science politique* 5 (1999), pp.97–109.

15. As another intermediary solution the Federal Council also envisaged a traditional agreement under GATT. However, this solution suffered from a major drawback: due to the most-favoured-nation clause, any tariff concessions offered to the EC should be extended to all countries belonging to the GATT.

16. In a survey conducted within the Vorort, the industrialists expressed their wish for preferential access to EC markets but not at the price of a surrender of trade policy.

17. In particular, agricultural products were not included in the free-trade agreement (P. Sciarini, *La Suisse face à la Communauté européenne et au GATT. Le cas-test de la politique agricole* (Geneva: Georg 1994), pp.109–11).

18. On 3 December 1972, the free-trade agreement was accepted by 72.5 per cent of the electorate, with a 52.9 per cent turnout.
19. C. Dupont, 'The Failure of the Nest-Best Solution: EC–EFTA Institutional Relationships and the European Economic Area', in V.K. Aggarwal (ed.), *Institutional Designs for a Complex World: Bargaining, Linkages, and Nesting* (Ithaca: Cornell University Press 1998), pp.124–60; see also Dupont *et al.*, 'Catching the EC Train'.
20. The Austrian government first opted for 'quasi-membership' and then for membership in the EC. See Dupont *et al.*, 'Catching the EC Train'.
21. Federal Council, *Message to the Federal Assembly regarding Switzerland's position in the process of European integration* (Berne: Feuille fédérale, 24 Aug. 1988).
22. The 1988 report itself was a response to a '*Postulat*' filed in 1987 by the Commission for Economic Affairs in the Lower Chamber, the National Council. Moreover, the various political and economic forces of the country were represented in this Chamber and, at that time, mostly focused on this channel to influence the policy of the government. See P. Sciarini, 'Le role et la position de l'Assemblée fédérale dans les relations avec la Communauté européenne depuis 1972', in Parlamentsdienste (ed.), *Das Parlament – 'Oberste Gewalt des Bundes'?* (Berne: Haupt 1991), pp.403–23.
23. Thus, in order to avoid distributive consequences at the domestic level, Switzerland wanted to exclude the sheltered sectors of the domestic economy (like agriculture) from the bargaining process.
24. Agence Europe, Doc. no 1542/1543, 26 Jan. 1989.
25. For a detailed analysis of the EEA, see C. Dupont, *Domestic Politics, Information and International Bargaining: Comparative Models of Strategic Behavior in Non-Crisis Negotiations.* (Genève: HEI 1994).
26. For example, Switzerland asked for a permanent derogation to the free movement of persons. In this case, as in others, Switzerland ultimately gained only a temporary derogation.
27. Occasionally, the Swiss negotiators tried to use their domestic constraints – and more especially the threat of a direct democratic vote – as a weapon in the negotiation. However, this strategy proved unsuccessful. See C. Dupont, 'Succès avec la SDN, échec avec l'EEE? Résistances internes et négociation internationale', *Annuaire suisse de science politique* 32 (1992), pp.249–72.
28. See, e.g., the declaration of the former EC Commissioner for external relations Willy de Clerq at the EFTA–EC meeting in Interlaken (Switzerland) in May 1987.
29. For instance, the Secretary of State and chief negotiator for Switzerland in the EEA process, Franz Blankart, declared in a speech in 1989 that 'Delors' initiative ... provides the chance of restructuring the Western European configuration and, if we take him at his word, of securing our co-decision rights ('*Mitbestimmung*') in the Western European area (F. Blankart, 'Integrationspolitische Lagebeurteilung', Zurich, Vortrag gehalten vor der Zürcher Volkswirtschaftlichen Gesellschaft, 14 Sept. 1989 – our translation). However, once it was agreed that the *acquis communautaire* would constitute the basis of the negotiation, a decision that occurred in autumn 1989, granting EFTA countries with co-decision rights was simply impossible, since this would give them a veto power on future EC legislation.
30. Dupont, *Domestic Politics, Information and International Bargaining.* For an argument that Swiss elites learned from the initial deadlocks, in the sense that they intended to use the EEA as a leverage for the restructuration of the domestic economy, see P. Sciarini, 'La Suisse dans la négociation sur l'Espace économique européen: de la rupture à l'apprentissage', *Annuaire suisse de science politique* 32 (1992), pp.297–322. Dupont, 'Succès avec la SDN, échec avec l'EEE?' demonstrates that this learning did not lead to major change in the negotiation tactics until late in the process.
31. The formal application for EC membership was submitted to the EC Commission in June 1992.
32. H. Kriesi *et al.*, 'Analyse de la votation fédérale du 6 décembre 1992 (EEE)' (Geneva/Berne: Département de Science Politique/GfS-Forschungsinstitut, Analyse-Vox No 47 1993).
33. 62% 'yes' in the National Council and 85% in the Council of States.
34. L. Marquis and P. Sciarini, 'Opinion Formation in Foreign Policy: The Swiss Experience', *Electoral Studies* 18/4 (1999), pp.453–71.

35. Survey results show the impact of the linguistic, rural-urban, class, and education cleavages in the voters' decision (Kriesi *et al.*, 'Analyse de la votation fédérale du 6 décembre 1992'; P. Sciarini and O. Listhaug, 'Single Cases or a Unique Pair? The Swiss and Norwegian "No" to Europe', *Journal of Common Market Studies* 35/3 (1997), pp.407–38). They also reveal that two antagonist conceptions of the country and its future clashed that day: While supporters of the EEA wanted to promote an open Switzerland, the opposition wanted to defend the traditional Switzerland that stands for its myths and values the virtues of isolation.

36. The status quo was not considered as a credible option either, since it would lead to the economic and political isolation of Switzerland.

37. Dupont *et al.*, 'Entre cohérence et efficacité'.

38. On 21 May 2000, 67.2% of the Swiss People said yes to the bilateral agreements with a 48% turnout.

39. This characteristic made it easier for the Swiss government to sell the package to the people, but might reveal its limitations in the near future.

40. P. Sciarini, C. Dupont and S. Hug, 'Example, Exception or Both? Swiss National Identity in Perspective', in L.-E. Cedermann (ed.), *Defining and Projecting Europe's Identity. Issues and Tradeoffs* (Boulder, CO: Lynne Rienner 2000).

41. The accession vote to the EC would require a double majority of voters and cantons.

42. K. Hanf and B. Soetendorp, *Adapting to European Integration: Small States and the European Union* (London: Longman 1998). See also K. Armingeon, 'Herausforderung eines Beitritts zur Europäischen Union: Interessenverbände und politische Parteien in der Schweiz', in T. Cottier and A.R. Kopse (eds.), *Der Beitritt der Schweiz zur Europäischen Union. Brennpunkte und Auswirkungen* (Zürich: Schulteiss Polygraphischer Verlag 1998), pp.273–92; W. Linder, 'Erfordert die Mitgliedschaft in der Europäischen Union eine Anpassung des schweizerischen Regierungssystems?', in T. Cottier and A.R. Kopse (eds.), *Der Beitritt der Schweiz zur Europäischen Union. Brennpunkte und Auswirkungen* (Zürich: Schulteiss Polygraphischer Verlag 1998), pp.427–48.

Abstracts

Consensual Government in a Heterogeneous Polity, *by Ulrich Klöti*

The Swiss system of government is renowned for its high stability which is traditionally related to institutional arrangements such as direct democracy, federalism and proportional representation. A more detailed analysis shows that the unique mix of presidential and parliamentary elements of consensual and competitive processes and of collegial and departmental structures may lead not only to stability but to problems of co-ordination and inefficiency as well. Considering the tensions between the various contradicting principles, basic reforms of the governmental system prove to be most difficult to achieve.

How Does Direct Democracy Matter? The Impact of Referendum Votes on Politics and Policy-Making, *by Yannis Papadopoulos*

This article outlines the effects of direct democracy on the Swiss political system. It deals with referendums initiated by petition 'from below' and with their indirect impact on politics and policy-making. Political elites sought to craft integrative strategies in order to tame the conflictual potential of these inherently majoritarian mechanisms. It is argued that this adaptive behaviour took three forms, the first two aiming to *prevent* recourse to direct democracy, and the last to *steer* the processes it engenders: widening the executive formula, to encompass all parties likely to make efficient use of the referendum if not co-opted as partners in the governing coalition; anticipation of the veto risk by negotiating *ex-ante* with opponents to policy reforms that were triggered by government and parliament; *ex-post* negotiation when the use of direct democracy could not be prevented, as in the case of popular initiatives. Finally, the limits of this neo-institutionalist approach are explored, before concluding with an assessment of the validity of the traditional functions of direct democracy today.

The Federal Parliament: The Limits of Institutional Reform, by Hanspeter Kriesi

The Federal Assembly, according to the Constitution the supreme political authortiy, is weakened by several structural features of the Swiss political system. The specific coalitional structure that has emerged in the National Council, however, prevents the incongruent composition of its two chambers from paralysing the political process. The position of the Federal Assembly has been reinforced in the more recent past by procedural reforms but there are increasing difficulties in finding pre-parliamentary compromises. Structural reforms to strengthen the position of the Federal Assembly have been in discussion for years, but decisive steps to improve the position are not in sight.

Towards the Judicialisation of Swiss Politics? by Christine Rothmayr

There is a moderate trend towards the judicialisation of Swiss politics. The Swiss Federal Supreme Court has strengthened the protection of rights and expanded its power of review due to, among other factors, the European Court of Human Rights. However, recent attempts to introduce the power to review federal laws, as part of the total revision of the federal constitution, were defeated in parliament. The federal constitution, therefore, still requires that the Federal Supreme Court apply all federal laws, even if the court believes the law to be unconstitutional, thus clearly limiting the power of constitutional review. The Swiss Federal Supreme Court is, nevertheless, a relevant player in public policy-making despite its limited power of constitutional review.

Institutions and Outcomes of Swiss Federalism: The Role of the Cantons in Swiss Politics, by Wolf Linder and Adrian Vatter

The analysis of Swiss federalism today focuses upon the role of the cantons and the strategies they engage in to protect their interests. In the first part an account is rendered of how the most important institutions of Swiss federalism operate and the outcomes they promote. Taking advantage of the growing empirical research on Swiss federalism, the second part presents new findings on the variations in the 26 cantons in terms of institutional structures, and it probes the impact of the differences between the cantons on policy outcomes. In the final part, the need for and possibilities of reform of Swiss federalism are discussed.

Swiss Political Parties: Between Persistence and Change, by Andreas Ladner

The Swiss party system has long been noteworthy both for its large number of parties and its stability. The parties themselves are considered to be weak with a low level of professionalisation and a high degree of internal fragmentation. This analysis questions these assumptions on a broader empirical basis. It takes up the recent electoral success of the Swiss People's Party, which seriously disturbs traditional arrangements of power sharing. For a better understanding of the ongoing changes, it also takes a closer look at developments on the level of the party organisation. The focus is not only on the national party system and its parties, but also includes the very important cantonal level. There have been significant changes affecting the Swiss parties, and a reorganisation of the party system has become more likely.

Institutionalising the Swiss Welfare State, by Klaus Armingeon

The Swiss welfare state over the last 50 years has moved towards the Western European model of a welfare state characterised by strong liberal traits, but a full convergence has been delayed by various socio-economic, political and institutional factors. Since the 1980s, however, the Swiss welfare state has begun to accelerate towards the Western European model. This process is due to decisions taken in the past bringing about gradual reform of existing schemes, to increasing demands on the welfare state because of demographic and economic developments, and to the inability of Swiss institutions – once responsible for stalling welfare state development – to prevent convergence.

The Growth of the Public Sector in Switzerland, by Jan-Erik Lane and Reinert Maeland

Switzerland has experienced a rapid expansion of its public sector, which is not in line with the traditional image of the country as primarily a market economy and not a welfare state. The public sector may be decomposed into allovative and redistributive components. Both types of public sector programme have grown faster than the rate of economic growth, but it is especially the redistributive programmes that have expanded very rapidly. The Swiss welfare state is one of the largest in Western Europe today, and it presents a problem of financing for both the federal and the cantonal governments. Allocative programmes grew much faster up to the oil crisis than after 1974, but redistributive programmes still display considerable increases. At certain specific time-points decisions were taken that increased public expenditures considerably, meaning that the expansion process of the welfare state has not taken a continuous linear process of growth.

The Political Economy of Switzerland: A Monetarist Success?
by Jan-Erik Lane

The Swiss political economy has become internationally renowned due to its exceptionally low unemployment numbers in an affluent and open economy. These have been seen as the indication of a successful corporatist regime. However, another interpretation is more plausible, namely the strong influence of the independent Swiss National Bank upon the economy by means of a classical monetarist regime, favouring a low level of inflation in a long-run perspective upon the growth in output.

Switzerland and the European Integration Process: Engagement without Marriage, by Cédric Dupont and Pascal Sciarini

Among Western European countries Switzerland currently has the most restricted, and most insecure, access to the EC Single Market. How can one explain this uncomfortable position? In contrast to the widespread interpretation that focuses on the blocking role of core domestic political institutions, this study provides a more nuanced analysis of the sources of variation in foreign policy making, carefully examining the influence of perceptions on the design of policy lines. Switzerland's stance toward the process of European integration, from the late 1950s to the late 1990s, has been the result of trade-offs between perceived risks and opportunities, with no clearly predetermined outcome from domestic political structures. Misperceptions about the range of feasible options at the external level have often reinforced domestic political difficulties and even at times overshadowed them. Domestic institutional reform is not a prerequisite to marriage with the EC in the near future. But there is an urgent need for a government with a firm steering capacity and willingness.

Notes on Contributors

Klaus Armingeon is Professor of Political Science at the University of Bern. His research concentrates in particular on the fields of comparative economic and social policy, corporatism and labour relations. Amongst his most recent works are 'Corporatism and Consociational Democracy', in H. Keman (ed.), *Comparative Politics. New Directions in Theory and Method* (2000); 'Introduction: From the Europe of Nations to the European Nation?' in H. Kriesi *et al.* (eds.), *Nation and National Identity* (1999); and (with M. Freitag) *Schweiz, Österreich, Deutschland. Die politischen Systeme im Vergleich. Ein sozialwissenschaftliches Datenhandbuch* (1997).

Cédric Dupont is Assistant Professor of Political Science at the Graduate Institute of International Studies in Geneva, and Associate Editor of *Business and Politics*. He has written on the political economy of international economic institutions, on bargaining theory and international negotiations, regional integration processes in Europe, Asia and the Pacific region, and on Swiss foreign policy. Recent publications include (co-author) 'Goods, Games, and Institutions', *International Political Science Review* (1999); and 'The Failure of the Nest-Best Solution: EC-EFTA Institutional Relationships and the European Economic Area', in Vinod Aggarwal (ed.), *Institutional Designs for a Complex World: Bargaining, Linkages, and Nesting* (1998).

Hanspeter Kriesi is Professor of Political Science at the University of Geneva. He is the author of several books and articles on the Swiss political system, in particular on direct democracy and the comparative analysis of social movements in Western Europe. Among his publications are: Kriesi *et al*, *New Social Movements in Western Europe. A Comparative Analysis* (1995); 'The Transformation of Cleavage Politics – The 1997 Stein Rokkan Lecture', *European Journal of Political Research* (1998); *Le système politique Suisse* (2nd edn 1998).

Andreas Ladner is Lecturer at the Institute of Political Science, University of Bern. His research focuses on political communities, political participation and political parties. His most recent work includes 'Local Parties in Switzerland: An Active Pillar of the Swiss Political System', in M. Saiz and H. Geser (eds.), *Local Parties in Political and Organization Perspective* (1999).

Jan-Erik Lane is Professor of Comparative Politics at the University of Geneva. He has taught at various universities around the world. His publications range over political theory, public management and comparative studies.

Wolf Linder is Professor of Political Science and Co-Director of the Institute of Political Science at the University of Bern. He was previously Professor at the Institute des hautes études en administration publique in Lausanne. His main research fields are the developments of Swiss politics and its institutions of direct democracy. He is author of *Schweizerische Demokratie. Institutionen – Prozesse – Perspektiven* (1999); *Swiss Democracy. Possible Solutions to Conflict in Multicultural Societies* (1994); and of numerous articles on Swiss Politics.

Reinert Maeland works in the Department of Statistics at Lund University. He specialises in probability and game theory, publishing on the power indices (together with Jan-Erik Lane).

Yannis Papadopoulos is Professor of Swiss Politics and Public Policy at the University of Lausanne and Director of the Institut d'Etudes Politiques et Internationales. He is the author of *Les processus de décision fédéraux en Suisse* (1997) and *Démocratie directe* (1998). He edited *Présent et avenir de la démocratie directe* (1994), *Elites politiques et peuple en Suisse* (1994) and recently co-edited the *Handbuch der schweizerischen Politik* (1999). He has published articles on direct democracy and on Swiss politics in various journals and in several edited volumes.

Christine Rothmayr is Lecturer in the Department of Political Science at the University of Geneva. Her most recent publications include *Politik vor Gericht. Implementation und Wirkungen von Entscheiden des Schweizerischen Bundesgerichts in den Bereichen Fortpflanzungsmedizin, Lohngleichheit von Frau und Mann und Sonntagsarbeit* (1999).

Pascal Sciarini is Professor of Political Science at the Graduate Institute of Public Administration (IDHEAP), Lausanne. He has written on Swiss politics (direct democracy, political parties, European policy), political behaviour, European integration and comparative political economy. Recent publications include (co-author) 'Referendums on European Integration. Do Institutions Matter in the Voter's Decision?', *Comparative Political Studies* (2000) and (co-author) 'Opinion Formation in Foreign Policy: The Swiss Experience', *Electoral Studies* (1999).

Adrian Vatter is Lecturer in Swiss and Comparative Politics at the Institute of Political Science, University of Bern. He is author of *Eigennutz als Grundmaxime in der Politik?* (1994) and *Partizipative Risikopolitik: Theorien und Fallstudien* (1998). He has published articles in, for example, the *Journal of European Studies, European Journal of Political Research* and *Politische Vierteljahresschrift*.

Index

conflict 49; protection of high moors 109; ratchet in social policy 160; xenophobic 40
popular votes, welfare state retrenchment and 160
Portugal 146, 192–3, 195–6
post-modern society 3, 14
power, decline of parliamentary 60
pre-parliamentary procedures 41–2, 102; compromise and 61; energy policy and 71; parliament and 70; referendum challenge and 103
President of the Confederation, *primus inter pares* 27
presidentialism 3
private welfare organisations 107
privatisation 30, 112, 189
professionalism, increase 134–5
proportional representation 22–5, 24, 63, 80, 127
public goods and infrastructure, growth rates 184
public sector productivity 185
public services 116–17

Quarterly Bulletin 204

Radical Democratic Party 123–4, 127, 130, 132, 135–6, 138–41; Catholic-Conservative cantons and 46; concrete review and 81; EEA (1992) agreeement and 224; in government 11, 13, 22, 39–40, 80, 96; magic formula and 23; reforms and 47
Rae Fragmentation Index 124–5
referendum mechanism, amicable agreement and 17; application of 16; pressure from below 35; reforms and 52; types `from below' 36
referendums, actors' behaviour and 41; blocking mechanisms 6; campaign, EEA treaty 224; Catholic-Conservative Party and 39; democracy 3–4; deterrence and 43; effect of threat of 42, 80; mandatory 21; support for government policies 40; veto groups 49; the vote and 43; `votes of control' 36
'*referendumsfähig*' actors, bills and 38
refugee programmes 108
religion, federal councillors and 23
rent-seeking 12
'La Republique Helvetique' (1798) 11
repos 201–2
'responsibility clause' 73
restrictive measures, social policy and 161
Rieder, A. 87

Riklin, A. 60, 71
'rise of the tax state' 176
road transportation 225–6
Rokkan, S. 132, 134
'Role of government' survey (1996–98) 151
Rothmayr, C. 7

Sager, Fritz 98
St Gallen canton 9, 126, 128, 130
Sartori, G. 124
Savioz, M. 114
scandal of secret service 71
Scandinavia 10, 150, 163, 184; corporatism 191–3, 197
Schaffhausen canton 9, 126, 128
Schengen agreement 226
Schmidt, M.G. 148, 191, 194, 196
Schumpeter, J. 185
Schwyz canton 9, 126, 128
Sciarini, P. 17
self-censor, 'blackmailing power' 41
'semi-direct democracy matters' 37
Shapiro, M. 90
shift-point defined 172
Siaroff, A. 192
Siegel, N. 147
Single European Act (SEA) 212, 220–21
Single Market 211, 221
social assistance 173
social care 178–80, 182
Social Democrats (SP) 13, 22–3, 25, 64–5, 82–3; concrete review and 81; in Federal Assembly 69; funding 136; governments at cantonal and federal level 157; industrial and urban regions 101; magic formula and 123–4, 139; National Council and 66–9; party membership 137–8, 141; political left 96, 140; protection of weak and environment 131; reliance on Green Party 100; results for 127; welfare state and 151
social insurance expenditure, growth rates 179
social policy, public–private mix 107; retrenchment 159–60
social security, growth rates in charges (1961–96) 186; welfare state and 179
Socialist Party (SPS), challenged by part of the Right 51, 131; EEA (1992) agreement 224; funding 135; optional referendums and 50
Socialists 39–40
Solothurn canton 9, 126, 130
Sonderbund war 39, 99
sovereignty of the people 88, 91
Spain 146, 192–3, 195–6

For Product Safety Concerns and Information please contact our EU
representative GPSR@taylorandfrancis.com
Taylor & Francis Verlag GmbH, Kaufingerstraße 24, 80331 München, Germany

www.ingramcontent.com/pod-product-compliance
Lightning Source LLC
Chambersburg PA
CBHW050416280326
41932CB00013BA/1886